OTHER RSN TITLES FROM SEARCH PRESS

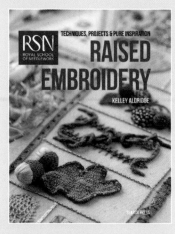

Raised Embroidery
by Kelley Aldridge
978-1-78221-189-1

Embroidered Boxes
by Heather Lewis
978-1-78221-652-0

Goldwork
by Emi Nimura
978-1-78221-703-9

RSN ESSENTIAL STITCH GUIDES

Crewelwork
by Jacqui McDonald
978-178221-922-4

Stumpwork by Kate Sinton
978-178221-923-1

Whitework by Lizzy Lansberry
978-1-78221-921-7

Goldwork by Helen McCook
978-1-80092-017-0

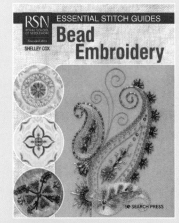

Bead Embroidery
by Shelley Cox
978-178221-930-9

Blackwork by Becky Hogg
978-178221-932-3

Canvaswork by Rachel Doyle
978-1-78221-931-6

Silk Shading by Sarah Homfray
978-1-80092-018-7

FINE WHITEWORK

DEDICATION

This book is dedicated to my parents, Janet and John Adin, whose inspiration, support and belief in me allowed me to fulfil my desire to become a professional embroiderer. To my husband Wayne and daughter Iona for their endless patience and support. To the RSN and my whitework tutor there, the late Sally Saunders, for passing on the exquisite art of fine whitework to me.

To Janet Every for her endless encouragement and belief that I could make this book happen.

ACKNOWLEDGEMENTS

My students, friends and colleagues for kindly loaning their work and collection pieces to be photographed; to my students past and present for the talents and inspiration; Mandy Ashton for proofreading; Mandy Ewing for assisting with sampling; Blair Castle for the use of the images of Lady Evelyn Stewart Murray's work; John Draper for his beautiful wren images.

First published in 2023

Search Press Limited
Wellwood, North Farm Road,
Tunbridge Wells, Kent TN2 3DR

Text and illustration copyright © Jenny Adin-Christie, 2023.

Photography by Mark Davison for Search Press Studios: pages 1, 3, 5, 9, 10, 11 (bottom left), 12, 13 (bottom right), 15, 16–17, 19, 20 (bottom left), 21 (bottom right), 22–30, 33, 36 (bottom right), 37, 39, 40, 71, 74–76, 79–80, 90, 94, 99–102, 104–107, 109, 118 (bottom left), 119, 120–122, 123 (bottom right), 124–127, 129, 130 (bottom three), 131 (top two), 145 (bottom right), 170 (bottom right), 171 (middle right), 180 (top right), 181 (bottom right), 183 (bottom three), 184–187. Photographs by Paul Bricknell for Search Press Studios: pages 20 (top right, bottom-right two); 21 (bottom left). Photograph by John Draper: page 128 (top right). Lucy Margolius: page 123 (top left).

Photograph on page 11 (bottom right) courtesy of Blair Castle, Perthshire.

Diagrams and all other photographs by Jenny Adin-Christie.

Design copyright © Search Press Ltd 2023.

ISBN: 978-1-78221-702-2
ebook ISBN: 978-1-78126-629-8

Suppliers

For details of suppliers, please visit the Search Press website: www.searchpress.com

For more information about the RSN, its courses, studio, shop and exhibitions, see: www.royal-needlework.org.uk

For information about the RSN degree programme, see: www.rsndegree.uk

Extra copies of the templates are available from: www.bookmarkedhub.com

Author's note

All the designs contained in this book are also available as pre-printed fabric or as full working kits. For all supplies and equipment, you are welcome to visit the author's website at: jennyadin-christieembroidery.com

Publishers' note

All the step-by-step photographs in this book feature the author, Jenny Adin-Christie, demonstrating fine whitework. No models have been used.

FINE WHITEWORK
TECHNIQUES, PROJECTS & PURE INSPIRATION

JENNY ADIN-CHRISTIE

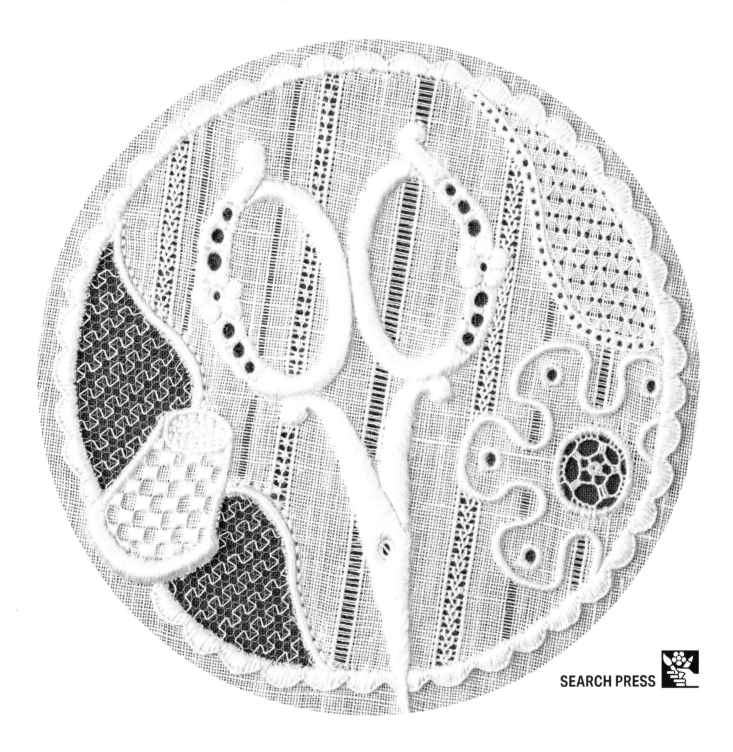

SEARCH PRESS

CONTENTS

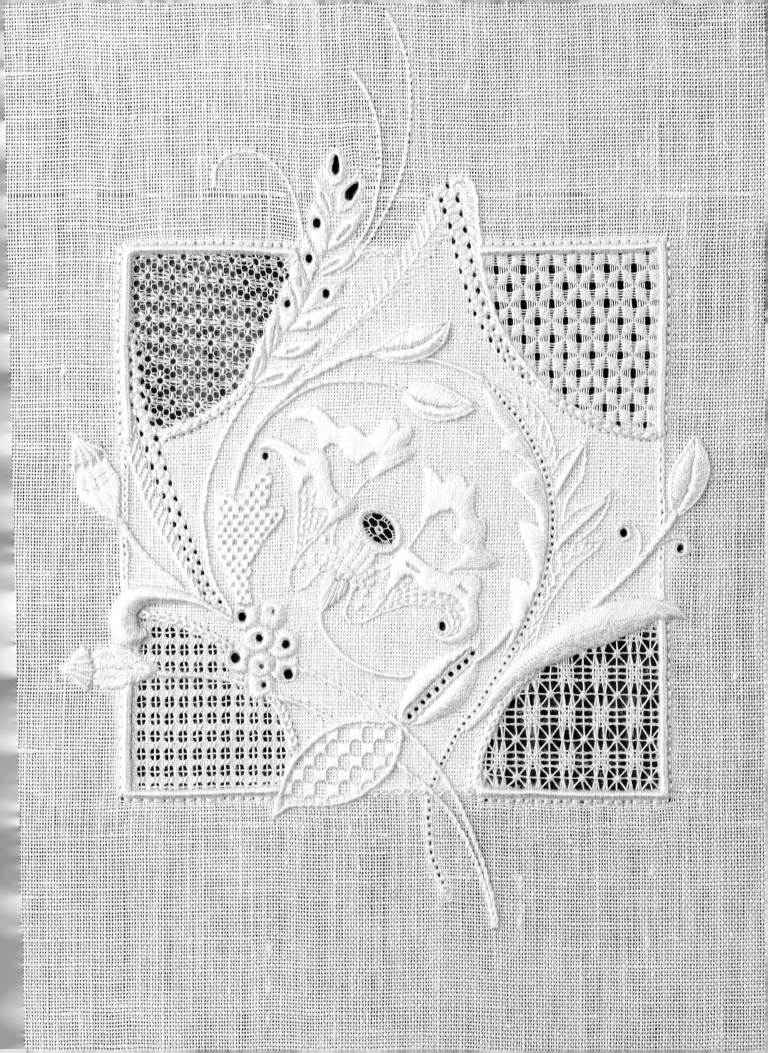

THE ROYAL SCHOOL OF NEEDLEWORK

Founded in 1872, the Royal School of Needlework (RSN) is the international centre of excellence for the art of hand embroidery. It is based at Hampton Court Palace in west London but also offers courses across the UK, in the USA and Japan. Today it is a thriving, dynamic centre of teaching and learning, and believes that hand embroidery is a vital art form which impacts on many aspects of our lives from clothes to ceremonial outfits, and from home furnishings to textile art.

To enable and encourage people to learn the skill of hand embroidery the RSN offers courses from beginner to degree level. The wide range of short courses includes introductions to each of the stitch techniques the RSN uses, beginning with Introduction to Embroidery. The RSN's Certificate and Diploma in Technical Hand Embroidery offers students the opportunity to learn a range of techniques to a very high technical standard. The Future Tutors course is specifically designed for those pursuing a career in teaching technical hand embroidery. The RSN's BA (Hons) Degree course is the only UK degree course solely focussed on hand embroidery and offers students opportunities to learn core stitch techniques, which they are then encouraged to apply in contemporary and conceptual directions. Graduates can go on to find careers in embroidery relating to fashion, couture and costume; to interiors and soft furnishings or in the area of textile art including jewellery and millinery.

At its Hampton Court headquarters, the RSN welcomes people for all kind of events from private lessons to bespoke stitching holidays, intensive Certificate and Diploma studies, tours around our exhibitions, which comprise either pieces from our own textile collections or students' work, or study days looking at particular pieces or techniques from our Collection. Since 2020, the RSN also teaches online, offering short courses and the Certificate and Diploma, as well as a series of talks and presentations. We also offer bespoke classes and private lessons online. For those who wish to work at their own pace there are a series of Distance Learning courses where a tutor takes you through a particular design step by step.

The RSN Collection of textiles comprises more than 2,000 pieces, all of which have been donated, because as a charity the RSN cannot afford to purchase additions. The pieces were given so that they would have a home for the future and to be used as a resource for students and researchers. The Collection comes from all over the world, illustrating many different techniques and approaches to stitch and embellishment.

The RSN Studio undertakes new commissions and conservation work for many different clients, including public institutions, places of worship, stately homes and private individuals, again illustrating the wide variety of roles embroidery can play, from altar frontals and vestments for churches to curtains, hangings and chair covers for homes and embroidered pictures as works of art. Over the last few years the RSN has worked with a number of prestigious names including Sarah Burton OBE for Alexander McQueen, Vivienne Westwood's Studio for Red Carpet Green Dress, Patrick Grant's E Tautz, the late L'Wren Scott, Nicholas Oakwell Couture for the Great Britain Exhibition, the Jane Austen House Museum, Liberty London, the V&A Museum of Childhood and M&S and Oxfam for Shwopping.

Most recently, the RSN created a den for HRH The Duchess of Cambridge's garden at the RHS Hampton Court Garden Festival and a portrait of the RSN Patron, HRH The Duchess of Cornwall, in blackwork technique.

For more information about the RSN, its courses, studio, shop and exhibitions, see www.royal-needlework.org.uk, and for its degree programme see www.rsndegree.uk

Hampton Court Palace, Surrey, home of
the Royal School of Needlework

INTRODUCTION TO FINE WHITEWORK

Whitework is an umbrella term spanning what is probably the largest array of individually unique embroidery techniques under one heading. In their traditional forms, many other embroidery techniques are far narrower in their characteristics and definition: blackwork being counted stitches on an evenly woven ground, silk work using silk threads to shade imagery generally on a silk ground, crewel work using crewel wools on solid linen twill, and so on.

Whitework techniques are unified in their use of white or neutral thread on a white or neutral ground fabric. Beyond this, they are eclectic in the individual stitches, materials and threads employed, their applications and their histories. The blanket heading covers the diverse and rather poetically named techniques: Hedebo, Hardanger, Schwalm, Carrickmacross, Broderie Anglaise, Reticella, Ayrshire, drawn thread, pulled thread and Dresden work, to name but a few. As the names suggest, these techniques have developed around the globe, resulting from people wishing to beautify and embellish cloth in its purest form – sometimes because undyed thread and undyed fabric was the most readily available; sometimes because undyed fabric symbolized purity, cleanliness and beauty; or because undergarments still required embellishment but did not warrant the use of more expensive silks and dyed threads.

Each individual whitework technique has its own design style and typical motifs, which result from the taste at the time it was developed – each beautiful in its way. However, due to the depth which can be achieved through this medium, the broad spectrum of whitework processes can provide a stunning palette of textures and tones. This palette can thus be used to create graphic, illustrative designs with tremendous depth and character.

This book could not possibly cover the intricacies of each historical technique – each is worthy of a book in itself. Instead, it aims to demystify the most vital stitch techniques, organizing them into grades of tone and texture, a formula by which unique pattern-based and pictorial designs can be created. Whitework may be basic in its pure, simple beauty and lack of colour, yet the challenge of working with white thread on a white ground has provoked some of the most ingenious, technically challenging and celebrated forms of stitchery ever to have existed. Consider the complex and exact nature of counted Dresden work on the finest sheer muslin, or the utter precision of the satin sprigs and spider-like webs seen in Ayrshire whitework. This form of embroidery cannot call upon colour to captivate the viewer: it must rely purely on the key textile design elements of texture and tone. Thus, whitework succeeds by exploiting the incredibly rich variety of textures which can be achieved with needle and thread – whether knotted, twisted, smoothed, pleated or plaited. The character of each stitch is seen in its purest form without shading and colour to distract, relying on the height to which the stitch is built against the ground. Thus, highlight, shadow and tone are created, and the varying twists and turns of the plied threads catch the light in different ways, breaking up the effect into hundreds of variables.

Furthermore, the manipulation of the weave of the fabric itself, using stitch, adds vastly to this tonal scale of whitework techniques. The even weave of cloth can be pulled open using stitches to reveal specks of the colour or light behind, creating a darker tone. These stitches can be worked in repeating rows on the weave of the cloth, creating myriad patterns and combining stitch textures, which contrast against holes of varying sizes.

The threads of the woven ground can be extracted, withdrawn from the weave, creating larger open spaces and revealing lattice grids, which demand to be strengthened and embellished, wrapped, knotted and woven into intricate lace-like forms.

Perhaps when a worker first snipped their fabric by mistake, and instead of darning the hole, decided to make it a little bigger and bind around it to strengthen, they noticed the stark beauty of these holes. More were then added to make a pattern and the beauty of decorative voids, contrasted by textured stitchery, was born. Because these holes were potentially considered too stark, embroiderers began to develop ingenious ways to partially refill the holes with mind-boggling needlelace patterns, adding a layer of mystery to the view through the holes, as a lace curtain or spider's web crossing a window.

Whitework has come to exploit every element of textile, from adding to and embellishing the surface and manipulating the weave of the base cloth, to extracting sections of this base to reveal the world beyond. The ingenuity of whitework has captured the imagination of worker and wearer for centuries. It has a pure, timeless beauty, which has spanned the generations and will hopefully continue to do so.

FINE WHITEWORK

In this book, the term 'fine whitework' refers to a specific technique taught by the RSN over many generations. Worked on a fine linen batiste, fine whitework allows the full spectrum of whitework stitches to be combined into one illustrative design, exploiting all of the tonal and textural contrasts possible within the spectrum and resulting in a piece with great depth, life and graphic realism. It includes: surface embroidery, pulled thread work, drawn thread work, cutwork and eyelets, insertion of darned net and application of a second layer of linen to achieve a shadow appliqué effect, and much more.

Fine whitework will not be everyone's passion to stitch due to its exacting nature, but its beauty can always be admired and the formula for design provided here – using the tonal and textural scale – is hugely relevant, if not fundamental, to all other forms of embroidery.

RSN Training School sampler
L. H. Fleming, 1925

This is a beautiful, classic example of a training piece of fine whitework produced by a student at the RSN. The same techniques are still taught to today's trainees.

THE HISTORY OF FINE WHITEWORK

The history of whitework embroidery is as encyclopaedic as the subject matter itself and each niche technique is worthy of its own book. Here, I look at the techniques I feel have contributed most significantly to the development of the Fine Whitework technique at the RSN, which have influenced my own work and which continue to provide inspiration for today's white-on-white embroiderer.

Detail of a baby's gown embellished in Ayrshire whitework
Beneath the gown is a vintage photograph of the skirt panel of another typical gown.

DRESDEN WORK

In 1600, Queen Elizabeth I granted a charter to the East India Company to trade in Indian treasures, one of which was muslin, a cotton fabric woven by hand for the Mughal Court, and of a fineness never seen before in Europe. The company sent the first muslins to Britain in 1670.

In the fifteenth to seventeenth centuries, lace produced by bobbin or needle, was prized and tremendously expensive. Muslin, with its ethereal fineness and exotic origins, could equal the luxury of lace.

European embroiderers developed techniques to adorn the muslin, working counted pulled thread patterns, combined with outline stitches, solid surface stitches and layering of the base cloth, effectively simulating lace.

Dresden in Germany gained recognition in the eighteenth century for producing the best quality embroidered muslins, becoming known as Dresden work. It adorned items such as fichus, sleeve ruffles, caps, lappets and aprons. Demand grew rapidly and work was exported throughout Europe. Cheaper to produce than lace, Dresden work became accessible to the growing merchant classes.

Muslin remained highly fashionable through the century, providing the perfect fabric for the neoclassical styles of the late 1700s and early 1800s. Kerchiefs, long scarves, bonnets and entire dresses continued to be embroidered in great detail. Pulled work began to decrease in intensity and combinations of delicate satin stitch and eyelets began to proliferate, with considerable use of tambour work (a method of rapidly producing outlines resembling chain stitch, worked with a hook rather than with a needle).

AYRSHIRE WHITEWORK

The Scottish Borders were a famed centre for weaving linen. The invention of the Spinning Mule in 1779 allowed the production of fine thread to equal Indian muslin, and Scottish weavers soon adapted to its manufacture. In 1782, a professional Italian embroiderer, Luigi Ruffini, travelled to Edinburgh and established a school to teach tambour whitework to women and girls, aiming to establish a commercial production line. Work spread rapidly and by the turn of the century, the region had a skilled workforce and a ready source of fine fabric.

In 1814, Lady Mary Montgomerie (daughter of the 11th Earl of Eglinton) returned to Scotland from travelling in Europe, bringing home a baby gown displaying intricate needlelace fillings. She showed this to a Mrs Jamieson of Ayr, who studied the techniques and established a school. The model was copied throughout the region and a major cottage industry developed. By 1856, there were 50 firms dealing in Ayrshire whitework in Glasgow (i) and the workers (age nine upwards), known poetically as 'Flowerers', numbered 25,000 in Scotland and 200,000 in Ireland (ii).

Ayrshire work developed a unique style with elegant designs minutely worked in padded satin stitch, trailing, drawn work and open eyelets filled with famously delicate needlelace. The work adorned items such as adult collars, caps, chemisettes and pelerines, and bonnets and gowns for babies.

i. Information from S. Tuckett, 'The needle crusaders: the nineteenth-century Ayrshire whitework industry', *Journal of Scottish Historical Studies*, University of Glasgow, 2016;
ii. As above.

An example of a lappet in Dresden work combining intricate pulled thread fillings with the heavier areas worked by applying a second layer of base fabric, secured with tambouring.

The Ayrshire industry declined rapidly after the 1860s as the industry became too large, standards dropped and demand reduced. A simpler form of whitework continued with eyelets remaining unfilled, forming the bold, dramatic patterns of Broderie Anglaise.

The hand-worked whitework industry was finally crushed by the invention of machines capable of accurate simulation.

CARRICKMACROSS LACE

This embroidered lace developed in Ireland in the early nineteenth century. Margaret Grey Porter, wife of the rector of Donaghmoyne, near Carrickmacross, County Monaghan, brought back pieces of applied lace from Italy. It became her wish to establish schools which would allow girls to earn their living by producing lace. Ireland already had a strong tradition for hand-lace-making by bobbin and needle; however, the applied lace would use the now readily available muslin, layered together with nets produced by John Heathcote's bobbin net lace machine, patented in 1820. The intricate designs were outlined by whipping a heavier cotton thread with a very fine thread, binding the layers together. Areas of the muslin could then be cut away exposing the tulle, with pattern stitches then darned into the net structure.

Carrickmacross was quicker to produce than conventional lace. It became fashionable and brought essential income for poor families, particularly during the potato famine (1845–1852). Further schools were established and attracted attention at national and international exhibitions, drawing wealthy clients including Queen Victoria.

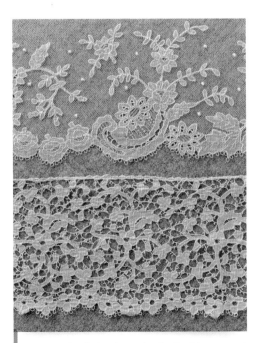

An example of a border worked in Carrickmacross lace (top) and a border worked in Carrickmacross guipure (bottom), wherein the net ground was removed and the bound cotton shapes joined by whipped bars or 'brides'.

Carrickmacross has long been valued by the British Royal Family. The RSN gave HRH Princess Diana a length from its collection for her wedding dress in 1981, and the lace panels for the wedding dress of HRH the Duchess of Cambridge, thirty years later, were crafted by the RSN, emulating the style of Carrickmacross using minute motifs cut from a machine-made lace, applied to a ground of tulle.

LADY EVELYN STEWART MURRAY

Lady Evelyn (1868–1940), daughter of the 7th Duke of Atholl) was born into one of the most aristocratic families in Scotland, at Blair Castle, Perthshire. The expectations of her class were to be educated as a fine lady, with the purpose of finding the right husband. However, Evelyn was highly strung and fiercely intelligent. Her refusal to conform set her at odds with her family and she became so difficult that, for fear of public embarrassment, she was sent away to Switzerland in 1891, and later to Belgium. There, she began to study embroidery, taking lessons, visiting museums and purchasing pieces to study and copy. She became highly skilled and her work was praised by the embroidery schools whose approval she sought.

In 1905 she commissioned the Atholl Arms to be worked professionally. The workroom mistress was not happy with the standard produced by her embroiderer and tore the piece in front of the distraught worker. It is said that this episode inspired Lady Evelyn's mission to work the British Arms in whitework.

It took Evelyn and a companion around seven years to complete, working on glass cambric in fine cotton, and resulting in arguably the most exquisite piece of whitework ever created. It is still housed at Blair Castle, alongside Evelyn's collection of around 120 pieces, half of which she worked herself.

The British Arms in whitework
45 × 38cm (17¾ × 15in)
Worked by Lady Evelyn Stewart Murray and companion.
Photograph courtesy of Blair Castle, Perthshire.

Ayrshire babies' bonnets, from the RSN collection.

Ayrshire piece depicting Tam O'Shanter and Souter Johnny (after Robert Burns).

A PERSONAL HISTORY

I first gained a love of whitework when training as an Apprentice at the Royal School of Needlework. I found my first year in training incredibly hard: as a perfectionist, I wanted to achieve precision in all my work, and yet as a professional embroider, I also had to be swift in thought, creativity, design and stitch. I found this balance terribly hard: my work was beautiful but I feared I would never earn a living or work in a professional studio if I did not learn to agonize less and work more swiftly.

Whitework was introduced at the end of my first year. Here was a technique wherein the colour was removed and I no longer had to make decisions on it – simply on tone and texture. I began to speed up, I received praise and therefore fell in love with the art. I loved its variety, precision and beautiful intricacy.

I adored a box in the RSN collection which was filled simply with tiny babies' bonnets (shown top left), each puffed out with tissue paper and nestled together like frosted jewels. Many of these were Ayrshire bonnets, each packed with the most intricate concoction of tiny pin tucks, minute sprigs of satin and complex needlelace fillings. I could happily study this box for weeks, fathoming the intricacies of each design and stitch. As a result, I was inspired to form my own collection of historical whitework, found in antique and vintage fairs, charity shops and through the donations of students who knew my love of this form of work.

One of my most treasured possessions is a small rectangular piece of Ayrshire whitework found in a vintage textile warehouse in the docks of Glasgow. Huge boxes of vintage textiles, including crates of whitework garments and baby dresses, were tipped out onto the floor for me to pore over. In a small office were haberdashery drawers of the 'better' items, which were shown one at a time. I could not resist the charming and rather rare Ayrshire piece I found there, depicting Tam O'Shanter and Souter Johnny from the Robert Burns poem of the same name (see left). This includes what may be the only pint of beer ever depicted in tiny whitework stitches! The piece sums up the magic of whitework, where, on a ground of exquisitely fine and translucent cotton lawn, the characterful figures and scene are depicted with perfect graphic clarity, simply by using basic white cotton thread to form carefully planned contrasting stitch textures and weights. The piece is further enhanced by the floral border, including some of those iconic delicate needlelace fillings.

Another momentous find was a long lappet of Dresden work (see page 10) discovered screwed up in a basket of lace oddments in a Hampton Court antique shop and sold for £3. Every scrap of the extremely fine muslin is adorned with such perfectly counted pulled thread stitches and eyelets that it had obviously been assumed to be machine-sewn. I treasure each of these pieces and they are a unique window on, and source of, the stitches and techniques of centuries gone by, many of which were not recorded in books.

As the very last training project of my Apprenticeship, I worked a piece of 'fine whitework', like generations of trainees before me, inspired by dragonflies and Art Nouveau book cover designs (see 'Dance of the Dragonflies', below). I loved every minute of pushing fine linen cambric and white stranded cotton to achieve the most intricate of designs, perfection of stitch clarity and lace-like open webs. This was the pinnacle of my RSN experience and really set me on the road of pursuing whitework as one of my embroidery passions.

In 2012, I was asked to design and work a piece of fine whitework for the RSN's selling exhibition at Leighton House, London (see below, right). My design was based on the stone carved frontage of the Natural History Museum and sold for £4,800. This proved to me that whitework can be celebrated and appreciated as a work of art, not just disregarded as a domestic technique used on petticoats and doilies.

Over the years, I have been able to research, develop and master my approach to fine whitework. My hope is that this book inspires readers to embrace and explore this magical field of embroidery further and realise its rightful place as art, and its workers as artists. It has been my endeavour over the last twenty or more years to revive and keep alive many of its techniques, which may otherwise be lost to the pressures and distractions of modern living, so that others can enjoy using them in their own work, and through practice will also understand and value the skills of past generations of embroiderers.

Many of the stitches which may seem unique to whitework are also highly applicable to other forms of embroidery and I love to experiment with these combinations, using the fabric-exploiting qualities of whitework to add greater depth to coloured embroidery. I have always felt that whitework, if it were not so technically challenging, should ideally be taught before coloured forms of embroidery, since this would allow a thorough understanding of texture and tone, much as in drawing, when tone and mark making are learnt before painting.

Dance of the Dragonflies
12 × 19cm (4¾ × 7½in), mounted: 18 × 25cm (7¹⁄₁₆ × 9¾in)
Jenny Adin-Christie

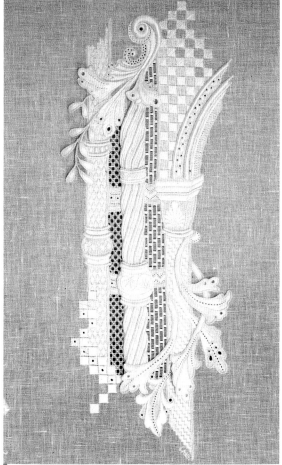

Study in White
20 × 30cm (7⅞ × 11¾in)
Jenny Adin-Christie

MATERIALS AND TOOLS

Whitework embroidery does not require a huge range of materials, threads and equipment. However, it is important to source high-quality fabrics and threads in order to achieve the best results. Traditional fabrics and threads have become increasingly hard to locate but a good number of specialist manufacturers around the world are still producing high-quality options, if in a smaller range than in the past.

The tools employed are of ancient design and yet still perform the same roles today. Many are bespoke items created by skilled craftspeople in wood and metal and are a joy to use.

FABRICS

Consider the following when selecting your fabric:

Do you want to work counted stitches? Be sure you can see, count and push your needle between the fabric threads easily. If you plan to work counted pulled thread work stitches, you must check that there is enough movement between the fabric threads to allow them to be pulled together, creating holes between the stitches. Check whether the fabric is an evenweave or not (i.e. does it have the same number of warp threads to weft threads within a defined measurement). If not, counted threads may appear skewed, i.e. a satin stitch square will look slightly rectangular. This may or may not be important within your design.

Do you want to work drawn thread work? Try removing the threads. Do they slide out easily without shedding excessive amounts of fibre? Are the threads they leave behind clean and sufficiently strong on which to work patterns?

Do you want to work sculptured stitchery? Is the fabric dense enough to support the weight of this and to ensure that the edges of design shapes are crisp? The fabric weave should not distort easily around the edges of a padded shape. If a fabric is too openly woven, it can be difficult to create solid edges as there is insufficient fabric for the needle to bite into.

Do you want to work with more than one layer of fabric? Try placing other fabrics behind the main fabric: is the additional weight effective, and does it provide distinct contrast?

Do you want to work cutwork or eyelets? The fabric must be sufficiently densely woven to support the strain which this will cause. An open weave may collapse when cut open.

You may wish to combine the above techniques so your fabric will need to answer all the relevant criteria.

SUITABLE FABRICS FOR WHITEWORK

Linen batiste (linen sheeting) A fine, evenly woven, smooth fabric which varies considerably between different suppliers. It is an excellent base for a wide variety of whitework techniques; it has good strength and density to support raised work, combined with pulled, drawn and openwork techniques. Usually not an evenweave.

The first sample shown (opposite) is a smooth, densely-woven batiste, highly suitable for surface work and cutwork but less suitable for counted work. The following two samples show two weights of linen batiste which are particularly good for working fine whitework techniques. These are still very fine but have a slightly more open weave, allowing for counted work to be combined with solid surface stitching: fine (approximately 55 threads/in, or 21 threads/cm) and very fine (approximately 65 threads/in, 25 threads/cm).

Evenweave linen These linens have the same number of warp threads as weft threads, usually counted by the centimetre or inch. The more threads per cm/inch, the denser the linen. They are ideal for working pulled thread and drawn thread as the threads are usually easy to see and count. A square stitch will remain square. Threads usually withdraw smoothly and easily, leaving strong threads behind. Linens with a higher thread count are good for sculptured stitchery but those with a lower thread count can be trickier to work with as there is insufficient fabric to ensure crisp edges are achieved.

Organza and organdie Sheer translucent fabrics, ideal for shadow work and layering with themselves or with other fabrics. Densely woven and surprisingly strong, they can support sculptured stitchery effectively. Organdie is stiffer, and made from 100 per cent cotton whereas organza is softer, and may be silk or synthetic.

Cotton lawn/batiste A beautifully delicate, semi-translucent fabric, useful for shadow work and for working with layers. Sufficiently strong and dense to support low relief sculptured stitchery and delicate openwork/cutwork/eyelets. This is the traditional fabric for Ayrshire whitework.

'Bisso' linen A beautifully fine, sheer linen with a reasonably open weave and yet a crisp, firm finish. Excellent for fine pulled thread and drawn thread and for layering.

Net/tulle Machine-made net was first created in the nineteenth century, and it was soon discovered that counted darning patterns could be worked onto its structure, creating an effect reminiscent of hand-worked bobbin or needle-made laces, but with much greater speed. Fine nylon tulle, created for use in conservation work, is a beautiful base for this as the patterns worked in fine cotton thread appear to be suspended in air, as the net structure is so fine. This is beautiful for combining with fine linen or cotton batiste to fill voided areas, or for shadow work behind organza. However, this is very fine to work. Cotton tulle is also available but appears much coarser, the stitches having less clarity since the weave of the net is more distracting. Cotton net can be useful for practising net patterns before moving to finer net.

Natural coloured linen A fine, densely woven linen which is superb as a subtle fabric colour to use behind completed whitework pieces to enhance their beauty. This can also be used as a ground fabric for white embroidery if a contrast is preferred.

Lace (machine/handmade, not shown) This can be a lovely addition to shadow work, placed behind a ground of organza. Useful for experimental work.

Densely woven linens (tablecloth weight, not shown) These are usually too dense to work pulled thread but can be used for bolder sculptured stitching and cutwork/openwork/eyelets. They are often too dense for a second layer to be applied behind. Threads can be withdrawn for drawn thread work.

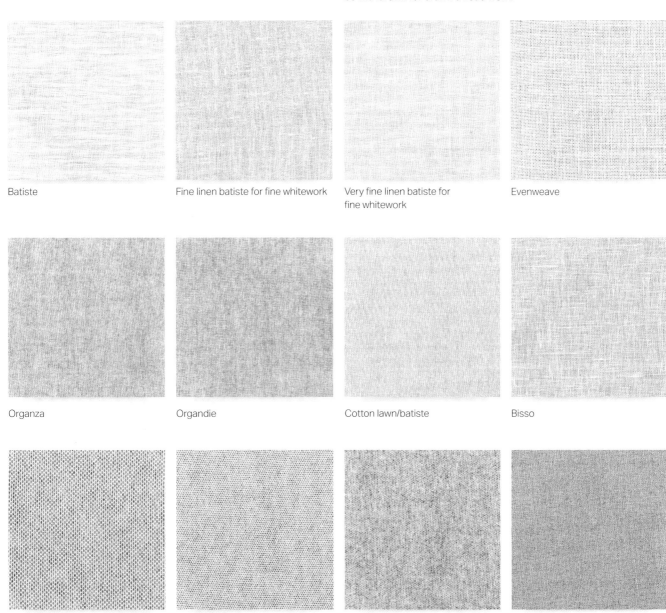

Batiste

Fine linen batiste for fine whitework

Very fine linen batiste for fine whitework

Evenweave

Organza

Organdie

Cotton lawn/batiste

Bisso

Cotton net, heavy

Cotton net, fine

Conservation net (tulle)

Ground fabric (natural linen)

From left to right: Retors d'Alsace (sizes 8 and 12); Floche à Broder; perlé cotton (5); Coton à Broder; perlé cotton (8 and 12); lace threads and polyester tacking threads.

THREADS

This list is not definitive and many other threads can be employed for whitework to produce creative effects. The addition of beads, pearls, crystals, buttons and fine metallics can also complement some designs. Just be cautious of those which distract from the clarity of the embroidery.

Please take note of the abbreviations shown here in brackets, which will be used throughout the book.

Stranded cotton (ST)   This is one of the most versatile threads for whitework. Six strands are plied together but can be withdrawn for individual use. A soft, fine, glossy thread with enough twist to maintain good condition during work but without causing stiffness. Excellent for surface embroidery. Less suitable for pulled and drawn thread work due to lack of strength and slightly fibrous quality, which can lack clarity.

Floche à Broder (F)   A slightly glossy, lightly twisted thread which has the approximate thickness of two strands of stranded cotton. Very useful for surface embroidery where stitches are required to blend together such as in satin stitch, and for those wishing to work less finely. Excellent as a thread for all types of padding. Not suitable for drawn and pulled techniques due to lack of strength and its fibrous quality. Floche is purchased in a long hank. When used as a surface thread, it should be used in relatively short lengths as it can wear more rapidly.

Retors d'Alsace   Glossy mercerized cotton threads with a clear twist structure. Available in sizes 12 (finest) and 8 (heaviest). Excellent for a bold, sculptured effect in satin stitch and for bolder surface textures such as for French knots or bullion knots (see page 37). Also suitable for heavier forms of drawn and pulled work. Retains strength and smoothness over long periods of use, resulting in a crisp finish.

Perlé cotton   Very similar to Retors d'Alsace and with equivalent thread sizes (also available in heavier size 5). These can be used as an alternative thread for the same purposes since they are more widely available.

Coton à Broder   A reasonably glossy, very smooth thread with a slight stiffness. Useful for working surface work stitches which require a crisp finish and where the individual character or structure of the stitch needs to be clearly visible, such as fly stitch, feather stitch and French knots. Less useful when stitches are required to blend together, such as in satin stitch.

Cotton lace threads (L)   Fine, high twist, ultra-smooth threads traditionally used for lace making. In whitework these are excellent for work requiring fine precision such as pulled and drawn thread work, ladder stitch, tiny eyelets and needlelace fillings.

Polyester tacking thread (TACK)   Used for marking out straight design lines worked along the straight grain of the fabric and for basting layers of fabric together. Avoid fibrous sewing threads, which may leave coloured fibres on the surface of your work.

Important note:

If combining various types of white threads, be sure to use those produced by the same company – the level of whiteness can vary significantly between manufacturers. Lace threads will always be produced by different companies from the heavier threads, however, and these can safely be combined with surface threads.

Always ensure that you purchase sufficient thread to finish a project, since batch shades can also vary.

NEEDLES

Three key types of needle are used for this form of whitework embroidery:

(A) Embroidery/crewel   These needles have sharp points and reasonably long eyes. They are easy to thread and are used for the majority of surface embroidery where the fabric needs to be pierced to produce an accurate stitch.

(B) Chenille   These have sharp points like crewel needles, but have longer eyes like tapestry needles. In larger sizes (24, 22, 20), they are excellent for use with heavier threads such as when plunging the core threads when working trailing. Finer chenille needles (26, 28) serve as a good alternative to embroidery/crewel needles if you struggle to thread the latter, due to the larger eye.

(C) Tapestry   These are blunt-tipped and have a longer eye. In whitework they are used for all stitches where the needle must push cleanly between the threads of the fabric, rather than piercing it, for example, pulled thread work, counted satin stitches and drawn thread work.

SELECTING THE NEEDLE TO USE

Your chosen thread should slide easily through the eye of the needle without dragging or wearing on the fibres.

When suspending the thread, the needle should not slide down the thread rapidly unaided as this will result in the needle slipping constantly during stitching.

The needle chosen should also make a large enough hole in the ground fabric to allow the thread to slide through easily without drag or wear. Too small a needle, and therefore hole, will cause a thread to wear rapidly.

There are no absolute rules governing which needle to use (apart from sharp for surface work and blunt for counted work), and it is ultimately best to sample stitches first and opt for the needle you find most comfortable to work with.

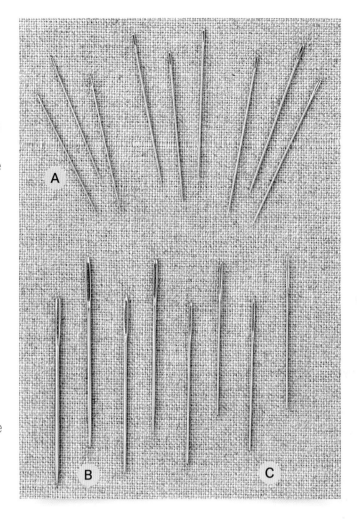

BEADS AND EMBELLISHMENTS

Embellishments can give extra dimension and life to some fine whitework designs. Tiny clear seed beads and glass pearls can add subtle sparkle. Small glass beads can also be used as a base for beautifully precise satin stitch dots. These must have a large hole in relation to their size to take the bulk of the satin stitches. Fine wire enamelled in white is used for edging three-dimensional embroidered shapes which are worked on a separate fabric, cut out and applied to the main design.

ESSENTIAL EQUIPMENT

Fine whitework requires the use of some traditional tools, most of which are easy to source or will already be found in your workbox.

Using high-quality tools will always be of benefit to the finished result.

(A) Acid-free tissue paper   Required for protecting and covering your embroidery whilst working.

(B) Blue plastic file divider   A thin, flexible sheet of coloured plastic sheeting (such as a file divider or folder) is required to create a barrier between linen and net layers in fine whitework, to allow the safe removal of linen to reveal the net insertion. The plastic should be sufficiently soft to allow a needle to pass easily through it.

(C) Tyvek   This fabric-like material is made from 100% high density polyethylene fibres. It is also extremely useful for protecting and covering your embroidery, but unlike tissue, will not tear, is water resistant yet breathable and is washable so can be used for long periods of time.

(D) A plain dark coloured cloth   To place over your knees to aid seeing the fine work.

(E) A plain white cloth   This can also be placed over your knees to aid seeing design lines.

(F) Stiletto   An essential tool for working eyelets. These are a smoothly tapered, usually metal tool, with a sharp tip, used to create round openings in the ground fabric. A stainless steel tool is highly recommended since it will not discolour the fabric. Antique stilettos in steel or bone are beautiful but care should be taken in use as they can often cause discolouration.

(G) Screwdriver   Used for tightening a ring frame.

(H) Thimble   An essential tool for all embroiderers but particularly so when working highly padded whitework.

(J) Tweezers   These are very useful for pressing and manipulating threads and stitches into place. Those with a curved or bent tip are very effective. Do not use those with a serrated tip, which can mark stitches.

(K) Mellor   This tool with a flat paddle at one end and a tapered blunt point at the other, originates from the field of goldwork embroidery but is superbly useful for whitework too. It too can be used as an effective laying and burnishing tool and is excellent for manipulating threads and stitches in tight places. Select a stainless steel mellor to avoid any risk of thread discolouration.

(L) Embroidery scissors   A pair of very fine, very sharp scissors with a smooth cutting action is essential for all whitework. Curved-tip scissors are highly recommended since these allow access to intricate points and curve away from the ground fabric when trimming ends and so on, avoiding risk of damage. Excellent for close trimming of fabric edges which are very often curved.

(M) Lobe-tipped lace scissors   These still have fine blades but one has a lobed tip. These are traditionally used for working Carrickmacross lace or similar, where layers of fine cotton lawn must be trimmed away in confined pockets without snipping the layer of tulle beneath. These are essential for cutting layers in fine whitework. The lobed tip can be safely pushed between the layers where the view is obscured.

(N) Awl   This term is sometimes used as an alternative to stiletto. However, here we are referring to a similar tool but with a very finely tapered tip and a sharp point. These are superb for opening up fine holes in whitework such as those in ladder stitch and pulled thread work.

(O) Aficot   These are a beautifully contoured embroidery tool, usually made in wood. They were originally based on a lobster claw and used in lacemaking for smoothing and burnishing. In embroidery and whitework they serve as an excellent laying tool. The larger end is held in the hand while the fine tip guides and tensions the working thread as it slides through the fabric, helping to keep stitches smooth, prevent tangling and keep threads in good condition.

They can also be used to burnish and smooth completed satin stitch and similar sculptured stitches.

(P) Pins   Very fine and smooth pins for use with delicate fabrics without leaving a mark. Always check that your pins are clean before using them on white fabrics.

EMBROIDERY HOOPS AND FRAMES

Working whitework embroidery on a beautifully taut base fabric is essential to a successful outcome. Here we will discuss the two key types of frames recommended for this style of work.

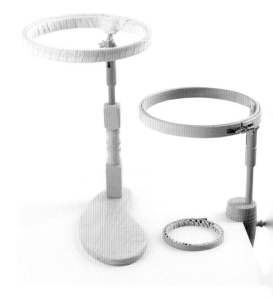

EMBROIDERY HOOPS/RINGS

For smaller projects an embroidery hoop works well. The hoop should have deep edges (about 2cm, or ¾in) and should be used with some form of stand. The latter is almost essential for whitework, allowing both hands to be free for working rather than holding the hoop.

Both rings of the hoop should be bound with cotton tape, bias binding, bandage strips or strips of cotton fabric, secured with stitching at the end. This protects the working fabric from possible abrasion or discolouration from the wooden hoop. It also helps to keep the fabric a great deal tighter. The tape can be replaced over time as required.

Deep-edged, bound hoops will ensure a very good working fabric tension for small pieces. Use a screwdriver to ensure the tensioning screw is as tight as possible. However, for larger, complex pieces or those which you will work on over a long period of time, a slate frame is highly recommended to ensure perfect tension.

BINDING AN EMBROIDERY HOOP

Apply a strip of narrow double-sided sticky tape to the outer edge of the upper section of the hoop.

Starting close to the screw, adhere the tip of your cotton tape to the edge. Proceed to bind the tape firmly and neatly around the perimeter of the hoop as shown. The tape should overlap slightly with each wrap, but not excessively, since this will cause bulk.

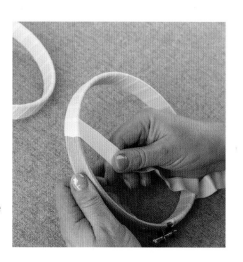

On completion, cut off the excess tape, fold over the end (on the outer rim of the hoop) and secure with neat oversewing. Secure the starting end fully with oversewing too.

Repeat for the inner ring of the hoop, this time applying the tape to the inner rim (thereby avoiding bulk between the two rings) and starting the binding at the joint. Be sure to cross the wrapping over the wood at the joint so that none of the wood rim remains exposed.

FRAMING UP A RING FRAME

It is essential to place the fabric into the hoop with care and ease it taut to a drum-tight tension, using the following method:

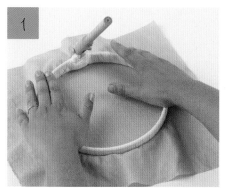

1 Remove the outer hoop and place this on a flat surface. Lay your fabric centrally over the top. Use two hands to press the inner hoop into the middle of the outer hoop, so that the fabric is trapped between them.

2 Gently begin to ease your fabric taut, taking care not to distort the fabric grain. Ease the screw of the hoop a little tighter using a screwdriver and then re-adjust the fabric to drum-tight tension. Finally, tighten the screw to its fullest extent to lock the tension in place. The hoop should remain tight whilst you work but from time to time may need another pull to maintain tension.

SLATE FRAMES

Slate frames are a traditional type of embroidery frame with two rollers, each with strong webbing tape applied along their length, and two corresponding arms. The top and bottom ends of the fabric are stitched to the webbing tape on the rollers. The arms slot into holes in the rollers; the rollers are pushed apart and the fabric is tensioned by slotting pegs into the holes in the arms on either side. The sides of the fabric are tensioned using lacing.

Slate frames are the best way to ensure beautiful and consistent tension across a fabric for embroidery. They retain tension well over a long period of time. They should be considered essential for working intricate and time-consuming whitework designs. They take time to prepare but this work pays back tenfold.

Ultimately, beautifully taut fabric makes working the embroidery much more pleasurable and results in a superior finish which is so vital for the success of a piece of whitework.

Slate frames tend to be named according to the length of webbing on the rollers; i.e. a '15in slate frame' has 15in- (38cm-) long webbing along its rollers. The length of webbing governs the maximum width of fabric which can be applied to the frame.

The fabric cut for a design should always be at least 8cm (3¼in) larger than the finished design to allow excess fabric for mounting on completion. Hence you should select your slate frame to have webbing at least equal too or slightly longer than this measurement.

Above, a slate frame supported on trestles.

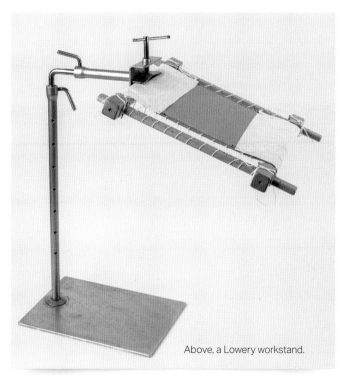

Above, a Lowery workstand.

SUITABLE STANDS FOR SLATE FRAMES

A slate frame must be supported by a suitable stand to allow the worker to use both hands for the embroidery. Traditionally, this would be in the form of trestles (above), which support even a large slate frame, allowing room for the worker to sit between. Smaller-size slate frames can be used on trestles by placing two slats/strips of wood across the trestles and resting the frame across these.

Trestles however can be quite an investment and take up a lot of space. Alternative stands are available such as the Lowery workstand pictured left, allowing a smaller slate frame (up to 38cm or 15in) to be clamped effectively along one edge. These allow greater flexibility in terms of sitting position, and are portable.

FRAMING UP

FRAMING UP A SLATE FRAME

Measure out your fabric. The selvedge of the fabric should run parallel with the length of the design. Allow 1cm (⅜in) excess on all sides to allow for the framing up process. Cut your fabric following the straight grain as closely as possible. Pull a thread of the fabric weave along each cut edge until you achieve one continuous thread. Trim away any excess fibres. This ensures that your fabric is absolutely straight to the grain line which is vital for many forms of whitework and is generally good practice.

YOU WILL NEED:

- Your chosen ground fabric (note that we have used blue fabric for clarity in these photographs
- Slate frame
- Dressmaking scissors
- Pins
- Strong buttonhole thread
- Acid-free tissue paper or Tyvek
- Nylon cord (of the type used for blind and light pulls)
- Sewing machine threaded with pale coloured or white thread
- A very large needle with an eye large enough to take the nylon cord (such as a packing needle)
- Stiletto

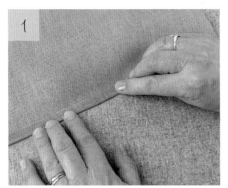

1 On a clean work surface, fold over 1cm (⅜in) along each side edge of the linen, following the straight grain as closely as possible, and finger press in place.

2 Take a length of fine nylon cord and lay along the side edges, placing this inside the fold made, just like a piping cord. The nylon cord should overhang at each end by about 2cm (or 1in). Pin in place.

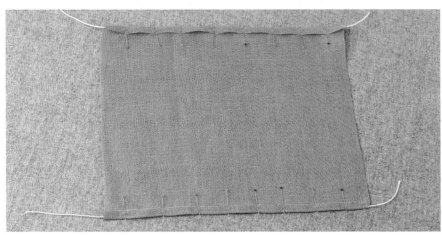
The fabric with cord threaded through on both long edges.

3 Use a straight machine stitch and the zipper foot to secure the cord inside the fold. Then work a zigzag to trap and seal the fabric edge.

4 Fold 1cm (⅜in) over along the top and bottom edges of the fabric, again following the straight grain, and finger press in place. Fold over the piping cord at the ends too.

Tip
If you don't have access to a sewing machine, use a hand-worked backstitch and strong buttonhole thread instead.

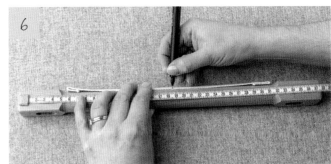

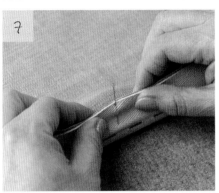

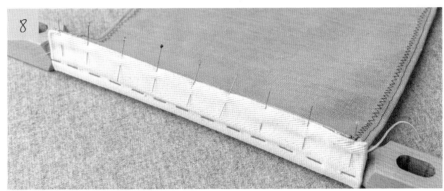

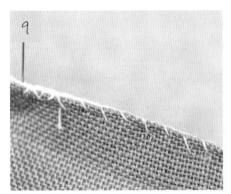

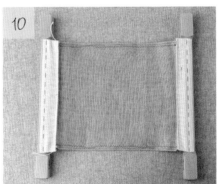

5 Fold the whole piece of fabric in half, bringing the two piped edges together, allowing you to find the centre point of the top and bottom edges. Mark these two centre points with pins.

6 Use a tape measure to measure the centre of the two wooden rollers of your slate frame, measuring from the outer tips of the roller (rather than just measuring the webbing itself). Mark these two centre points on the outer edge of the webbing attached to the rollers, using tacking or pencil.

7 Take the first roller; the folded bottom edge of the fabric will be matched to the edge of the webbing, the raw fabric edge being hidden between the roller and the fabric. Start by matching the centre point in the fabric to the centre point in the webbing. Pin together with the pins pointing vertically.

8 Continue to pin out to the sides, smoothing out the fabric and adding a pin every 2cm (or 1in). Repeat for the second roller.

9 Use strong buttonhole thread to oversew the folded edge of the fabric to the edge of the webbing, starting from the centre and working out to the left. Repeat from the centre out to the right. The oversewing stitches should alternate between about 1–2mm (1/16in) to 2–3mm (1/8in) deep and should consistently be about 3 4mm (1/8in–3/16in) apart. Pull them tight throughout. Oversew through the folded piping at the left and right ends to secure. Secure the working thread with tight oversewing stitches.

10 Repeat for the second roller and the top edge of the fabric.

11 At this point it's a good idea to attach a piece of protective fabric (Tyvek) or tissue paper, to be trapped into each roller. Cut two pieces of Tyvek or tissue paper to fit the width of the fabric and, working from the reverse of the frame place the Tyvek or tissue paper in position as shown and secure in place at each corner with a few stitches. If using Tyvek, it should be placed so that its shiny face will be drawn round the roller to sit face-to-face with the embroidery surface.

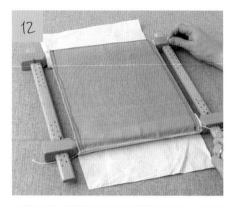

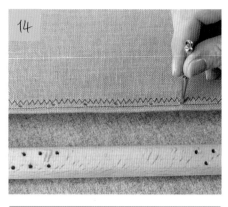

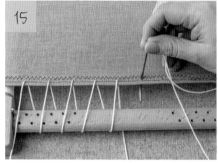

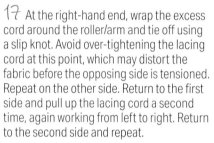

12 Roll any excess fabric onto the rollers and insert the arms. Stretch as much as you can by hand, inserting the pegs at the corresponding positions on either side to hold the tension evenly.

13 If required, the gentle pressure of a foot on each end of one of the rollers can be used to stretch the fabric further.

14 The sides can now be laced to tension further. Use a stiletto to ease a hole in the fabric at 2cm (¹³⁄₁₆in) intervals along each side edge. The holes should sit just between the straight stitch machine line and the zigzag.

15 Starting from the left-hand side, using a long length of fine nylon cord and your large needle, lace through the pre-made holes in the fabric, wrapping around the arm.

16 Tie off the left-hand end. Then ease up the slack a little in the lacing cord working from left to right.

17 At the right-hand end, wrap the excess cord around the roller/arm and tie off using a slip knot. Avoid over-tightening the lacing cord at this point, which may distort the fabric before the opposing side is tensioned. Repeat on the other side. Return to the first side and pull up the lacing cord a second time, again working from left to right. Return to the second side and repeat.

Your fabric should now be beautifully taut, even and straight, ready for work.

The fabric should now be straight, square and as tight as a drum. It should remain tight during work for a considerable time but if it does slacken, simply repeat the process of easing up the slack in the lacing, always working from left to right on each side.

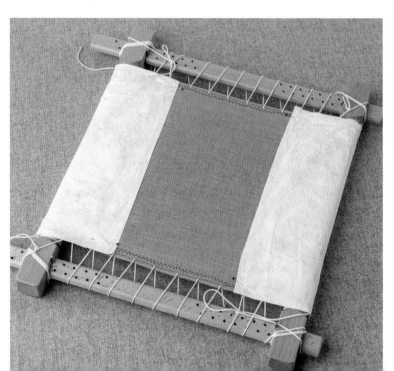

DESIGN INSPIRATION

Inspiration for whitework design can come from many sources and should only be limited by your imagination. However, sources which already show a sense of design stylization and perhaps also offer a combination of negative and solid spaces juxtaposed together, can provide excellent keys to captivating designs. For example:

- Carved plaster, stone and wood suggest the three-dimensional nature of whitework.

- Wrought iron is an excellent source for looking at the balance of negative against solid space.

- Designs of antique lace offer beautiful stylization and solid and open areas with the addition of patterns formed within.

- Stylized monograms are often traditionally worked in white-on-white; their bold, crisp forms serve beautifully as inspiration.

- Study the way in which plants and flowers are interpreted by wallpaper designers, printmakers, jewellers and engravers and the way in which they engage with simplified forms, textures and lines, with an absence of excessive colour.

If you choose to work from photographs, they do not have to be amazing. Sometimes simple, even blurry pictures can be useful; too much detail or information can be confusing, making it hard to extract those vital, beautiful shapes.

25

Design inspiration from my collection: antique whitework design books, carved printing blocks, needlework tools, photographs of stone carving, monograms and buttons.

CLARITY AND PRECISION

Traditionally, whitework techniques would be worked in pure white on pure white, ivory on ivory or beige on beige. Many of these techniques look at their absolute best when the thread colour matches the ground colour. If they vary, this can be distracting. We look at the thread colour instead of the tonal effects of the light catching the textured stitches set against the ground fabric.

One key aspect of white embroidery is that whatever stitches are worked, they must be worked with clarity and precision. Misaligned and distorted stitches, worn threads and so on cannot be hidden in a sea of colour. The work is stark and crisp, and anything which draws the eye away from this can immediately make the work look dull, discoloured, lifeless and confused.

The same is true in terms of clarity of stitch selection. An attempt to use an eclectic range of complex textured stitches to depict, for example, the varied plants of a garden, in white-on-white will turn to sludge. The design motifs first must be refined, stylized and simplified and the 'fuss' removed. Trying to depict a garden realistically in whitework, as you would in stumpwork for example, will not work. The key forms of each plant need to be extracted carefully and reduced to their beautiful essential and characteristic features. The spaces between them should be equally beautiful. This is much the same way as a printmaker would work to extract key design shapes to be depicted through the simplified layers of a wood block.

Then the stitches need to convey each part of the motif clearly and cleanly, choosing each with careful thought as to how it will convey the motif and how it will be juxtaposed against its neighbours without confusion. Less is always more and clutter is the curse of good whitework. You should always test your planned stitches on your fabric before embarking on a larger piece.

SOLID AND OPEN

One of the key aspects of whitework design which does not apply to other forms of embroidery is the balance of solid areas of stitching with areas where the fabric has been cut away, revealing open voids. Always consider the following:

• Open areas should generally be used for design features which make sense as a negative space – such as the sky behind a scene, water, background between leaves and flowers. Rarely do negative spaces work for design motifs which we would naturally think of as being solid, for example a section of a human figure or animal, the body of a butterfly, the frontage of a building. This is less applicable to a pattern-based design.

• Open areas tend to dominate whitework and naturally catch the eye, drawing us into a design. They therefore need to be carefully balanced throughout a design.

• Open areas can be planned to draw the eye on a journey through a design and into the distance beyond the embroidery's surface, so can be a powerful tool for creating a sense of depth and life.

Design inspiration for the *Small Birds May Fly High* project (see pages 128–187), showing the initial sketch through to the refined final drawing.

Design equipment

PREPARING THE DESIGN ON PAPER

The first step in preparing a design is to draw on paper with pencil. You may prefer to sketch freehand or to trace using a lightbox or tracing paper.

Once you have some initial drawings, stand away and view them from a distance, and live with them for a few days: pin them to a board or the fridge so that you can glance at them from time to time. This will help you understand what is working and what is not, and to see whether the design flows, or is crowded and needs elements to be removed.

- Lay tracing paper (or thin cartridge paper on a lightbox) and gradually refine and re-work the design. Keep standing back.

- Always include the final composition of the piece rather than just the motifs. For example, will a motif sit within a rectangle, a circle, or an organic shape? Look at the world around your design motifs and your composition, rather than seeing them just within the context of a sheet of paper. Often, the clever placement of design motifs will create interesting background shapes which call out for openwork techniques as a foil to solid forms.

- Once you are happy with the design, trace off a copy with clean, fine lines, simplifying as much as possible. Draw over these lines using a fine line marker so that you can place the design directly behind your white fabric without risk of pencil being transferred.

- Add vertical and horizontal straight centre lines using a set square. These will help to align the design with the straight grain of the fabric, if necessary for your design.

'The most important element in successful work is the choice of design… While inferior work can be tolerated for the sake of the design, if that is good… excellent work on a worthless design must be cast aside as labour lost… design is the very soul and essence of beautiful embroidery…' – May Morris, *Decorative Needlework*; Joseph Hughes & Co., London; 1893 (page 79).

THE TONAL AND TEXTURAL SCALE OF WHITEWORK

All key whitework stitches and techniques can be organized into a 'tonal and textural scale'. This scale runs from those which add the greatest extra body, height and whiteness to the ground fabric; to those which add low-relief texture and some additional whiteness; to those which open the fabric, to allow a little of the colour behind to penetrate (therefore appearing darker); and finally to those which allow removal of the fabric to create negative spaces and dark hollows.

It is fundamental to consider this scale when planning a whitework design and the stitches with which it will be worked; careful placement of the stitches will result in a design with a sense of depth, life and realism.

THE FINE WHITEWORK TONAL SCALE

'Whitest' design areas and areas of highest relief

1. Three-dimensional shapes (wired or soft). These may be needlelace, organza or embroidered fabric.

2. High-relief padded satin stitch, padded with laid bundles of thread.

3. Padded satin stitch, padded with satin or split stitches. Can be slanted, straight, voided or encroaching.

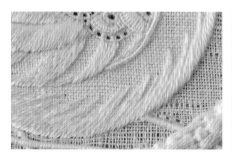

4. Dense surface stitches such as: fishbone, natural shading, closed fly stitch, closed buttonhole, French knots and bullion knots.

5. Counted satin stitch patterns

6. Seeding

7. Trailing: Tapered, bobbly, multiple rows.

8. Plain areas of double linen (shadow appliqué) and shadow work.

Background colour shows through the most and design sections become negative spaces, and so fall away from the eye.

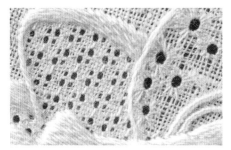

9. Pulled thread fillings.

10. Ladder stitch

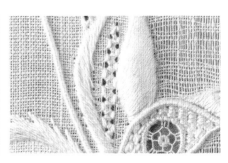

11. Three-sided stitch

12. Beading

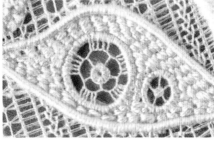

13. Single eyelets of various shapes and sizes, possibly filled with needlelace.

14. Drawn thread fillings with the threads removed vertically or horizontally only, or in both directions to create a grid.

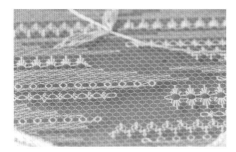

15. Net insertion with darned patterns.

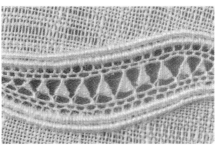

16. Open voids created using cutwork (possibly with the addition of needlelace fillings).

FINALIZING THE DESIGN OF THE STITCHES

Once you are happy with your outline design, you can then begin to plan the stitches using the Tonal and Textural Scale (see pages 28–29) as a guide.

Fill your design using tones of one colour, to illustrate the tonal grade created by the various stitches – you may like to use the colour you are considering placing behind the design on completion. This process will give you a better sense of the balance of the design, how the stitches are working with each other and how the positive and negative spaces are balanced and contrasted.

In the example given here:

• **White** is used for areas of surface stitching and double linen;

• **Very lightest shade** for areas of single linen;

• **Light shade** for areas of pulled thread work;

• **Medium shade** for areas of drawn thread work;

• **Darkest shade** for areas of net and the holes in eyelets, ladder stitch, three-sided stitch, beading and so on.

Use a fine pencil or pen to map in the directions of work for stitches such as satin stitch, natural shading and drawn thread. This will help you to ensure that these directions work together to create a fluid movement throughout the design. It can be helpful to make several copies of your coloured design and try drawing the stitches in different directions to see which works best.

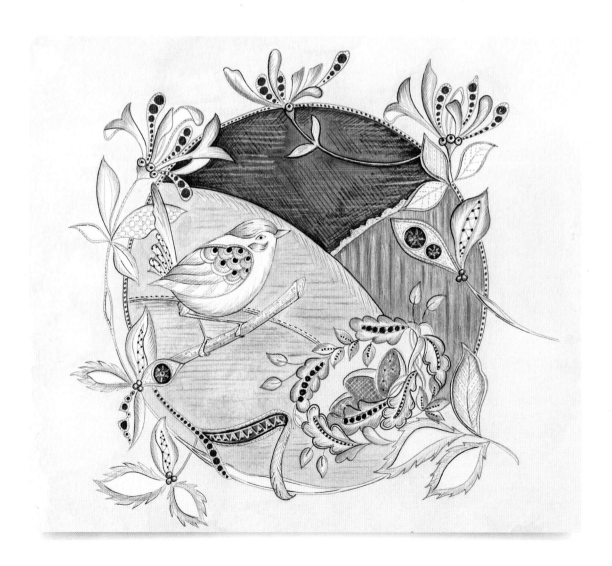

DESIGNING FOR FINE WHITEWORK EMBROIDERY

When designing for fine whitework specifically, there is a range of other points to consider to ensure the design will be visually effective and technically strong:

• Symmetrical designs can be very challenging, but can be stunning if you are happy to take on the added complexity of making the two halves the same.

• Creating a perfectly circular design can also be challenging, but it can often be helpful to break the circle with another design shape in order to distract the eye from concentrating on the circle itself – see the design shown opposite, which forms the basis of the *Small Birds May Fly High* embroidery on pages 128–187.

• Creating long, perfectly straight lines on fabric in stitches such as trailing can be difficult, for architectural subjects for instance. You can either accept that lines inevitably move a little when worked on fabric, or create distractions by lapping design motifs over the lines. Alternatively, use a softer technique to create lines – a line worked in scattered French knots and free eyelets may look straighter than a length of straight trailing.

• Areas of net insertion and drawn thread work should not be too small and intricate as this can make cutting the fabric away very difficult.

• Areas of net insertion should not be too large, else they may stretch, distort or tear. Distortion can be a great deal more apparent if the design shape has straight sides.

• Consider the direction and scale of pulled thread patterns and how these will enhance the flow of the design.

• Consider also the direction and scale of drawn thread patterns. Drawn thread has either a strong linear or grid structure so must be placed carefully within a design. Its bold lines can help to draw the eye through a design in the desired direction.

• Areas of net and drawn thread must be surrounded by strong stitching to allow the fabric threads to be cut away, without risk to the surrounding work. If this is trailing, there must be two rows, or one row with another stitch next to it (such as chain stitch, backstitch, chain with backstitch, stem stitch or ladder stitch), on the side furthest from the openwork. The border to the openwork could also be satin stitch; however, if this is worked directly against drawn thread, the satin stitches can be disturbed by the removal of the threads. It is therefore a good idea to edge the satin with trailing in these circumstances.

• Avoid applying a second layer of linen next to a voided area of net insertion. This would mean that linen has to be trimmed away both on the front and reverse of the work around the delicate net area, resulting in a distracting double rim of trimmed fabric.

• Avoid trapping the double layer in tiny 'pockets' of the design where you eventually want to have single linen/net. It will be very fiddly, and therefore time consuming and risky, to remove the second layer in these areas.

ORDER OF WORK

The order of work in fine whitework is very important to ensure maximum visual effect, to avoid trapping the second layer of fabric unnecessarily and to ensure the design is technically possible and is strong on completion, despite the removal of fabric.

The following pages describe the best order of work. Colour-shade the key stages on copies of your drawn design, as demonstrated – this will help you to plan the construction, and highlight any possible issues before starting. These illustrations will also serve as an invaluable reference while stitching.

1 Frame the linen and draw on the design on a taut frame (see page 35).

2 Work the net darning patterns onto the tulle.

3 Apply the tulle to the reverse of the linen on a slackened frame. This allows the net to be thoroughly bound into the design as the embroidery is completed, providing extra strength.

4 Work all areas of pulled thread work (shown here coloured in pale blue).

Small Birds May Fly High

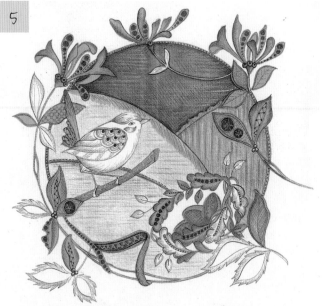

5

Small Birds May Fly High

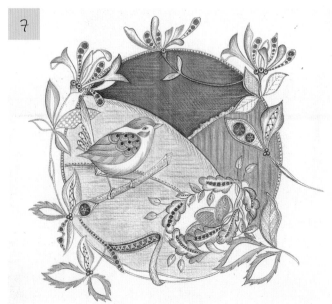

7

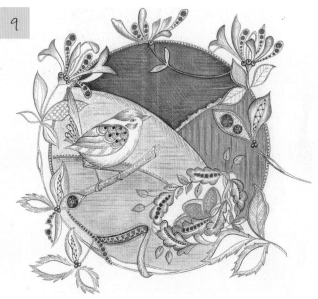

9

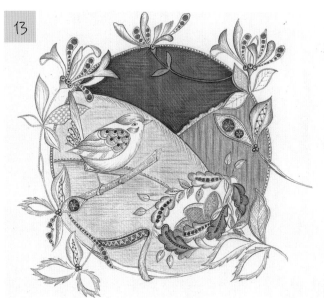

13

5 Work all the surface embroidery stitches, eyelets, and so on, which are to be worked on a single layer of linen (i.e. they have single linen on either side of them and are not required to secure a second layer) – shown here in pink.

6 Apply the second layer of linen on the reverse of the work on a taut frame.

7 Work all surface embroidery required to secure the second layer of linen in place and that sitting within the double layer design motifs (as shown here, shaded in lime).

8 Cut away the excess linen around the motifs on the reverse.

9 Work the drawn thread work: remove the threads on a slack frame and tighten again to work patterns, as shown here in yellow.

10 Add any surface embroidery required over the top of the drawn thread work.

11 Wash the work while still on the taut frame (see page 177).

12 Slacken the frame to cut away the linen, revealing the net. Tighten the frame very gently.

13 Work any final details which may cross the net and apply any three-dimensional embroidered shapes (shaded green, right).

TRANSFERRING THE DESIGN TO FABRIC

Transferring a design for whitework is perhaps more difficult than for other forms of embroidery, due to the delicate nature of the stitching and fabrics, and the need to be sure that lines will be covered successfully. Usually, whitework fabrics are sufficiently fine to allow a design to be traced on from the original printed outline. Some designs can be seen easily through the fabric, while others require the assistance of a lightbox.

My preferred medium for tracing onto fine white fabrics (linen, cotton, silk and silk organza) is a very fine, 0.1mm diameter pale grey marker pen, the Pin, currently produced by uni-ball (shown right). These are also available in sepia and a slightly darker grey in 0.1mm, and in 0.05 and 0.03mm in black. They produce a beautifully delicate line and do not bleed. The lines are permanent so must be covered completely by your embroidery. The pens are water-resistant so are not affected by washing your work at the end of a piece.

If you do not wish to use a pen, try using a pale blue, non-water-soluble pencil crayon or blue propelling pencil but ensure that the point is kept very sharp at all times while drawing. The pencil crayon can also wear away while working the embroidery so keep the lines covered to prevent this. Avoid using pencils with a very soft tip, which can smudge easily. I recommend the permanent 'Pablo' series by Caran D'Ache in shade Sky Blue 666.141.

Avoid using graphite pencils as these will tend to discolour your white threads. Water-soluble and 'friction' pens are also not recommended as they are temperamental and colour can reappear over time.

KEY FACTORS IN TRANSFERRING A DESIGN SUCCESSFULLY

It is important that a whitework design is planned and is carefully and accurately drawn on paper before attempting to transfer this to the fabric. The minimum of design lines required to work a piece should be drawn onto the fabric and tiny details, or shapes which could be worked successfully by eye, should be avoided.

For example a spray of tiny eyelets may just require a central dot to mark each position. Two parallel design lines close together may just require one line to follow. The fewer the lines the better.

- The outline design on paper must be clear and crisp, ideally drawn using a permanent black fine-liner.
- Be sure that all pencil is removed as this can cause discolouration of the fabric.
- The fabric must be very taut and smooth.
- Your hand must be steady: practise on spare fabric until you feel confident that you can maintain clean lines. Do not forget to breathe whilst drawing! Tension leads to wobbly lines.
- Avoid hesitation, which can lead to heavy lines. Move quickly and with confidence.
- Using the natural pivot of your hand to draw into curves will assist with ensuring these are smooth. Use a pair of compasses, which will hold a pen, for larger circular lines.
- Place clean tissue paper under your hand while drawing to keep the work clean. Cover the excess fabric surrounding your design with tissue to prevent marks in the wrong place.

Tip

If you don't have a lightbox, try using a piece of glass or perspex, supported between two tables, with a spotlight placed behind.

Tip

A plastic template for drawing circles of all sizes is an invaluable tool for drawing eyelets.

TRACING ON SMALLER DESIGNS WHEN USING A HOOP

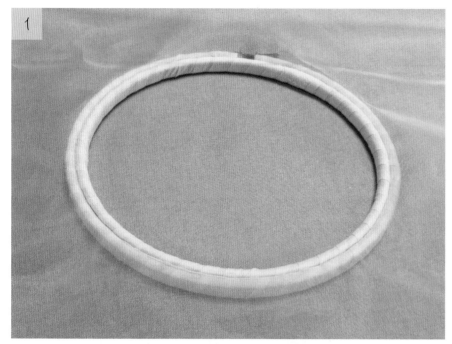

1 Frame up a shallow-edged hoop with your fabric (here, silk organza), following the instructions on page 20.

2 Photocopy the design template (here, the scabiosa shown on page 189), and place this flat on your work surface, securing with tabs of tape. Place the organza centrally on top, the fabric pushed flat against the design. Align the straight grain of the fabric through the centre of the design. Holding the hoop steady, carefully trace the design lines using a very fine marker pen. Keep all lines as delicate as you possibly can.

3 Use the pen in a pair of compasses to make drawing circles more accurate. Once drawn, release the screw and remove the fabric from the hoop.

4 Turn the fabric over and place in your deep-edged hoop, ready for work. The drawn lines will be uppermost. Ease the fabric taut carefully, taking great care not to distort the design lines. Lock the tension in place by tightening the screw fully.

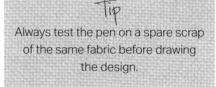

Tip
Always test the pen on a spare scrap of the same fabric before drawing the design.

TRACING ON DESIGNS WHEN USING A SLATE FRAME

This method is suitable for larger designs and those which require the design to be aligned accurately to the straight grain of the fabric.

1 Frame up your piece of linen in your slate frame as described on pages 22–24.

2 Using a clean tape measure or ruler, measure the vertical centre of the fabric.

3 With a length of pale coloured tacking thread, work a running stitch vertically down the centre of the fabric, following the straight grain of the weave. While stitches should be approximately 5mm (³⁄₁₆in) long, accuracy of length is not important here but the tacking must be kept straight. The length of the tacking line need only span the depth of the design.

4 Measure the horizontal centre and repeat the tacking process again in this direction to form a cross through the centre of your fabric. Again, this needs only to be long enough to span the design.

5 Place your taut slate frame upside-down over a lightbox, with the reverse of the fabric facing you. Your outline design should also have horizontal and vertical centre lines drawn clearly using a set square.

6 Turn your design upside-down so that the reverse is facing you. Place this over the taut linen, aligning the printed vertical and horizontal design lines with those tacked onto the fabric. The alignment does not have to be exact but should be as close as possible.

Tip

If you have difficulty aligning the tacking with the printed lines, this is often because the tension of your slate frame is not even. Try adjusting the tension of the side lacing to straighten and align the design.

7 Use tabs of low-tack sticky tape to secure the design to the reverse of the linen. It is vital that you align your design with the straight grain of the linen at the start of a project: many whitework designs include the use of counted pulled and drawn thread work, which must follow the grain.

TRACING THE DESIGN

1 Turn the slate frame back to the right side. Working over a lightbox, carefully trace the design using a pale grey fine-liner pen. Start at the top and gradually work down over the design towards your body. Place a piece of tissue paper beneath your hand as you work so that you are not leaning directly on the fabric.

2 Place your free hand beneath the frame as you work, to push the printed design up against the reverse of the fabric, enabling you to see the design lines more clearly.

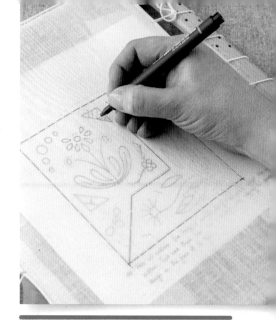

TACKING DESIGN LINES

If your design contains a lot of straight lines, you can tack the major lines onto your linen, following the straight grain, prior to drawing on the curved lines and more detailed sections. This is particularly important if the design is to include counted pulled and drawn work patterns which must be aligned with the straight design areas.

• Begin by working bisecting centre vertical and horizontal lines as described on page 35. Place your printed outline design under your taut fabric.

• Use fine pins to mark the positions of a few of the key design lines.

• Take away the printed design and use pale coloured tacking thread to work running stitch lines between your pins.

• Keep replacing the design and adding further pin markers before tacking again, until you have created a framework of the key straight design lines.

• Draw in, rather than tack, any small, intricate design lines to avoid confusing the working process.

• Trace the rest of your design following the method described on pages 34–35. When you place your printed design in position, take great care to align this with your tacking lines. However, remember that the tacking is not permanent – if some areas do not align fully, you can adjust the placement when you work the embroidery.

USING A PRE-PRINTED DESIGN

Many people find drawing directly onto fabric intimidating and difficult. If this is the case, seek professional help to apply the design for you, or purchase a pre-printed linen. The accurate application of a whitework design is vital to its success so it is advisable to use this option if you have any concerns.

Note

If you are working a design where you are unsure how a design area will be stitched, or whether an outline will be worked around the design shape (covering a design line), it is useful to tack the shape of these elements rather than drawing them. This will give you a chance to adjust the shapes if required.

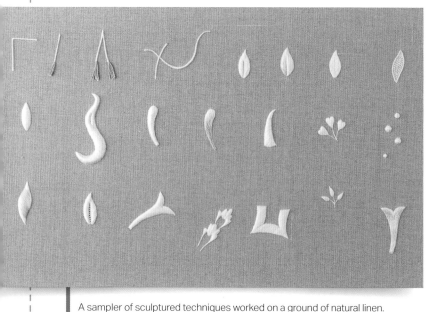

A sampler of sculptured techniques worked on a ground of natural linen.

WORKING A PREPARATORY STITCH SAMPLER

The following chapters, beginning on page 38, provide in-depth instruction for working all of the fundamental techniques of the whitework tonal scale, which can be used to produce effective fine whitework, and indeed all whitework, designs. These techniques have been divided into five key sections according to their position in the tonal scale and as an aid to their suggested use: sculptured, translucent, filigree, fretted and voided. Working the suggested samples of each technique will provide an invaluable body of experience as a preparation for working full designs and for working whitework embroidery as a whole.

Fine whitework requires accuracy and dexterity of workmanship to produce beautiful results. Hence, practice via sampling should be considered essential.

These samples can produce a beautiful body of work in their own right, which can be presented as an attractive sampler. The samplers of previous generations of whiteworkers are equally as fascinating and beautiful as the finished products.

ESSENTIAL STARTING TECHNIQUES

THE WASTE-KNOT TECHNIQUE

Generally all threads are started using the waste-knot technique (WKT).

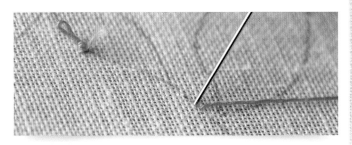

1 Knot the thread and take the needle down through the fabric from the front of the work, near to where you will start stitching. Place the knot on a design line or within an area of the design which will be covered by stitching – on plain fabric, it may leave a mark.

2 Work two tiny backstitches side-by-side along a design line, or within a design area. Begin your embroidery, then cut away the knot and tail neatly once the thread is fully secured. Curved-tip scissors are very useful for doing this.

Tips

Avoid carrying threads between worked areas as these will show through. As many areas of whitework will be worked using 'openwork' techniques, take extra care when placing starting and finishing stitches to ensure that they are hidden.

If you run out of places to work the two backstitches, turn to the reverse of the work and instead work two tiny oversewing stitches into the back of the existing stitching.

FINISHING THREADS

Work two backstitches on a design line or within a design area, bring your thread to the surface of the work and cut away the tail close to the fabric. If you no longer have space in which to do this, turn the work to the reverse and pass the thread through the back of your stitching for about 0.5cm (¼in), or work a couple of small oversewing stitches into the reverse of existing stitching. Cut away the excess thread.

ESSENTIAL STITCHES

WORKING A FRENCH KNOT

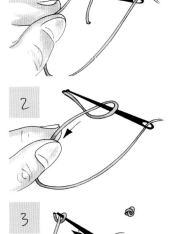

1 Bring the needle up where you wish the French knot to sit. Hold the needle parallel to the ground fabric. Wrap the thread around the needle once.

2 Pull the needle back and pivot it around until you can insert the tip next to the point at which the needle originally emerged. Pull the working thread as shown, easing the loop/knot formed down until it sits snugly against the fabric.

3 Keep hold of the taut working thread whilst you push the needle down and through with the other hand. Let go of the working thread at the last minute and ease the remaining thread through to the reverse. You should have a neat plump knot, as shown.

WORKING A BULLION KNOT

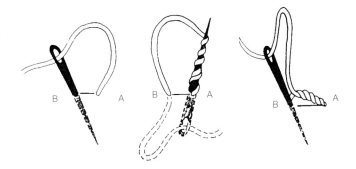

1 Bring the needle up at A and down at B: this is the finished length of the knot.

2 Bring the needle up again at A and, with the needle remaining half in the fabric, wind the working thread around the needle in an anti-clockwise direction. Add enough twists so that, when compacted, they fill the space chosen in step 1. Lay the needle down to check this. Don't pull the twists too tight.

3 While gripping the twists lightly with your finger and thumb, pull the needle up to emerge through the twists. Keep hold of the twists while you pull all of the excess thread through. The twists will tighten to fit the space as shown. Manipulate the thread until the twists sit smooth and neat across the space. Take the needle back down through the fabric to complete the knot.

SCULPTURED TECHNIQUES

Techniques which create sculptured form and textured relief on the fabric surface are fundamental to whitework embroidery: they create height and a sense of depth, enhanced further by their juxtaposition against open or translucent areas.

Textured and sculptured forms should have a strong sense of definition in terms of shape and clarity of workmanship – without this, the design may be difficult to read. Any stitch which creates a texture can be worked in white thread on a white ground. However, whether a sculptured stitch is effective or not in white-on-white will depend on several factors:

- **Choice of thread and ground fabric** In terms of both texture and weight – a feather stitch worked in very fine thread on a coarse, loosely woven fabric may not be discernable, but can be very effective if worked densely on a closely woven fabric. Generally, sculptured techniques work best on fabrics with a fairly dense weave, since this supports the heavy work effectively.

- **Size of stitch** Tiny, sparse seeding stitches may be invisible if worked in white thread on a white ground, but could have significant impact if worked, closely packed, in a bolder thread;

- **Clarity and efficiency of working technique** Padded satin stitch worked with uneven edges and at uneven angles may cause the overall design shape to be lost and can appear rough and ragged where there is no colour to catch the attention. In contrast, satin stitch worked smoothly with flowing stitch angles and precise edges captures the light and appears to look like sculptured plaster or icing.

The following chapter provides an effective palette of sculptural textures for whitework and advises the best way to work these techniques to achieve maximum clarity and effect. These methods can be applied to many other forms of embroidery.

COUNTED SATIN-STITCH PATTERNS

Counted satin patterns are composed of blocks of straight stitches, worked vertically, horizontally or diagonally to form organized patterns on the weave of the ground fabric. They add the density of satin stitch to the fabric without creating significant height, while also adding texture and pattern.

Experimenting with changing the size, density and orientation of traditional, existing patterns can produce varied results; new patterns are also easy to create. Blackwork darning patterns and canvaswork stitches can provide good sources of ideas.

Fabric: Counted satin stitches require a fabric wherein the warp/weft threads can be easily seen and counted – not too open, not too dense. These samples are worked on an evenweave linen which is 12 threads/cm (30 threads/in).

Thread: The working thread should generally be slightly heavier than an individual thread of the ground fabric. Threads with a degree of twist – perlé cotton, Coton à Broder or stranded cotton – are also more suitable than loosely spun threads. These samples are worked in Retors d'Alsace, no. 12.

Needle: Use a blunt-tipped tapestry needle to push between the threads of the woven ground fabric, rather than piercing them.

Tip

All counted satin stitches must be worked in a continuous pattern and with a wrapping motion which encircles the reverse as well as the front of the fabric. This ensures that the satin will appear plump and rounded, resulting in maximum effect.

If you are working a stitch to fill a rounded shape, adjust the length of the satin stitches to fit to the curved edge as closely as possible.

A SELECTION OF COUNTED SATIN-STITCH PATTERNS

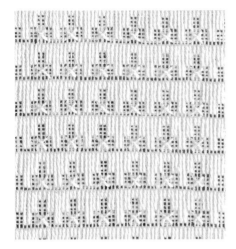

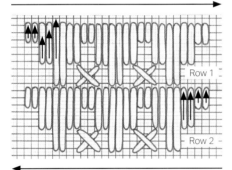

Work two vertical stitches over two threads of the linen, following the direction of the arrows. Work all stitches with a wrapping motion. Then work two stitches over four threads of the linen, followed by two over six; return to two over four. Repeat along the row.

Work the second row below the first as shown above.

Add cross stitches over three by three linen threads in the spaces left between the rows.

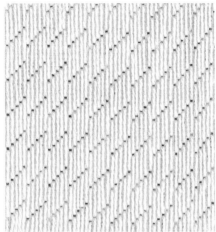

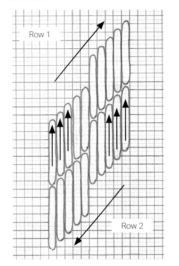

Work a vertical satin stitch over eight linen threads, following the arrows. From the base of this stitch, move one thread right and one thread up and repeat the stitch over eight. Repeat to form a stepped block of five stitches each over eight. All stitches are worked in a wrapping motion.

Move one thread right and four threads up to work the next vertical stitch over eight linen threads. The new stitch therefore aligns with the halfway point of the previous stitch. Work the block of five stitches in the same fashion. Continue.

The following row slots up against the first row as shown. It is always best to work the stitches of the new row towards those of the first row so that the needle goes down into the shared holes.

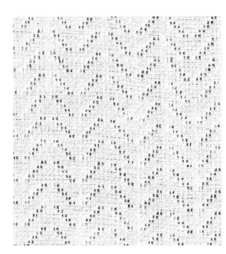

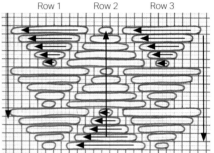

Work a horizontal stitch over 10 linen threads, following the arrows. Work a further horizontal stitch directly below and central to the first, but this time over eight threads. Work further stitches over six, then four, then two directly below, forming a triangle. Repeat these triangles to form a vertical row.

Leaving one linen thread between the rows, work a new row of triangles in the opposite direction, each stitch falling in line with those of the previous row. The triangles will interlock together with a narrow space between.

Leaving one linen thread between the rows again, repeat row 1 to create row 3.

THREADED SATIN STITCH HONEYCOMB

SATIN BLOCKS

Work a small block of vertical satin stitch: work four stitches, each over four threads of the linen, each worked from bottom to top. This ensures a wrapping motion to the stitches. Each stitch has one thread of the linen between it and the next.

Once one block is complete, move diagonally down to work the next block to the right.

Continue to work the blocks in a diagonal row. On reaching the bottom of the row, work back up to the top with a second diagonal row so that the blocks form a chequerboard pattern. When working back to the top, work all stitches from top to bottom, again to ensure a wrapping motion.

Continue to work diagonal rows back and forth until the design shape has been filled.

THREADING

Once the design has been filled with satin stitch blocks, these can be threaded in horizontal zigzagging rows, as the diagram, left, shows.

The threading lifts and compacts the satin blocks, giving them greater prominence and definition, and creates the beautiful honeycomb effect.

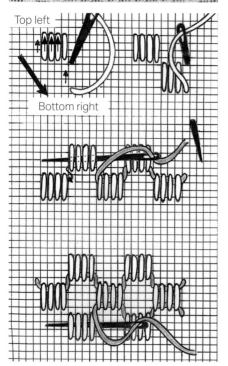

Top left

Bottom right

FREELY WORKED SATIN-BASED TECHNIQUES

These techniques are fundamental to the art of fine whitework, to most forms of whitework, and indeed to many other forms of embroidery. They create sumptuous surface design textures with great clarity and therefore serve as an excellent drawing medium for portraying some of the boldest and most eye-catching structures within a design.

Fabric: Traditionally, dense linens or cottons are used – these may be heavy or fine, but must be densely woven. In practice, any fabric which can support the weight of this heavy form of stitching without puckering is suitable. Even organza can be used if held taut in a frame.

Thread: A reasonably soft thread without excessive twist is preferable, allowing the stitches to blend smoothly for an overall sculptured effect wherein individual stitches are not visible. Stranded cotton for fine work and Floche à Broder work very well. For slightly bolder, heavier work and sampling, perlé cotton, Retors d'Alsace, Coton à Broder and knitting cotton are also effective.

Needle: Sharp embroidery needles for fine threads, or chenille needles for heavier threads, can be used.

The pattern shapes can be found on page 188.

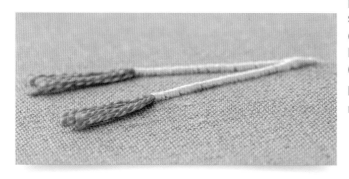

TRAILING

Trailing is a method of couching – applying thread to the ground fabric by working binding stitches over the top. In trailing, the thread being couched (the 'core thread') is completely covered by dense couching stitches, producing a beautiful sculptured cord effect. The thickness of trailing can be tapered to produce undulating lines.

Trailing has excellent drawing qualities, producing, crisp, clear lines, either curvilinear or straight. It is strong and durable and, as such, has been used in many forms of whitework embroidery; it is excellent for sealing together layers of fabric.

The first sample shown below is worked in perlé cotton no. 8 – please note that the coloured threads are for clarity of photography only.

The template for this sample can be found on page 188.

The template for this sample can be found on page 188.

Tip

Stranded cotton makes an excellent core thread for finer work. This thread contains six divisible strands. If using it as a core, it is best not to separate these strands, as the twist in the threads helps to keep the trailing firm. However, if you wish to use more than six strands, you can add further individual strands to the bundle.

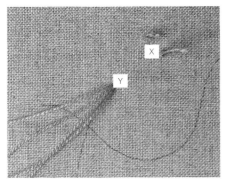

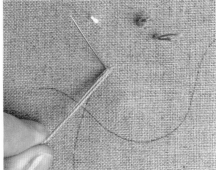

STARTING THE CORE THREADS

When working a design, the initial knot should be positioned on a design line, or well away from the working design area, to ensure that the surrounding fabric is not damaged.

Take your chosen number of core threads – here, four strands. Take two of the strands and knot them together at the end. The needle descends through the fabric a short distance from the starting point of the trailing (X). The needle emerges at the starting tip of the trailing (Y).

Repeat for the remaining pair of core threads. Each should emerge at a slightly different point at the start of the trailing, to avoid making a large hole in the fabric.

Finer threads may be brought to the surface at the start of the trailing in small groups rather than individually. Heavier threads should always be worked individually.

STARTING THE TRAILING

Take a length of your stitching thread and secure this with two tiny backstitches, at the tip of the design line, beneath your core threads. To begin the trailing, pull the anchored threads to tension them. The working needle emerges as shown, angling it out from beneath the core threads at approximately 45° to the ground fabric. It then descends on the far side, tucked at an angle towards and under the core threads, again at 45°. Pull the stitch down to sit snugly around the core.

The cross-section diagram below shows these correct working needle angles, which ensure a lovely, rounded appearance to the finished effect, The diagram also shows that the needle does not emerge and descend in the same hole beneath the trailing. Instead, a small amount of fabric is pinched into the stitch below. This stabilizes the trailing, allowing it to sit firmly and to be used as an effective stitch to secure fabric layers together.

Continue to bind the core threads in the same fashion. All stitches sit perpendicular to the line of the trailing and are positioned close together so that the core thread is fully obscured. Avoid over-packing the stitches, however, as this can cause distortion.

Maintain tension on the core threads to ensure a smooth trailing. The core threads should always lie along the design line rather than being moved from side to side.

Far left, the correct stitch angle, producing a rounded profile; left, an incorrect needle angle, producing a flattened profile.

FINISHING THE TRAILING

Approximately 5mm (³⁄₁₆in) before you reach the tip of the section of trailing, take each core thread in turn and proceed as follows. If there is nowhere convenient to allow the core threads to emerge like this, plunge them at the tip and hold them taut on the reverse of the work while finishing the trailing.

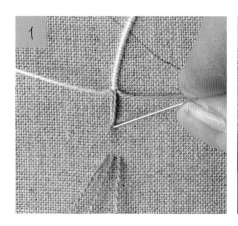 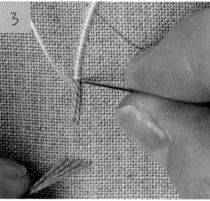 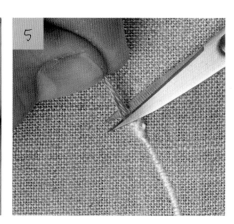

1 Plunge each core thread in turn down at the tip of the trailing line.

2 Bring the needle up a short distance away.

3 Once all the core threads have been treated in this way, continue the trailing to the tip of the design line. Apply tension to the core threads as you work.

4 At the end, turn the work to the reverse and secure the stitching thread by working two tiny oversewing stitches, caught into the reverse of the trailing.

5 Trim the core threads flush to the end of the trailing. It can be helpful to cut one thread away at a time to ensure a very neat finish. Curved-tip scissors can be helpful here.

There is no need to leave any excess core thread on the reverse as the threads are thoroughly sealed in place by the dense surface binding.

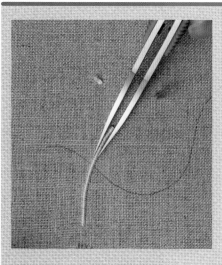

Tips

If you find it difficult to see where the last trailing stitch was placed (which can be an issue in white-on-white), move the core thread slightly to the side each time you place a new stitch. You will then be able to see clearly where the angle of the core thread changes and place your new stitch snugly against the previous one.

It is not essential to bind the trailing in the direction shown. If you are more comfortable binding in the opposite direction, this is no problem. If you wish to change the direction of binding halfway along a section, work a tiny locking stitch in the fabric beneath the trailing before doing so.

Use tweezers to pinch along the trailing: this will help smooth any slight distortions.

WORKING TAPERED TRAILING AND CROSSING BEHIND EXISTING TRAILING

STARTING THE TRAILING

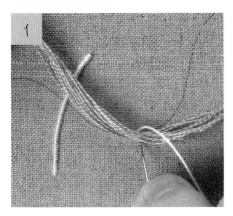 

1 Take a bundle of core threads (here, 10 lengths of perlé cotton). Lay this along your design line where you intend the heaviest section of trailing to be. Begin your stitching thread with two tiny backstitches beneath this point. Then begin trailing as before, angling the needle out from beneath the core threads as it emerges, and down beneath them as it returns.

2 Keep tension on the core thread as you work.

TAPERING THE TRAILING

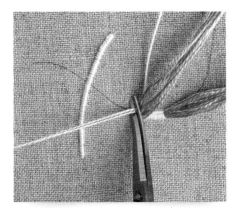

Fold the core thread back on itself. Separate out the number of strands to be removed (in this case, two). Push your scissors in tightly beneath the core thread and cut the threads away very close. Curved-tip scissors are useful for this process. The core threads are then laid back along the line and the trailing continues.

Repeat this process of removing core threads as you work along this section: the trailing gradually becoming thinner. By the time the trailing meets the existing perpendicular section, the core should be reduced to four threads only.

Note

There are no strict rules to suggest how many strands you should remove at any point of a piece of trailing. It is dependent on how fine the core threads are (finer threads, and those in large bundles, can be removed in larger groups as the effect will be less dramatic), how long the design line and how dramatically you wish to taper the thickness along that line. If in doubt, work tentatively: remove fewer threads, then work a couple more trailing stitches.

If the diameter remains too heavy, remove more threads. Selecting how many threads to take, and where to take them from, develops with practice.

PLUNGING BENEATH AN EXISTING PIECE OF TRAILING

As you approach the existing trailing, thread each remaining core thread into a needle and tuck it down against the existing trailing. It will emerge on the other side, again tucked close to the trailing.

Where one section of trailing bisects another in this way, the upper section of trailing should be worked first, as instructed here; the lower section then passes behind it. If the lower section of trailing is worked first, it will be difficult to judge how large a space to leave, for the upper section to cut through it.

FINISHING THE TRAILING

Continue the trailing on the far side of the crossing point, tapering further if required. The trailing is finished in the manner previously described on page 42.

Complete the remaining section of trailing in the same manner, tapering as you wish.

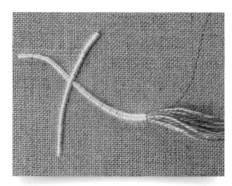

WORKING 'BOBBLY' TRAILING

Along the length of a piece of trailing, a large needle (such as a tapestry needle) can be inserted, every so often, beneath the core thread. Trailing stitching continues on the other side. A small loop of core thread is formed, creating a 'bobbly' effect to the trailing.

Working bobbly trailing.

WORKING A SECOND ROW OF TRAILING

If you wish to work a second row of trailing against an existing one, bring the needle up, to the outside of the second row, and take it down again, angled towards the existing row. This ensures that the second row is pulled snugly up against the first.

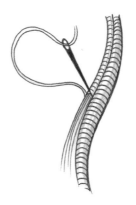
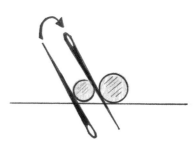

Working a second row of finer trailing against an existing line to create a tiered effect.

Cross-section to show the correct angle of the emerging and descending needle.

TRAILING AT AN ACUTE POINT

It is ineffective to bend trailing around an acute point, as this will result in an awkward, heavy finish. It is more effective to work two separate lines of trailing and blend them together at the acute point.

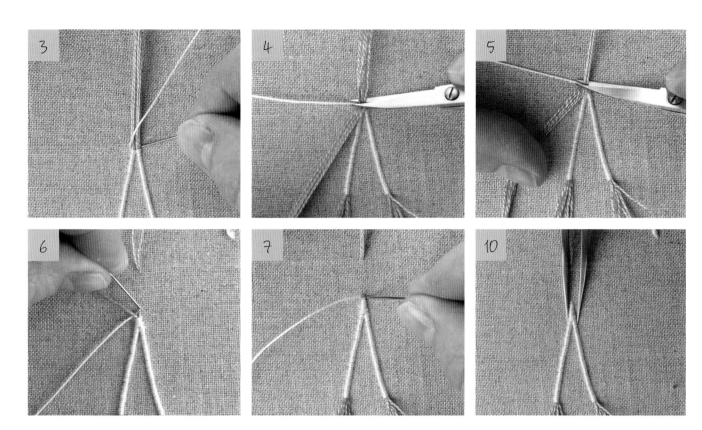

1 Work the two sections of trailing leading into the acute point (here, each bundle has five strands of no. 8 perlé cotton). Stop just short of the point as the two lines of trailing begin to touch each other.

2 Take one of the two stitching threads out of work, leaving it to the side (this can be finished on the reverse later).

3 Take a stitch over the two bundles of core threads to draw them together. Take care not to pull this in too tight, in order to maintain the smooth edges.

4 Peel back the core threads and use curved-tip scissors to closely snip away a few of the combined strands from the bottom of the pile (here, four).

5 Work a further couple of trailing stitches over the remaining strands. Then peel the core threads back again to remove a few more (here, two).

6 Plunge the remaining core threads down one at a time at the tip of the point, bringing each up again a little further away. Distribute the points at which you plunge each thread so that they do not all go through the fabric at the same point, thus helping to make the point sharper and finer.

7 Complete the binding of the trailing to the tip, putting tension on the tails of core thread at the same time.

8 Turn to the reverse of the work and secure this and the other stitching thread by oversewing into the back of the trailing.

9 Cut off the excess core threads cleanly against the end of the trailing.

10 Use tweezers to pinch the end of the completed trailing to sharpen the point further.

STARTING TRAILING WITH A LOOP

This is another effective way to begin a single line of trailing. It has a slightly more prominent tip, which works well at the tip of a flower stem, for instance.

1 Secure the stitching thread at the tip of the trailing using the WKT (see page 37). Take your core threads (here, two) and fold in half. Take a stitch up through the loop of core threads and secure at the tip of the design line. Work a tiny locking stitch on the design line beneath the trailing to keep the loop in place.

2 Work three to four trailing stitches over the bundle of core threads, starting these just shy of the tip of the trailing. The tip of the trailing will not be covered at this point since if you begin trailing at the very tip, the stitches are likely to slip off the end.

3 Work back to the tip to complete this section. Continue with your trailing along the main design line.

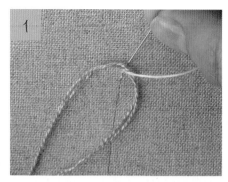
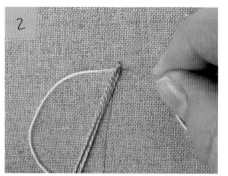
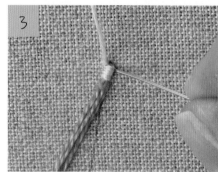

Adding a new thread into the trailing

If you have tapered your trailing to make it thinner, you may wish to increase the thickness again further along the line. This is achieved by knotting the core threads, taking the knot down at the side of the work and introducing a new thread to the main core, allowing them to emerge on the design line where they will join the base of the core bundle. In the photograph below, the addition of the new thread is shown in green.

TURNING CORNERS IN TRAILING

If trailing is simply turned around a corner, the finished effect is unlikely to be sharp and neat. This process is useful for right-angled corners (or slightly sharper) and obtuse angles.

1 Work your trailing along the design line towards the corner. At this point, your thread must be on the outside edge of the corner. If it is not, work a tiny locking stab stitch on the design line beneath the core threads.

2 On reaching the start of the corner, bring the needle up on the outside edge, slightly beyond the corner design line. Take it down, tucked at an angle, into the core threads, forming a short diagonal stitch which spans about two-thirds of the way across the core threads.

3 Bring the needle up at the outermost tip of the corner, again just outside the design line; take it down again, tucked into the core threads, this time a little shorter. This traps the core threads out to the corner, ensuring a sharp tip.

46

The finished corner.

4 Work a third stitch, again about two-thirds the depth of the trailing and pushing down into the core threads, beginning to push them around the corner.

5 Return to working a stitch around the full group of core threads. Push the needle tight in on the inside edge and pull the core threads round. This will form a sharp corner. Continue trailing in the new direction.

6 Use tweezers to pinch the trailing to straighten the new section and sharpen the corner further.

SLANTED SATIN STITCH

Slanted satin stitch is one of the most fundamental stitches in whitework and indeed many other forms of hand embroidery. Design shapes are bound with closely packed, carefully aligned stitches, usually with padding beneath, to produce a bold, sculptured, glossy effect. Slanted satin stitch is highly versatile and takes many forms.

Satin stitch must be worked well to look effective in whitework: uneven edges and misplaced angles diffract the light and can cause the work to look dull and discoloured. Achieving perfectly plump and smooth satin stitch takes practice but is a joy once mastered.

The following pages and design shapes provided explain the key forms of satin stitch in great depth, teaching you the skills required to achieve a professional finish with ease. The design shapes can be photocopied and then traced onto your chosen fabric using a lightbox (as described on page 35); they may be made larger or smaller as you prefer – adjust your thread choice accordingly. Each sample lists the threads used to create the original – you may adjust these to suit the threads you have to hand.

THE SLANTED SATIN STITCH RULE

Padded satin stitch looks at its best when it has smooth edges, harmonious flow and change of angle, consistent density and smooth, regular stitch tension. These effects can be achieved by following the **slanted satin stitch rule**, which is the working method described below and overleaf.

Following the diagram on the right, the satin stitch starts at the widest point of the shape where it is easiest to set a good angle (see red stitch). The stitch should always be at a 45-degree angle to the line of the shape. Here, we work an angle from top-left to bottom-right. It is a design decision as to whether the angle flows this way or in the opposite direction.

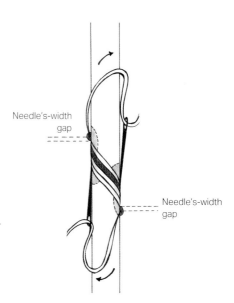

Needle's-width gap

Needle's-width gap

WORKING ABOVE THE CENTRAL STITCH

The needle ascends on the left-hand side of the design shape, leaving a tiny gap between this point and the previous stitch (see the red dot in the diagram, below, and on page 47). This gap is approximately equivalent to the width of the needle or thread in current use. This raises the left-hand end of the stitch, extending it upwards a little.

Note that the needle is emerging on the side at which the satin stitch forms an obtuse angle with the edge of the design (see diagram on page 47).

• The needle emerges from the fabric pointing straight upwards towards the sky at 90° to the ground fabric (the 'rocket ship angle' – see below).

• The needle descends on the right. It is tucked into the 'V' shaped slot created by the previous satin stitch – see right.

The needle is descending on the side at which the satin forms an acute angle with the edge of the design. The angle of the needle at this point is very important and is described on the right.

THE FUNDAMENTAL NEEDLE ANGLE (FNA)

The needle descends at a 45-degree angle to the surface of the ground fabric. This angle is known as the **Fundamental Needle Angle** (hereafter, the FNA):

• The needle should be aligned along, and lie parallel to, the edge of the design shape (usually outlined using split stitch).

• The needle should lie at 45° to the ground fabric.

• The point of the needle tucks towards and slightly under the previous satin stitch. This ensures that the angle of stitch is maintained and the edges of the satin shape remain smooth.

• The needle tip presses down onto the existing satin stitches at this right-hand end, squeezing them together slightly.

The result of this process is that the tiny gap slightly raises the stitch on the left while the pressure downwards lowers the stitch on the right, thereby ensuring the steep 45° stitch angle is consistently maintained.

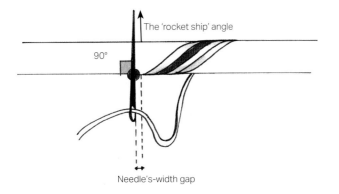

The 'rocket ship' angle

90°

Needle's-width gap

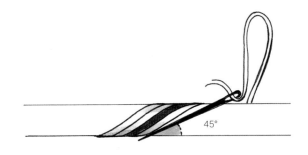

45°

WORKING BELOW THE CENTRAL STITCH

The process is the same. The needle emerges on the right-hand side of the shape, leaving a tiny gap between it and the tip of the previous stitch. The needle descends on the left tucking into the 'V'-shaped slot created by the previous satin stitch.

Employ the FNA again with the needle running parallel to the design outline, about 45° to the ground fabric and tucked towards and slightly under the previous satin stitch.

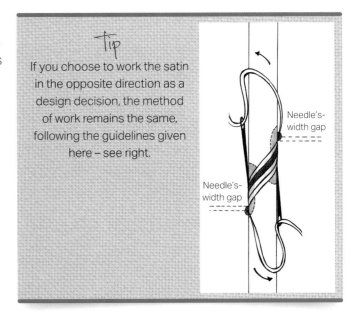

Tip
If you choose to work the satin in the opposite direction as a design decision, the method of work remains the same, following the guidelines given here – see right.

Needle's-width gap

Needle's-width gap

48

BREAKING THE RULE

When the satin stitches are worked in the opposite way to the rule, the needle 'squashes' the point of the stitches so that they appear flattened and do not flow around the shape (a).

When the rule is followed but the needle is angled towards the design outline, rather than using the FNA, the outline is squashed and damaged. The edges of the satin stitch become uneven and distorted (b).

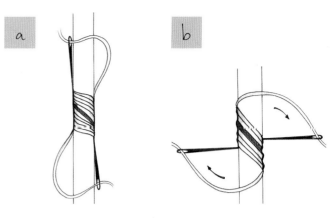

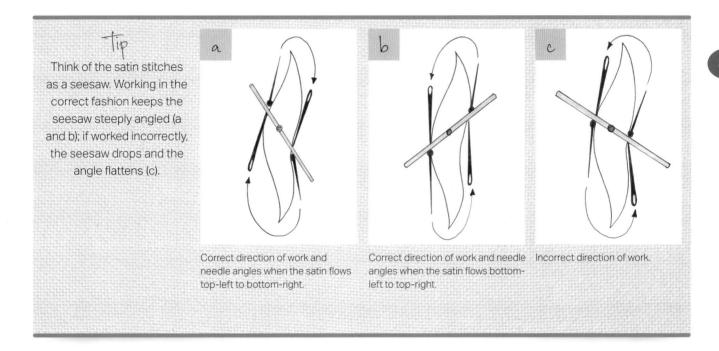

Tip

Think of the satin stitches as a seesaw. Working in the correct fashion keeps the seesaw steeply angled (a and b); if worked incorrectly, the seesaw drops and the angle flattens (c).

Correct direction of work and needle angles when the satin flows top-left to bottom-right.

Correct direction of work and needle angles when the satin flows bottom-left to top-right.

Incorrect direction of work.

THE 'Z' RULE

The 'Z' rule is a useful aid for remembering on which side the needle emerges and descends in slanted satin stitch.

On paper, draw the design shape in question and mark in your starting stitch at a 45° angle. Form a 'Z' shape as shown in red, using the stitch line as the diagonal of the Z and the two design edges as the top and base. Your needle will always descend into the acute angles of the Z.

Wherever you are working slanted satin stitch, you can use this guide to help you work out your stitch directions before using the satin stitch rule to maintain the angle while working the design shape.

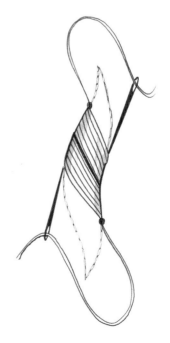

WORKING PADDED, SLANTED SATIN STITCH

SMALL, SIMPLE SHAPES

This technique is appropriate for small, simple, compact shapes. These are usually best padded with long, straight stitches.

To begin, the shape is outlined using a row of small, even split stitches, sitting on the drawn design line. This edge provides a framework to contain and support the satin stitch. Each stitch splits through the thread of the previous stitch at its centre point (see diagram below).

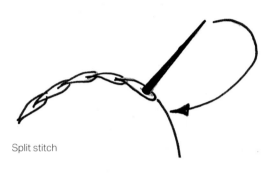

Split stitch

YOU WILL NEED:

THREADS

For thread abbreviations, see page 16.

Outline: split stitch, F (single)

Padding: F (single)

Surface: F (single)

The template can be found on page 188.

When starting to work the second edge, the needle re-emerges a short distance along the design line, and the first new split stitch is worked by tucking the needle towards and under the tip of the previous row, before continuing along the new edge.

This technique helps to give a crisp, sharp tip and should be employed at all points, rather than bending the split stitch around the point.

PADDING

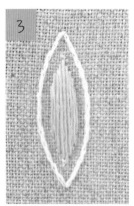

1 Work the first layer of padding stitches from the centre outwards, ensuring that they sit well within the split-stitch outline. Work all padding stitches in a back-and-forth motion, so that they do not cross the reverse of the work with a long stitch. The reverse should remain flat while the surface is raised.

2 The second layer of padding stitches are slightly bigger and should be worked back and forth over the top of the first layer.

3 A third layer can worked in the same fashion, getting closer to the split stitch outline.

4 Add a further four layers of padding, getting increasingly closer to the split stitch. Each layer should now be worked in a contrasting diagonal angle to the layer beneath. Work all stitches in a back-and-forth motion to ensure that the reverse remains flat.

5 The final layer of padding hugs close to the split stitch. Secure the working thread by passing it back up through the padding, then cut away the excess.

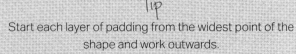

Tip
Start each layer of padding from the widest point of the shape and work outwards.

 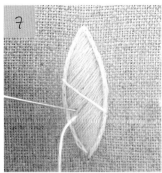  

6 Work a second row of split stitch around the perimeter of the shape: this should sit on top of the existing row and will redefine the edge, which may have been distorted by working the padding.

7 Secure the working thread using the WKT in the padding, close to the widest point of the shape. Start the satin stitch across the widest point of the shape, at a 45° angle. Once this stitch has been worked satisfactorily, secure with a locking stitch worked into the padding.

8 The satin stitch then follows the satin stitch rule (see page 47) as you work towards the upper end of the shape. The needle emerges on the left (leaving a tiny gap): take it down on the right, employing the FNA. Slide the needle along, parallel to the split stitch outline, and tuck it towards the previous satin stitch at a 45° angle. This maintains the stitch angle and keeps the edges of the shape smooth.

9 Continue working satin stitch towards the top of the shape. Aim to maintain the same angle, density and tension of stitch throughout, following the satin stitch rule.

Tips

Use a laying tool when working satin stitch, such as an aficot (pictured) or a mellor, or any similar blunt-tipped, highly polished implement.

Tensioning the working thread as it glides down through the fabric in this manner will help to ensure that each stitch lays beautifully smoothly and that the thread remains in good condition, preventing knotting and tangling.

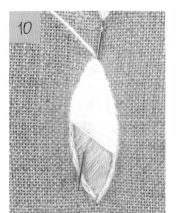 

10 To finish the shape, bring the needle up at the very tip, just beyond the split stitch, as if to work a further satin stitch. It descends, but instead of passing through the ground fabric, it slides back through beneath the satin stitch and padding, emerging in the padding. Cut away the excess and use a new thread for the lower half. This process sharpens and lifts the tip of the shape and allows the finishing thread to add to the bulk of the padding, rather than to the reverse of the work.

11 The lower half of the shape can be worked in the same manner as the upper half: reverse the direction of the stitches, and follow the satin stitch rule as before. The FNA is again employed. Finish the thread at the tip in a similar fashion: this time, the needle emerges through the satin stitch before being clipped away carefully, using curved-tip scissors.

FINISHING TOUCHES AND BURNISHING

On completion of a piece of satin stitch, burnish the surface and edges.

1 Use a clean, smooth tool such as an aficot or mellor. Support the work from beneath, using your fingers, while pushing the tool firmly across the satin surface several times, in the direction of the stitches.

2 If there are any dimples or hollows in the perimeter, slip a tapestry needle under the stitches at these points, close to the ground fabric, and gently lever them out a little.

Note
If you have stitched the perimeter stitches in the wrong place, levering the stitches (as shown left) will achieve nothing. However, dimples in edges usually result from stitches having been pulled a little tighter than neighbouring stitches. Easing them will achieve an even, smooth edge.

3 Finally, take a firm, blunt tapestry needle (or a tool such as a mellor), and press firmly around the perimeter of the satin. Take care not to score the ground fabric: just press the edge of the stitches. This will give a finesse and crispness to the finished edge.

The finished padded satin stitch shape from above and at an angle to demonstrate the height. The same shape can be worked with an opposing stitch angle (working from bottom-left to top-right), reversing the method of work accordingly...

BACKSTITCH SEEDING

Seeding involves the working of multiple, usually fairly densely worked stitches across the surface of the fabric. In many embroidery techniques, these stitches are worked in random directions. However, in whitework, seeding is worked in densely packed rows of tiny backstitches. Backstitch is much more effective than running stitch since its wrapping motion 'plumps' the individual stitches, giving them each a lovely raised appearance.

1 Cast on the thread using the WKT. Work a tiny row of regular backstitches around the perimeter of the design shape. Each stitch is about 1–2mm (¹⁄₁₆in) long. Pull the stitches a little so that it is easier to take the needle down in the same hole at the tip of the previous backstitch.

2 Continue to work further rows, spiralling inwards. Align the stitches with those of the previous row where possible. However, it will not be possible to do this continually since the rows will become shorter. Avoid making the backstitches themselves too much shorter, and instead maintain the stitch size, even if this results in misalignment. Work dense rows all the way to the centre.

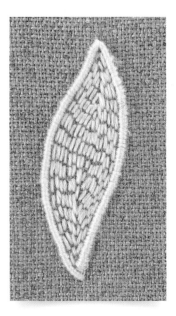

CURVILINEAR SHAPES

Long, narrow, curving shapes are common in whitework (such as in monogramming) but are difficult to pad using long straight stitches, as these do not turn easily. The most common padding for these shapes therefore employs rows and layers of line stitches, such as running stitch, chain stitch and split stitch. My preference is for long split stitch: it is swift and simple to work, yet creates high relief from the surface of the fabric, while leaving the reverse beautifully flat.

The shape demonstrated below teaches this type of padding and provides excellent practice for working with slanted satin stitch and manipulating it to fit to curved forms. The sample also teaches voided satin stitch, wherein the width of the satin is divided into two sections. This is a useful decorative feature and can reduce the length of unwieldy stitches in a wide design section.

The design shape is outlined using a row of small even split stitches, as for small, simple shapes (see page 50).

Long split stitch

YOU WILL NEED:

THREADS

Outline: split stitch, F (single)

Padding: F (double)

Surface: Perlé cotton No. 8

The template can be found on page 188.

Tip

Practise drawing directional lines on a photocopy of the outline design shape to indicate the flow of satin stitches around the design shape. Start with a line at 45° across the widest point and work out from there. This will help you greatly when you come to stitch the shape, as you will be able to predict where wedge stitches (see page 55) are required to turn the angle successfully.

PADDING

The padding is worked using long split stitch; these need to be as long as possible without compromising the curve of the shape. The needle splits the previous stitch at its tip rather than at its centre, which results in maximum thread on the surface and minimum on the reverse.

Use double Floche à Broder to build up the padding more rapidly. Thread a long length of cotton into your embroidery needle, double it over and knot together the two ends. The needle is thus trapped in the loop of the thread. Use a laying tool such as an aficot or mellor to keep the two threads smooth, and drop the needle from time to time to allow any twist to fall out.

1 Work a row of long split stitch along the shape, fractionally to the left of the centre spine. Finish at the tip and angle the needle towards and under the split stitch outline, tucking into the point of the shape. This will make the padding at the point sharper and more fluid.

2 Work a second row of long split stitch padding to the right of the first. The point at which the needle enters the fabric for each stitch should not be the same as that of the previous row: keep the stitches staggered to produce a smoother effect. Add further rows of split-stitch padding in the same manner; pack them snugly together. Work out from the centre, and back and forth along the design shape. Tuck the needle into the points at each end to ensure a smooth effect.

3 Continue until the shape is filled densely, right out to the split stitch outline. The background fabric should no longer be visible within the shape.

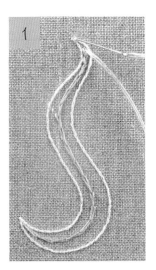
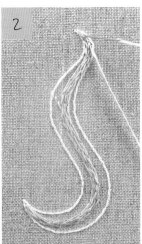

Once the first layer of padding is complete, work a second layer on top. This, again, starts with a row to the left of the centre line, followed by a row to the right of the centre line. Each row stops slightly short of the tip of the shape this time.

Continue to work the rows towards the edges, but do not allow them to reach the outline – a narrow space should be left around the edge so that a tapered, domed contour will begin to develop. The cross-section diagram below shows the domed effect of the three tapered layers, with the addition of a fourth layer (as below).

Now work a third layer over the second in the same manner. This time, each row finishes a fraction further in from the edge, to enhance the domed contouring.

When this third layer is complete, step back and look at the padding overall. Check for any areas which appear a little sparse or hollowed – go back and add further straight stitches or short sections of long split stitch into these areas, so that the domed shape is as smooth and firm all over as possible.

The second layer in progress.

The completed second layer of padding.

ADDING FURTHER HEIGHT

At this point, it will become increasingly difficult to pass the needle repeatedly through the dense padding stitches so I advise that you leave the padding at this point rather than adding more, as three layers of split stitch will produce sufficiently bold and solid padding.

However, if you do wish to add further height, padding can be added to the surface only, using double Floche à Broder.

1 Bring the needle up close to the tip of the design shape then pass it sideways, catching under the upper surface only of the existing padding stitches. Use similar stitch lengths to the long split stitches to work further 'catch stitches' slightly left of the spine of the shape, always passing the needle in the same direction. At the end of the row, pass the needle back down through the padding close to the tip of the design shape.

2 Work a further row of the surface padding to the right of the first. Direct the needle away from the first row to avoid catching into it (see above, right).

3 Further rows are added working from the centre spine outwards until the surface is covered almost right out to the split stitch outline (see right).

4 Finally, work a second row of split stitch around the perimeter, sitting on top of the original line but adjusting the line if required, to produce a smoother edge.

Starting to add further height with surface whipping.

Working further rows.

WORKING SATIN STITCH

1 Secure the working thread using the WKT in the padding, close to the widest point of the shape. The needle emerges outside the split stitch on the left and descends on the right, forming a stitch across the padding at 45°. Work a locking stitch into the padding to secure this first stitch.

2 Work towards the upper half of the shape first. Following the satin stitch rule, bring the needle up on the left and take it down on the right. As the needle emerges, it rises straight to the sky, leaving the tiny gap (see dot, diagram 2a). As the needle descends, the FNA is employed and it slides along parallel to the split stitch outline, to be tucked towards and under the previous stitch.

ADDING WEDGE STITCHES

To turn the angle of the stitch around the curve, inserting wedge stitches is essential.

1 At approximately three-quarters of the width of the design shape, the needle emerges through the padding at a shallow angle (the 'Superman angle'). This angle ensures that the stitch blends smoothly into the work. It then descends as normal on the outer edge before returning to work the next full stitch. The wedge will have turned the direction of work.

2 As the shape bends around the corner, more wedge stitches will be required between the full stitches. You can also work two wedge stitches together to make a slightly more dramatic change of angle but these should be slightly different lengths. Add as many or as few wedge stitches as appropriate: the aim of these is to maintain a 45° angle to the stitch in relation to the flow of the shape, at all times – wedge stitches should be used wherever required to ensure this.

3 The satin stitch progresses up the shape. Add wedge stitches on the right as required. The shape then begins to turn in the other direction: wedge stitches will now be required on the left-hand side. The needle rises on the left-hand edge as usual but now descends into the padding: the stitch length should be approximately three-quarters of the length of the full stitches. The needle descends at a shallow angle, pointing towards and under the previous stitch.

CREATING A VOID (OPTIONAL)

Drop the needle down along the line of the centre spine, between the rows of split stitch padding. Employ the FNA as the needle slides down between the rows of padding.

Continue working half-length stitches for as long as required, maintaining a 45° angle and adding a wedge stitch if necessary. Then return to full stitches.

Once you have completed the void, continue working satin stitch to the tip of the shape, maintaining a 45° angle. Again, add wedge stitches as required to achieve this.

FINISHING THE TIP

At the tip, the stitches will still be long, and lying at 45°.

At the very tip of the shape, bring the needle up slightly outside the split stitch edge. Then slide the needle back beneath a few of the satin stitches, emerging between them, as shown on the right.

This process finishes off the thread, and more importantly extends the tip of the shape to a very sharp point.

COMPLETING THE LOWER END

1 Using a new thread and following the satin stitch rule and the 'Z' rule, bring the needle up on the lower edge and down on the upper edge. Continue to add wedge stitches as required.

2 Complete the lower tip in the same way.

COMPLETING THE SECOND HALF OF THE VOID

1 Using a new thread, the missing section of satin stitch, to the right of the void, can now be filled. Starting at the top of the space and moving downwards, following the satin stitch rule, bring the needle up on the right and down into the void on the left.

2 Add wedge stitches, if required, to turn the angle.

3 Burnish the surface and stretch any stitches around the edge which may appear dimpled, as previously described (see page 52).

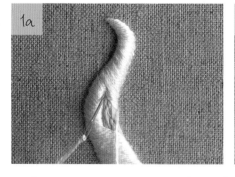 

Tip

Try reversing the design shape and working in the other direction to gain more practice with the satin stitch rule and in manipulating satin stitch to work effectively around beautiful curves.

56

HIGH-RELIEF PADDING WITH A ROUNDED TIP

This method uses a bundle of padding threads to create dramatic height which complements and supports long, narrow and curving satin-stitch shapes. It creates a bold statement and a sense of great depth.

PADDING

Outline the design shape using split stitch.

This sample used a bundle of approximately 54 lengths of Floche à Broder, all at least 5cm (2in) longer than the design shape at both ends. The initial quantity of padding used should be slightly larger than the shape itself. To gauge the amount of padding thread, place the bundle over the outlined design shape, pinching it in tightly. The padding should appear to bulge over the edges slightly and seem almost too big for the shape. When the stitching is worked over the top, the padding will be compacted considerably and should form a neat dome within the confines of the outline.

YOU WILL NEED:

THREADS
Outline: split stitch, F (single)
Padding: F (54 strands)
Surface: Perlé cotton No. 8

The template can be found on page 188.

1 Cast on a working strand of Floche à Broder in an embroidery needle using the WKT. Fold the bundle of padding threads in half and place the 'loop' at the rounded tip of the design shape.

2 Bring up the needle through the loop and take it down at the tip of the shape, biting slightly into the split stitch outline. This will help pull the padding tight against the outline. Work a locking stab stitch into the fabric within the design shape to secure this in place.

3 Work a stitch over the breadth of the padding at its widest point, the needle emerging and descending within the split stitch outline. As you pull this stitch into place, the padding should sink to fit snugly between the two split stitch outlines. If you have applied too much padding, remove a little at this stage; or add more if you've applied too little. Work a further locking stab stitch into the fabric to secure.

4 Work stab stitches into the bulk of the padding at the rounded end to smooth, secure and contour the form. Bring the needle up within the split stitch outline and down into the padding. Work further stitches into the end and across the span of the padding until the rounded tip is firm and smoothly contoured. Now begin to work the tapered stem of the design shape. Work a further binding stitch which spans the width of the padding, about 3mm (⅛in) below the starting point. Anchor the stitch by working a locking stab stitch into the fabric below the padding.

5 Peel back the upper layer of padding threads, separating a bundle at the base of the pile to be removed – this should be approximately one-third of the bundle, but judge this by feel rather than counting individual strands. Push your curved-tip scissors in tight under the padding and clip away the padding threads cleanly.

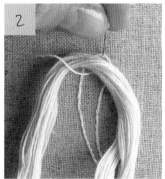

Tip

There are no rules regarding how many threads to remove: just proceed tentatively. Separate a small number, cut these away then take the next binding stitch over the padding. If the padding still appears to bulge beyond the split stitch outlines, or does not look tapered, remove further threads.

6 Continue to bind over the padding along the design shape, keeping the needle emerging and descending in the split stitch outline. It is preferable that the stitches are not straight and perfectly aligned, since the criss-cross effect produces a more even padding. Work some stitches down into the padding as well as over the top, to adjust and mould the contouring.

7 Approximately halfway along the design shape, remove more threads from the bottom of the bundle – about one-third of the bundle again.

8 Continue binding along the shape to three-quarters of the full length of the shape. Work a locking stitch before removing a further third of the bundle.

FINISHING THE END

1 Continue binding to a point 3–4mm (⅛–³⁄₁₆in) from the tip of the design shape. Secure the stitching thread with a locking stab stitch. Split the padding into two halves. Separate the upper half and clip away the lower half cleanly.

2 Lay the padding threads back down and bind over them to pull those remaining down over the cut ends, hiding them beneath. Secure with a locking stab stitch. Align the scissor blade along the bottom edge of the design shape and cut away the remaining strands.

3 Work stab stitches into the end of the padded form to secure the tip fully, the needle emerging on the design line and stabbing into the padding.

4 Work back along the padded form adding further stitches to smooth and compact the padding further. These should be angled differently from, and may cross over, those already worked, to produce a smoother effect. If the padding is falling away from the split stitch edge at any point, the needle can be taken down into the padding, angled towards the outer edge, and manipulated to ease the padding out towards the split stitch, as shown here.

5 View the padding from different angles to check for any uneven areas. Run a finger along the surface to check that it tapers smoothly, so that it will be easier to work the satin stitch. Finally, work a new row of split stitch around the perimeter to neaten.

SATIN STITCH

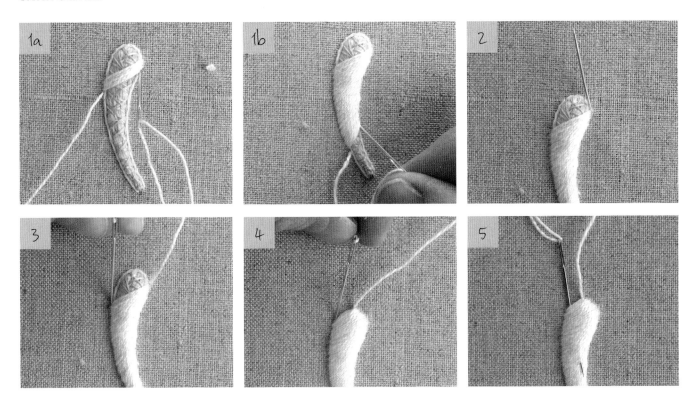

1 Take a stitch at a 45° angle across the widest part of the design shape. Begin to work the lower half of the design shape following the satin stitch rules and recommended needle angles. Add wedge stitches to adjust the angle as required.

2 On reaching the base, finish by sliding the needle beneath the padding as before. The rounded end of the shape is now worked. Following the satin stitch rule, the needle now emerges on the opposing edge. To form an effective rounded effect, the needle should be tucked up very tight against the previous satin stitch and emerge as if angled out from beneath this stitch. The line of the needle runs parallel with the split stitch outline and emerges at a 45° angle to the surface of the fabric (the FNA in reverse, or the 'Superman angle').

3 The needle descends as normal on the left-hand side, tucking into the acute corner formed between the satin and split stitch outline, using the FNA.

4 As you work around the curved tip, each time the needle ascends it will turn a little so that it always lies parallel to the split stitch outline. It descends in the same fashion. Angling the needle at both ends of the stitch like this pulls the stitch into a curved form. Imagine, as you work, that you are drawing a curve with the needle.

5 Work the final stitch across the peak of the curve. This time, slide the needle under the padding to emerge through the satin stitching where it can be clipped away. Burnish the surface and edges of the completed work as before, and use tweezers to pinch and mould the finished shape.

HIGH-RELIEF PADDING WITH A FLAT BASE

The method for working a flat-ended shape in high-relief padding is a little different from that for a rounded end. This sample uses 100 strands of Floche à Broder.

PADDING

YOU WILL NEED:

THREADS

Outline: split stitch, F (single)

Padding: F (100 strands)

Surface: Perlé cotton No. 8

The template can be found on page 188.

1 Outline the design shape using split stitch.

2 Place the bundle at the broad end of the shape.

3 Secure a strand of Floche within the design shape (WKT) and work a stitch spanning the breadth of the design shape, about 4mm (³⁄₁₆in) from the flat base, therefore at the widest point. Secure with a locking stitch.

4 Work up towards the tip of the design shape, cutting threads away from the base of the padding bundle in stages as you progress (as previously described). The needle emerges and descends in the split stitch outline.

5 At the tip, you should have approximately five strands of Floche remaining. Once these have been clipped away, work stab stitches down into the point to secure, before working back down the padding adding further stitches to smooth.

6 At the flat base, separate the padding into two equal halves and peel back the upper half.

7 With your scissors aligned with the flat base line, push the blades tight under the padding and clip away the lower half of the threads completely and cleanly.

8 Lay the remaining threads back in position. Work two or three further binding stitches over the top to pull the threads down over the cut ends beneath, taking the padding down to the bottom edge of the shape. Work a locking stitch to secure.

9 With the blade of the scissors aligned with the flat base of the shape, cut away all the remaining padding threads. When cut they should sit flush with the split stitch outline.

10 Work stab stitches of varied lengths into the end of the padding, across the breadth of the shape. Bring the needle up in the split stitch and take down into the padding. Check that the contouring is smooth before sealing off the working thread.

Flat-based shapes are always worked in this manner, removing half of the threads just short of the shape end and then pulling the remaining half down over, cutting these away and then sealing with stab stitches. This means that the padding shelves smoothly towards the flat base as well as towards the point.

SATIN STITCH

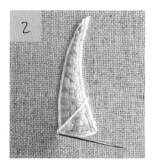 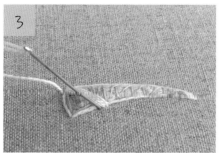  

1 The satin stitch begins by working a stitch across the design at its widest point and at a 45° angle. Use a locking stab stitch to secure. This creates a triangle shape at the bottom right corner. Stitching a triangle like this is similar to stitching the rounded end in the previous sample.

2 As you bring the needle up, you do not need to leave a tiny space between it and the previous stitch, as this would force the stitch off-line. Instead, the needle should be tucked very tight up against the corner satin stitch. It emerges as if angled out from beneath this stitch. The line of the needle runs parallel with the split stitch outline running across the base of the shape, and emerges at a 45° angle to the surface of the fabric (the FNA

in reverse, or the 'Superman angle'). Take the needle down as normal on the right-hand side, tucking it into the acute corner formed between the satin and split stitch outline, using the FNA.

3 Continue in the same fashion along the base of the shape until the triangle is filled.

4 At the corner, the needle emerges at the very tip before sliding back under the padding to emerge in the satin and be clipped away.

5 The satin is now worked in the upper portion of the design shape following the satin stitch rule to maintain the stitch angle in the normal fashion.

SATIN STITCH IN TWO HALVES WITH A CENTRAL CONTRAST VEIN

This is an extremely common form of satin stitch in many whitework designs. Splitting the satin stitch into two halves makes each half narrower and more manageable to work and the stitches less unwieldy.

The contrast centre adds life, depth, texture and interest. This may be an open centre as shown here using ladder stitch, eyelets or beading or may simply be a section of plain linen. The centre may be embellished after completion with a string of beads. This method is highly suitable for leaves and petals but can also be used to break up the width of sections of satin monograms.

PADDING

Work an outline using split stitch. Work the centre vein if required, stopping approximately 8–10mm (5/16–3/8in) from the tip of the shape. Pad the sides using a minimum of two layers of long split stitch padding. Re-work the split stitch outline on top.

YOU WILL NEED:

THREADS

Split stitch: Floche à Broder (single)

Padding: Floche à Broder (double)

Surface: Floche à Broder (single)

The template can be found on page 188.

SATIN

  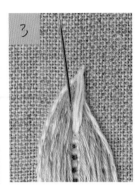  

1 Bring up the needle at the tip of the centre vein and down at a point a fraction outside the spilt stitch at the tip of the leaf. This helps to sharpen the tip.

2 Bring up the needle at the same point at the tip of the vein and make a stitch to the left of the central stitch. Take the needle down over the split stitch outline, using the FNA to ensure a smooth edge and sharp tip. Work a further stitch in the same manner to the right of the centre.

3 The angle of the stitch must now be turned to achieve an angle of approximately 45° to either side of the centre. This is achieved by working wedge stitches. Bring up the needle about two-thirds the

depth of a full stitch and angle it out from beneath the previous satin (the Superman angle). Take it down as normal on the outer edge (FNA). Follow this with a full-length stitch.

4 Continue to work further wedge stitches and full stitches combined on either side of centre, until the 45° angle is achieved.

5 Each half of the leaf is now worked in the same manner, maintaining this angle throughout using the satin stitch rule. At the base of the leaf, the angle should still be 45° and the stitch long. Add wedge stitches if required, to maintain this.

FISHTAIL IN NATURAL SHADING

This technique can be known as 'natural shading', 'silk shading' and 'long-and-short stitch shading'. The former terms provide the most accurate description. The process uses slightly varied lengths of densely packed, flowing straight stitches in overlapping rows, to produce smooth, solid, areas of stitching with a lovely sense of movement.

This technique is highly adaptable and provides an excellent alternative to satin stitch for shapes which may be too complex or broad to work effectively in satin, or where more movement and contrast of textural interest are required. It can be worked directly onto the ground fabric or over padding for a heightened sculptural effect.

The colours are used in the photographs overleaf simply to clarify the layers of stitch.

YOU WILL NEED:

THREADS

Split stitch: Floche à Broder (single)

Padding: Floche à Broder (double and single)

Surface: Floche à Broder (single)

The template can be found on page 188.

PADDING

1 Work an outline using split stitch. Work two layers of long split stitch padding using double Floche à Broder along the length of the shape leaving a tiny space between the edge of the padding and the perimeter split stitch.

2 Cover this with a layer of satin padding in the direction shown in the images opposite, using single Floche à Broder, working from the widest point outwards. This additional layer of padding is worked in a contrast angle to the shading to be worked on top. This is essential (particularly in white-on-white) to avoid the shading stitches sinking into the padding and to make it easier to see the flow of the stitches.

3 Re-work the split stitch outline on top if preferred.

SHADING

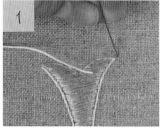 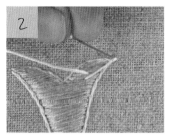  

   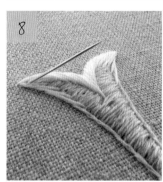

63

1 Starting at one of the two outer tips of the design shape, work a stitch about 7–8mm (¼–⁵⁄₁₆in) long, which emerges in the padding and extends out over the split stitch outline. Extend slightly beyond the split stitch outline to sharpen this peak point.

2 Work a second stitch a fraction shorter than the first to the left of the point. The needle descends at the FNA, tucking towards the point, smoothing the edge and sharpening the top.

3 Work a third stitch again a fraction shorter than the first to the right of the point. The needle descends at the FNA.

4 Work further stitches to either side of centre. All stitches remain around 6–8mm (¼–⁵⁄₁₆in) long, but vary to produce a slightly staggered effect. The FNA is employed on the outer edge throughout.

5 Stitching continues in the same fashion, adding wedge stitches as required (see page 55) to turn the angle sufficiently to be flowing straight down the spine of the design shape as the base of the centre 'V' shape is reached.

6 Return to the right-hand side and work further stitches to pull the shading down a little further over the split stitch outline. These stitches emerge just inside the split stitch edge, glide over the split stitch (almost parallel to it) and descend with the needle tucked towards the point (FNA).

7 The process is repeated for the left-hand point of the design shape.

8 The second layer of stitching now begins returning to the centre of the left-hand spike. Bring up the needle through the existing stitches, splitting the thread. It bites back into these stitches by approximately one-third to half their length. It is important that the stitches overlap existing stitches by a significant amount: this produces a rich, dense surface and allows a more subtle turning of the stitch angle. As the needle emerges, it should do so at a shallow angle, i.e. flowing in the general direction of the flow of the shading. The stitch length is about the same as those of the first row, around 6–8mm (¼–⁵⁄₁₆in). Some shorter stitches can be used, if required, to turn the angle.

Tip

As a general rule in shading, all perimeter edge stitches are worked with the needle emerging inside the design shape, within the split-stitch boundary, and descending out over the split stitch, using the needle angle to smooth and shape the edge. All internal stitches are worked in the opposite direction, the needle rising through and splitting the existing stitches and descending within the design shape.

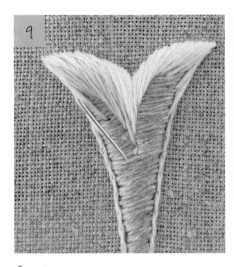

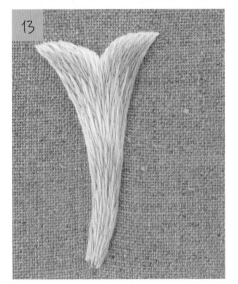

9 Now work further stitches around to the right and left. Each bites back into the existing row by at least a third to a half its depth (never less) but this is varied with every stitch. It is also effective for some stitches to bite much further back into the existing stitches since this provides more opportunity for varied splitting points, ensuring that the shading line is as softly staggered as possible. Stitch lengths remain approximately the same but appear staggered due to the varied emerging positions. The angles of the stitches are turned a little, gradually curving them so that they begin to flow fluidly along the design shape. The same method is used to the left of the point; thus, a soft, sketchy, blended effect is created.

10 Add further stitches at the left-hand edge to extend the work further along the design shape. Bring the needle up in the padding and take it down over the split stitch outline. Again, the edge stitches run almost parallel with the split stitch and the length of the stitch covers the edge. Further central stitches are also worked through the previous layer, pulling the shading down further into the design shape, following the method described above.

11 Repeat the process in the right-hand spike. The stitches should blend together in the centre of the shape, ready to pull the shading down through the centre spine.

12 The shading continues in the same fashion through the centre of the shape. Start at the centre spine and work outwards. At the edges, the stitch direction is reversed as before.

13 Further layers of stitch are worked to fill the shape, turning the stitch angle gently and covering the edges in the same manner. Burnish the surface and smooth the edges as previously described.

RAISED FISHBONE STITCH

Raised fishbone is an excellent stitch to fill narrow design shapes and is formed using overlapping cross stitches. It is ideal for feathers, leaves and fish due to the soft 'V'-shaped pattern formed.

YOU WILL NEED:

THREADS
Outline/split stitch: F (single)
Surface: F (single)

The template can be found on page 188.

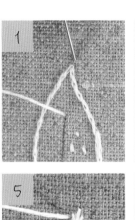

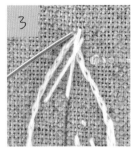
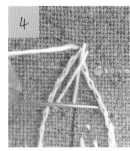

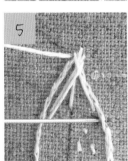

1 Bring the needle up on the centre vein line, roughly 7mm (¼in) down into the shape, and take it down at the tip of the leaf, extending just outside the split stitch outline, to sharpen the point.

2 Bring the needle up to the bottom-left, just inside the split stitch outline, slightly lower than the centre stitch. Take it back down at the top right outside the split stitch and tucked towards the central stitch. Employ the FNA to ensure a smooth edge.

3 Bring the needle out at the top-left, outside the split stitch, sliding out as if from beneath the centre stitch, parallel with the split stitch outline. The needle should emerge at a 45° angle to the ground fabric. This is the FNA in reverse.

4 Take the needle down at the bottom right, just inside the split stitch and level with the existing stitch. These two stitches form a long cross stitch, which will be repeated to form the fishbone pattern.

5 Work the next cross below, and overlapping, the first. As the needle emerges, a small space should be left between it and the tail of the previous stitch. The same applies as the needle descends at the base of the second stitch. At the top of the cross, the stitches are tucked tight against the existing stitches. Leaving a small space between stitches at the tail end of the cross and tucking close at the top helps to maintain the angle of the stitches; otherwise, the angle of the cross will flatten and the fishbone will appear stunted, rather than flowing.

6 As the leaf turns, add wedge stitches on the left-hand side, to change the direction of the stitch without needing to leave spaces. A wedge stitch is required whenever the base of the cross stitches is no longer level and the two stitches are out of sync, or when the fishbone stitches appear to be slipping over each other. The needle emerges as usual at the top left, outside the split stitch. However, the stitch is shortened to approximately three-quarters of its normal length and the needle is tucked towards and under the previous stitch. Follow this by working a full stitch from the top left to bottom right again in the normal way. The partial length stitch will have turned the direction of work and you can return to the normal pattern of working. The process can also be used to flatten the angle of the fishbone stitches if they become too steep.

7 The angle can also be turned on the right-hand side of the shape by working a wedge stitch as the needle emerges. The stitch should be three-quarters the normal length and the needle emerges as if out from underneath the previous stitch, descending on the outside edge outside the split stitch. The is again followed by working a full length stitch again.

8 Continue in the same fashion, adding wedge stitches if required.

9 Near the base of the leaf, the tails of the crosses gradually become shorter until there is no longer space to allow the stitches to cross at the centre. At this point, the remaining uncovered areas of the design at the sides are covered using satin stitches.

TRANSLUCENT TECHNIQUES

On a translucent base fabric, density, form and texture are created with the addition of stitch. Further depth can be created through appliqué and layering of additional fabrics and other items. These are highly versatile techniques, which can be worked rapidly, to maximum effect. Stitches have a superb drawing quality and can be used to create a great sense of depth.

CHOICE OF FABRIC

Traditionally: Cotton organdie, silk organza, fine linen batiste, cotton lawn.

In practice: Any fabric which is sufficiently sheer to allow the embroidery threads to be visible through it.

CHOICE OF THREADS

Traditionally: Fine cotton threads such as stranded cotton, Floche à Broder or lace threads.

In practice: Any, although generally finer threads are used such as stranded cotton, fine perlé cotton, lace threads, fine Retors d'Alsace, since these do not distort the fine ground fabric.

WORKING DOUBLE BACKSTITCH

Double backstitch is also known as 'closed herringbone'. Using a sheer ground fabric, backstitches are worked along both edges of a narrow shape, crossing from one side to the other. This creates a herringbone stitch on the reverse; the backstitches outline the design shape on the front. The herringbone is seen as a 'shadow' through the sheer fabric, adding both density and pattern.

A template for this straight band can be found on page 188.

> Tip
>
> Threads must be started accurately, otherwise this can appear distracting on a sheer fabric.

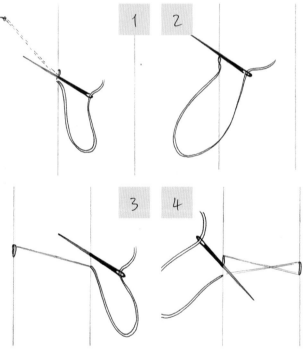

1 Draw two parallel design lines, roughly 12mm (½in) apart, using a fine marker pen. Begin with a knot on the surface, positioned away from your starting point, to the left of the design shape. Work two very tiny backstitches side-by-side along the design line.

2 Work the first of your embroidered backstitches over the top of the tiny backstitches, approximately 1mm (1⁄16in) long.

3 Jump across to the opposite side of the design shape and work a second backstitch.

4 Jump back to the left and work a third backstitch below the first. The needle descends at the tip of the first backstitch, sharing the hole. Jump back to the right and repeat.

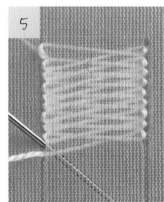

5 Continue down the design shape in the same manner. The pairs of stitches should continue to sit directly opposite each other throughout to maintain a pleasing herringbone pattern.

JOINING IN A NEW THREAD

The old thread is secured by working two tiny backstitches, to be covered not by the next embroidery backstitch, but by the one which falls below this. Bring the thread to the surface a little away from this point and leave it hanging, to be cut away on completion of the shape. The following steps show the neatest method of joining in a new thread.

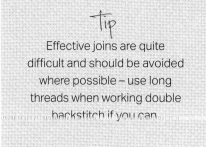

Tip
Effective joins are quite difficult and should be avoided where possible – use long threads when working double backstitch if you can.

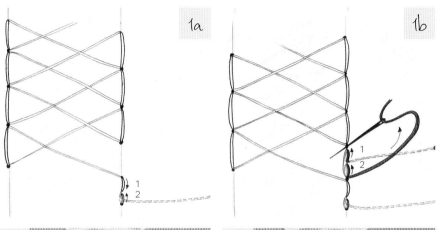

SHADING WITH DOUBLE BACKSTITCH

As you progress down the design shape, alter the length of the backstitches – this will change the density and effect of the herringbone, allowing you to create a sense of shading.

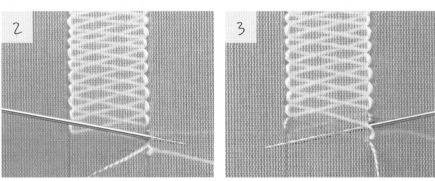

1 Take the new thread (see red in diagram, beige in photographs). Start with a knot on the surface of the work, a short distance from the joining point. Work two tiny backstitches inside the space remaining.

2 Cover these backstitches with a full embroidery backstitch.

3 The double backstitch now continues using the new thread. The backstitches neatly cover the finishing stitches from the previous thread.

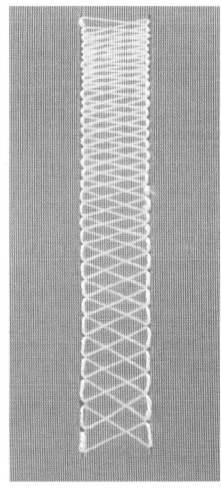

FINISHING THREADS AT THE END OF A SHAPE

The neatest way to finish a thread is to tuck two tiny backstitches invisibly beneath the last full backstitch. The working thread can then be cut away close to the work.

WORKING DOUBLE BACKSTITCH ALONG CURVED SHAPES

Double backstitch is worked effectively along narrow, curved shapes, by altering the length of the backstitches. Stitches become larger on the outside of the curve, and smaller on the inside. The trick is to keep the stitches on opposing sides of the shape level with each other on a perpendicular line, allowing the herringbone pattern to turn fluidly. A template for this shape can be found on page 188.

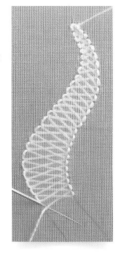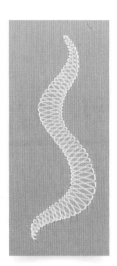

CIRCULAR SHAPES

These same principles can be applied to a circular design shape. Start at 1, and follow the direction of the arrows shown on the right.

If the double backstitches remain opposite each other all the way round the circle, they should meet up again exactly at the join.

A template for this shape can be found on page 188.

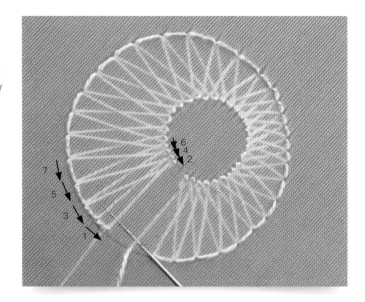

WORKING ADJACENT SHAPES IN DOUBLE BACKSTITCH

Broad shapes are difficult to work effectively in double backstitch, as the herringbone stitches become long and unwieldy. These shapes are often therefore divided into several narrow shapes. A double line of double backstitch between these shapes can be avoided – simply work the first section of double backstitch with normal size backstitches on the left and very tiny backstitches on the right.

Work the second section as normal. The backstitches on the left sit over the top of, and therefore hide, the tiny backstitches, producing a single line.

A template for these adjacent shapes can be found on page 188.

OVERLAPPING SHAPES

Work the top shape first. As you work the bottom shape, the thread can travel behind the upper one at the crossing point, with the existing stitching obscuring the thread.

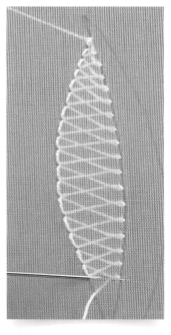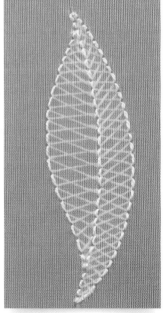

FILIGREE TECHNIQUES

PULLED THREAD WORK

In filigree techniques, the weave of the ground fabric is pulled open to allow light to penetrate the fabric. The weave is thus manipulated and distorted into pattern forms. The combination of holes and patterned stitches creates a huge array of textures and a great sense of depth and life. The viewer is drawn through the delicate holes and translucent lace-like texture to glimpse the world beyond.

CHOICE OF FABRIC

Traditionally: Cottons and linens with slightly open weaves; true evenweaves, i.e. those with an equal number of warp and weft threads within a measured gauge. Pulled work is also applied to cotton lawn and muslin in some finer forms of whitework.

In practice: Counted pulled thread stitches can be worked on any fabric wherein the weave is sufficiently open and clear to enable the individual fabric threads to be counted and pulled apart or together.

Some freely worked stitches (such as free eyelets) can be worked on denser fabrics. Linear pulled stitches, such as ladder stitch, usually require a denser weave to support their structure.

CHOICE OF THREADS

Traditionally: Fine, strong threads such as cotton and linen lacemaking threads.

In practice: Any, fine, strong, smooth thread such as fine Retors d'Alsace, perlé cotton, Coton à Broder and lacemaking threads can be used. The weight of the working thread approximately matches the weight of one thread of the ground fabric.

Avoid threads which are brittle or fibrous: these can break under the tension exerted, and can take away from the clarity of the stitch pattern.

Stitches which produce a higher percentage of thread on the upper surface of the work benefit from the use of a thread which is slightly heavier than that of the fabric weave.

Always test a thread before use to make sure it is strong enough to endure the strain of pulling the stitches tight, and to ensure that you like the effect.

THE STITCHES

There is a huge number of pulled thread work stitches although many are variants of the same basic structures. The following selection is useful for creating a variety of effects within whitework designs, and provide a range of distinctive, decorative textures.

When selecting a stitch, consider the following:

• **Do the direction and texture of the stitch suit the design?** For example, using geometric and linear stitches for architecture, and softer freer stitches for natural forms. Stitch direction can be used effectively to draw the eye through a design along a chosen path.

• **Does the stitch suit the size of the design area in terms of its scale and complexity?** Large, complex stitches require larger areas; simple stitches suit intricate areas and fine fabrics.

• Many pulled stitches can look similar in texture, particularly on fine fabric. It is important to choose stitches with textures which are significantly characterful to allow them to read clearly within a design.

• All stitches can be adapted, in terms of the size of individual stitches, to suit a design. Experiment with spare fabric before making a final selection.

These samples are worked on an evenweave linen with 12 threads/cm (30 threads/in), using Retors d'Alsace, number 12.

FREELY WORKED STAR EYELETS

Freely worked eyelets create a lacy, filigree effect on the ground fabric. They are not counted and are therefore relatively quick and easy to work. They can be worked in a variety of sizes and weights of thread, and these variations can create a shaded effect in terms of scale, weight and density. They are therefore one of the most versatile and useful pulled thread stitches.

STARTING THE THREAD AND WORKING THE FIRST EYELET

1 Begin the thread with a knot on the surface of the work. Carry the thread – approximately 2cm (1³⁄₁₆in) – behind the area you are about to work.

2 Choose a centre point for the eyelet and work the first stitches (red in the diagram below) by taking the needle down into this centre point.

3 Work stitches of varying lengths around the eyelet, each dropping down into the centre hole.

4 Pull the thread tightly to open the centre hole.

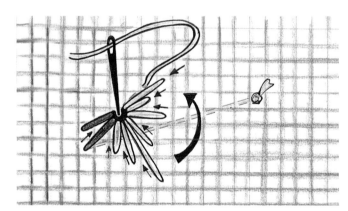

Tips

Maintaining an even tension is essential for working effective pulled thread work. Stitches must be pulled firmly and evenly to achieve a strong lace-like effect. Practice pulled stitches until you understand the stitch well and achieve a rhythm of work, before applying to a design, since this will ensure an even finish. However, varying tension can also be an effective means of creating shading in creative work.

Try to ensure you have sufficient thread to complete a full row of stitch. It can be difficult with many stitches to join effectively in the middle of a row. If a thread breaks in the middle, unpick back to the edge of the shape and finish the thread.

MOVING TO THE SECOND EYELET

1 Once the first eyelet is complete, ensure that the last stitch pulls away from the hole as you travel to the next eyelet. Otherwise, you may see the working thread travelling across the hole, thus obscuring it.

2 Work a tiny stitch over one thread of the ground fabric, shown by the green stitch in the diagram. This stitch holds the thread away from the eyelet hole, and will disappear into the fabric weave. You can then travel easily to the next eyelet without obscuring the hole in any way. It is not always necessary to work a locking stitch when moving to the next eyelet. This will depend on where you wish to work the next eyelet. This technique enables you to move safely between eyelets in any direction however.

3 As you begin the next eyelet (see red stitch in diagram), ensure that the first stitch wraps back towards the travelling thread from the first eyelet. This will ensure a good tension on the new eyelet, and the hole will open effectively.

Tips

You can work either clockwise or anti-clockwise around an eyelet.

You may also like to use a stiletto to open the eyelet hole further.

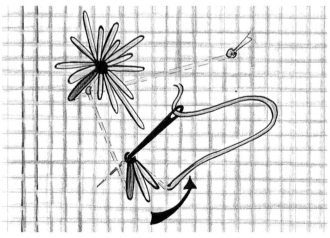

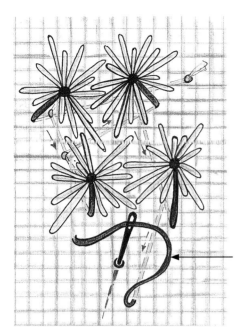

FURTHER EYELETS

Work more eyelets of random shapes, each locking into the shape of the existing ones. Alternatively, you may prefer to leave more ground fabric showing between the eyelets.

The green threads in the diagram, left, show the path travelled between eyelets on the reverse of the work.

The green stitches are the locking stitches (worked over a single fabric thread) which are used to secure an eyelet before moving on to the next

Beginning to work the fifth eyelet

The working thread wraps back towards the travelling thread from the fourth eyelet. This gives a good tension on the fifth eyelet and helps to open up the hole.

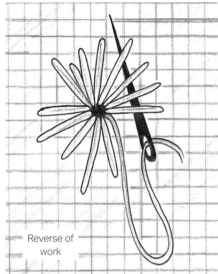

Reverse of work

FINISHING THE THREAD

To finish the working thread, turn to the reverse of the work and slide the thread through the back of a few of the eyelet stitches.

COUNTED HONEYCOMB STITCH

Honeycomb stitch is worked in horizontal rows across the fabric and produces a beautiful lace-like effect, reminiscent of hexagonal cells of honeycomb, punctuated by small holes.

Pulled thread stitches may be worked within a design area with a solid outline. If the shape has a solid line and will be outlined later, casting on the thread can be worked in the normal fashion using the WKT. Other stitches, such as the free eyelets shown previously, can be secured by working the embroidery over the casting on thread to secure. However, some pulled work patterns have minimal thread on the reverse, for which this technique is unsuitable.

If the shape is being created solely using the pulled thread stitch, with no outline to be worked, and the stitch has minimal reverse coverage, the following method can be used, hiding the casting-on process beneath the embroidery stitch.

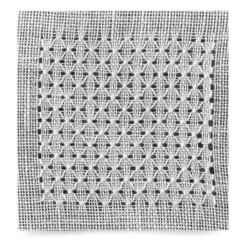

1. STARTING THE THREAD

Tie a knot in the thread. Take the needle down through the fabric close to the point at which you want to start the honeycomb.

As the diagrams show, the thread is secured by working three backstitches in a vertical row, each stitch being worked over a single thread of the ground fabric.

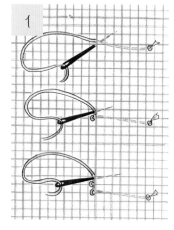
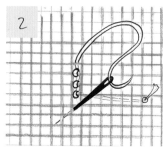

2. STARTING THE HONEYCOMB STITCH

(See right) The first stitch of the honeycomb pattern is a vertical stitch worked from top to bottom over five horizontal threads of the ground fabric. This covers and hides the starting stitches beneath.

3. WORKING THE HONEYCOMB STITCH

a Having worked the vertical stitch down over five ground threads, take the needle to the left behind four ground threads.

b Wrap the thread back over these same four ground threads; the needle then travels beneath them to the left again. Pull this stitch tight.

This process forms a wrapping stitch around the block of four vertical ground threads, pulling them up tightly and forming a hole at each end of the stitch.

c The thread then travels up over five ground threads again, before passing the needle beneath a further four ground threads to the left.

d The thread wraps back over these four ground threads and the needle repeats the stitch. Pull this stitch tight.

This process forms a second wrapping stitch around the block of four vertical ground threads.

e The diagram shows how the stitch continues in this pattern across the width of the row.

Each vertical stitch is laid up (or down) over five horizontal threads of the ground fabric. Each horizontal stitch wraps tightly around four vertical threads of the ground fabric.

At the end of the row, a tiny locking stitch is worked over a single thread of the ground fabric to secure the 'pull' of this row, before moving down to the next. This stitch is hidden beneath the last honeycomb stitch of the row, as shown.

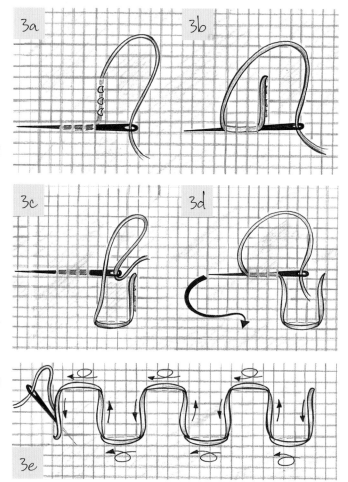

4. MOVING TO THE NEXT ROW

a A tiny locking stitch is worked over a single thread of the ground fabric, to secure the thread before beginning the second row. This stitch is covered and hidden by the first honeycomb stitch of this second row.

b The second row is a mirror image of the first row, and is formed of laid vertical stitches and wrapped horizontal stitches in the same way. Where the two rows join, the horizontal stitches become double. The tension of the stitches pulls the design into a hexagonal honeycomb pattern.

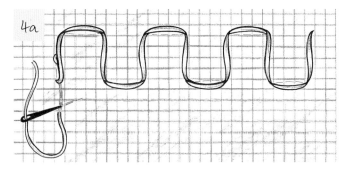

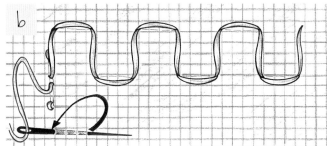

5. FINISHING THE THREAD

At the end of a section of honeycomb stitch, the thread is finished securely as follows (right): three tiny backstitches are worked, each over one thread of the ground fabric. These are hidden beneath the last honeycomb stitch.

Tip

Try altering the length of the laid vertical stitches to create a 'shaded' effect, as shown, below left.

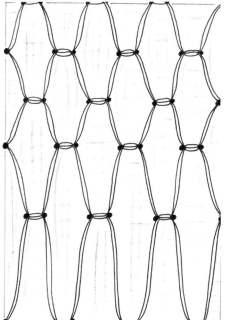

The overall pattern of the stitch and changing the depth of the stitch

Gradually changing the depth of the vertical stitches can produce an interesting shaded effect.

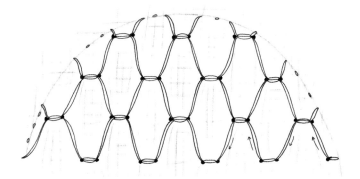

Fitting the stitch to a curved shape

This diagram shows how the stitches are adjusted to fit to the outline of a curved design shape. Tiny stitches, each worked over a single thread of the ground linen, are used to secure each row, and to travel from one row to the next.

If the vertical stitches are shortened at the end of the row, try to 'slant' them a little so that they look in keeping with the general pattern.

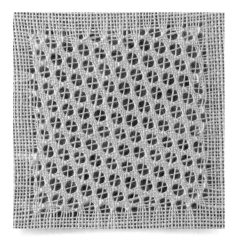

DIAGONAL DRAWN FILLING

This is a small, delicate stitch, useful for creating overall lacy backgrounds in small areas.

1 Cast on the thread as previously described. Work a vertical stitch northwards over four fabric threads. The needle then passes diagonally to the left by four vertical and four horizontal threads.

2 Work a horizontal stitch to the right over four fabric threads. The needle passes diagonally to the left under four horizontal and four vertical threads.

3 Repeat step 1.

4 Continue in this fashion to the end of the row, working a locking stitch over one thread of the fabric to complete the 'pull' of the row (see stitch marked in green). Work a locking stitch over one thread to begin the new row (see red stitch). The return row is a mirror image of the first, leaving a cross of one horizontal and one vertical thread between the rows.

5 Continue to work rows back and forth, pulling tightly. The threads left between the rows form crosses, which look like tiny windows.

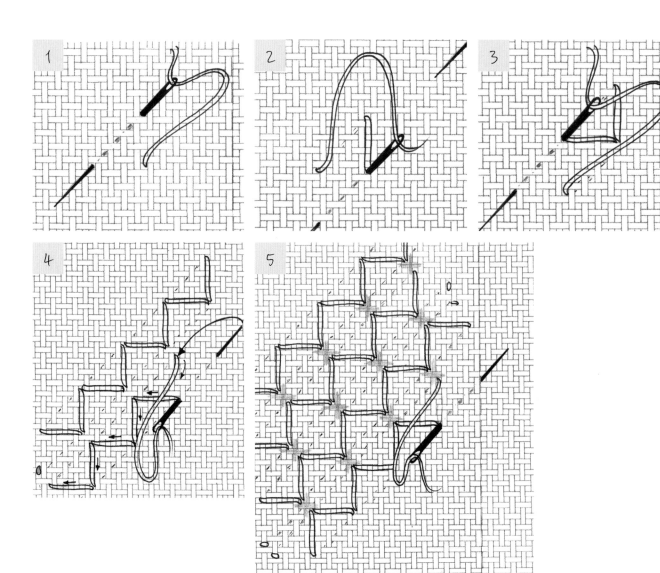

DOUBLE WAVE STITCH

This stitch produces horizontal rows of strong holes, which are effective for small areas.

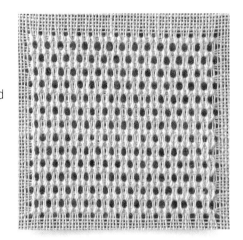

1 Cast on the thread as previously described. Note that this stitch will not cover the casting-on stitches in the same way. If the design shape is not to be outlined, start the thread leaving a long tail, which can be darned into stitches on the reverse upon completion. Work a diagonal stitch towards the top-right, two vertical threads over and four horizontal threads up. Stitch under four vertical threads to the left.

2 Repeat this stitch before passing the needle to the left under four horizontal threads.

3 Work the next stitch to form a triangle with the first two stitches.

4 Repeat this stitch and pass the needle to the left beneath four vertical threads. Continue in this fashion along the row.

5 Further rows are worked as mirror images of the previous rows. Pull tight throughout.

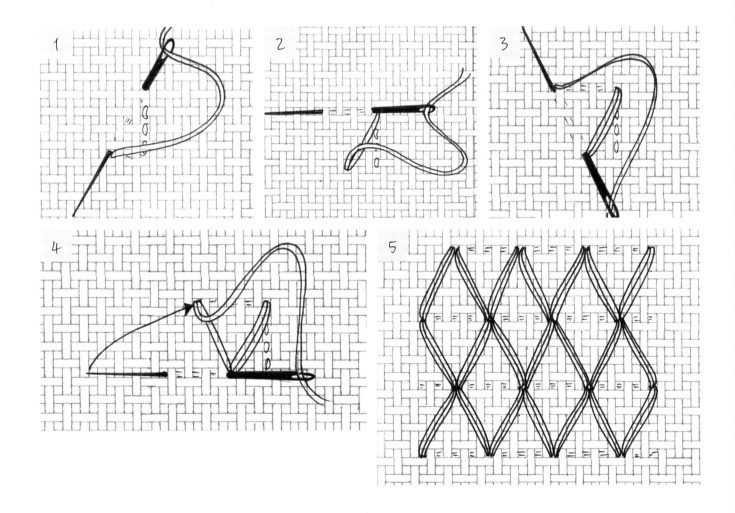

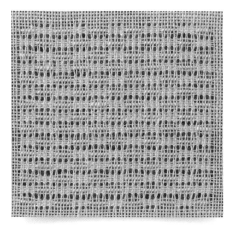

REEDED STITCH

This is a beautiful, delicate stitch combining bands of satin stitch with rows of double backstitch. The double backstitch forms a criss-cross herringbone on the reverse of the work, creating a sense of subtle density.

The stitch can be worked in formal rows or in a random pattern. The former is excellent for architecture, and the latter is particularly useful to produce sketched suggestions of texture, such as water, ground or tree bark.

1 Cast on the thread using a surface knot; pass the starting tail behind the first row to be worked. Work a band of five vertical satin stitches, each over two ground threads.

2 The needle emerges at X. Take a backstitch to the right over two ground threads. The needle emerges four threads up, ready to work a further backstitch directly opposite.

3 Work the second backstitch. The needle emerges, ready to work a third backstitch to the left of and in line with the first.

4 Complete a block of six backstitches, working from side-to-side and between each, forming a herringbone pattern on the reverse. The needle emerges, ready to work the second block of satin stitch.

5 Continue across the row, working alternating blocks of five satin stitches and six double backstitches. Work a locking stitch at the end of the row and the start of the next. Work the second row back to the right. This time, the blocks of satin and double backstitch alternate with those on the previous row.

This method of working can be adapted to form random combinations of satin, double back and backstitches, creating a softly textured effect – as shown on pages 128–187, within the *Small Birds May Fly High* design.

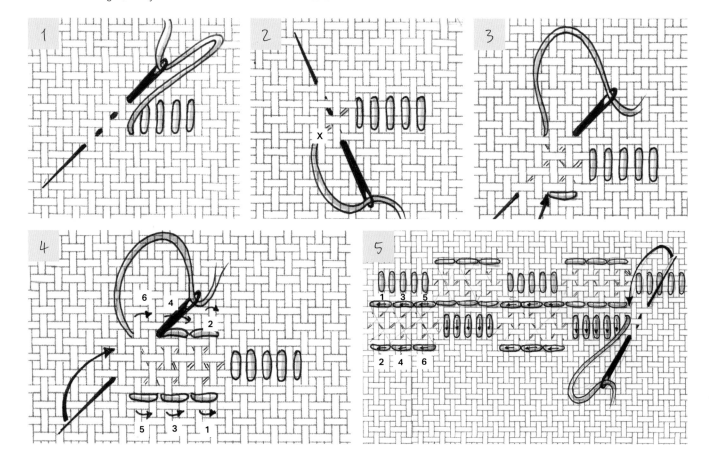

LADDER STITCH

Ladder stitch is a beautiful, useful pulled thread stitch, which forms a string of tiny holes with a firm couched boundary line. It is not counted and does not have to follow the straight grain of the fabric so can be worked along curved, organic lines. It is useful for opening up the work and drawing the eye through a design.

Ladder stitch must be worked with tightly twisted, strong, fine threads such as cotton lace thread for fine work, Coton à Broder, perlé cotton or one strand of stranded cotton for slightly bolder work. It is also possible to use a heavier thread (or even several threads) for the corded outline, compared with those used for stitching, to provide a bolder edge.

This sample was worked using Coton à Broder no. 25 with a cording thread of Coton à Broder no. 16.

Tip

When working ladder stitch, do not make the backstitches too small, else there will not be enough give in the fabric to complete the ladder stitch process, and the holes will become blocked.

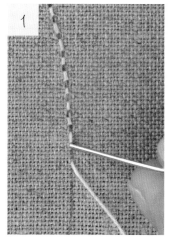
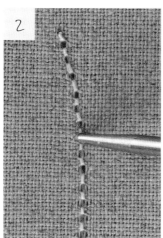

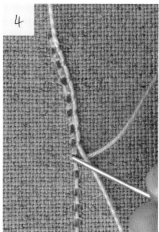

1 Cast on the thread (WKT) along the design line or close by. Work an even backstitch along the design line. Each backstitch should be 1–2mm (¹⁄₁₆in) in length. Pull each backstitch taut so that a small hole starts to open between them.

2 Push a fine awl into the holes between each backstitch to open them up and make them more evenly sized.

3 Take two further lengths: cast on both threads (using the WKT) close to the tip of the ladder. Bring up one thread to the right of the backstitch line and lay it simply alongside the backstitch as a cording thread. Use the second thread (here, shown in blue) to work a further backstitch over the top of the original backstitch (in white).

4 Bring up the thread in the fabric to the right of the cording thread and level with the next hole along the ladder. Then stitch it over the cording thread and drop it down into the hole, thereby couching the laid thread. Pull all stitches tight.

5 Work a backstitch over the top of the next (original) backstitch along the line and then repeat the couching stitch into the next hole. Repeat this process of backstitch, couching stitch, backstitch, couching stitch, all the way along the prepared backstitch line. Keep some tension on the laid cording thread to ensure that it sits smooth and taut. Push a fine awl into each of the holes on completion to make them more distinct and even.

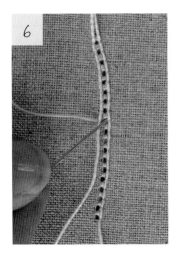

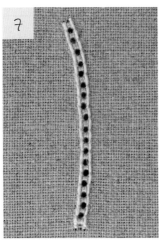

6 On reaching the bottom, secure and finish both couching and stitching threads, either by working stab stitches into an adjacent shape, hiding these under the laid edge of the ladder, or by turning to the reverse and oversewing into the back of the stitching, taking care not to obscure the ladder holes. The same process is now repeated along the left-hand edge of the ladder using new couching and stitching threads.

7 On completion, finish off each thread as described above, and open the holes with the awl again.

LADDER STITCH VARIATION

This is a slightly bolder and stronger version of ladder stitch, where the corded edge is thoroughly covered with binding stitches, rather than openly spaced couching. The stitch can also be used to seal the edges of open areas, such as for net insertion in fine whitework (see *Small Birds May Fly High* design, pages 128–187).

1 Where you would normally work one stitch into the open hole, work one or two stitches, depending on the size of the holes.

2 Wrap the centre bar with one stitch as normal.

3 Work two to three couching stitches to the left of the bar, into the fabric of the bar itself. Then bind into the next hole and so on.

4 Open all the holes at each stage using a fine awl.

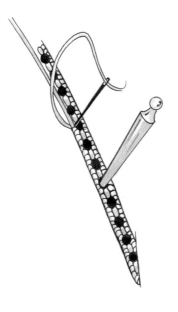

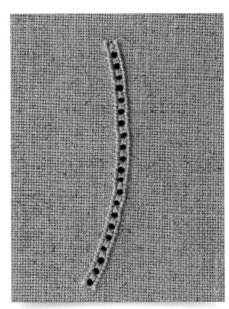

The finished stitch.

THREE-SIDED STITCH

Three-sided stitch is a pulled thread stitch closely related to wave stitch. It can be worked as a counted stitch along the fabric grain, but can also be freely worked along a curved line. When working the latter, the stitch placement and size are judged by eye.

It is a very effective stitch for opening up the fabric to allow light to penetrate and drawing the eye through a design, in the same way as ladder stitch.

This sample is worked in Coton à Broder 25 with a chenille 24 needle.

The completed three-sided stitch.

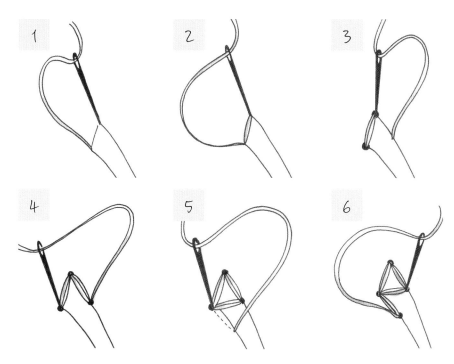

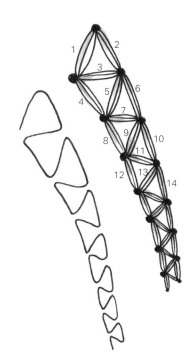

1 Work straight stitch across the end of the design shape. Pull the stitch tight, creating holes at each end.

2 Repeat this stitch, using the same holes. Pull tight again.

3 Take a stitch out along the right hand-edge of the design shape. As you place the needle, try to visualize this as forming an equilateral triangle shape with the previous stitches. Repeat this stitch again as before. Pull both tight.

4 Work the next stitch to form a triangle, connecting back to the starting point. Repeat this stitch again. Pull both tight.

5 Work a new stitch out along the left-hand edge, again visualizing a triangle with the previous stitch. Repeat the stitch and pull tight.

6 Work the next stitch to complete the second triangle. Repeat this stitch and pull both tight. Continue in this way along the design shape, working two stitches in every stitch position. Pull all stitches tight and try to maintain an even tension, thereby creating even-sized holes between the stitches, which should all be about the same length.

On completion, use a fine awl to open up and even out the holes.

The diagram above, right, shows the completed effect and the pattern of the stitch, which clearly links three-sided stitch to the structure of wave stitch. The diagrams on the right show how three-sided stitch can be adapted to fit a pointed leaf shape.

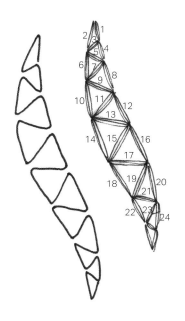

FRETTED TECHNIQUES

Fretted techniques exploit the structure of the weave of the ground fabric. The warp (or weft) threads of the fabric are withdrawn and removed, exposing the weft (or warp) threads in bands. Sometimes both warp and weft are removed, to create lattice mesh structures and larger voids, and to allow a greater amount of whatever is placed behind the work to show through. The remaining fabric threads can be manipulated, pulled and distorted into pattern forms by working stitching upon them and across voided areas.

Fretted techniques incorporate knotting to pull threads together or apart; twisting the fabric threads over themselves to form patterns; and needleweaving to recreate areas of density. The dramatic open spaces, contrasted by the delicate, lace-like designs, create a great sense of depth and texture – reminiscent of fretwork.

These techniques are commonly referred to as 'drawn thread work'.

CHOICE OF FABRIC

Traditionally: Cottons and linens with reasonably even structures and strong warp and weft threads. These are sometimes 'evenweaves' (with the same number of threads per defined measurement in the warp and weft).

In practice: Any fabric whose warp (or weft) threads can be removed, leaving threads of sufficient strength to remain intact and withstand further stitching and distortion.

CHOICE OF THREADS

Traditionally: Fine strong threads with a reasonably high twist, such as cotton and linen lace threads.

In practice: Any, fine, strong thread such as fine perlé cotton, lace threads, Retors d'Alsace or crochet thread. The weight of thread should roughly match the weight of one thread of the ground fabric; or can be slightly heavier for a bolder effect. Avoid threads which are fibrous, lightly twisted or break easily under tension.

FABRIC FOR SAMPLES

The following samples are worked on linen with 12 threads/cm (30 threads/in) using no. 12 Retors d'Alsace.

WITHDRAWING THREADS FROM THE FABRIC (DRAWN THREAD WORK)

Due to the nature of the fabric weave, withdrawing groups of threads usually forms vertical (or horizontal) bands of openwork in the fabric, which therefore create a bold, geometric feel.

In order to remove fabric threads, the surrounding fabric must first be secured. The following diagrams show how to secure the fabric at both ends of a band of fabric threads to be withdrawn.

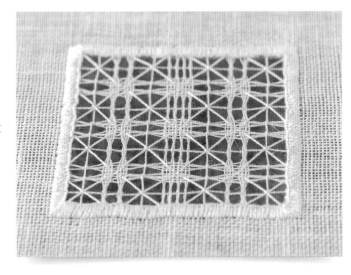

SPLIT STITCH PREPARATION

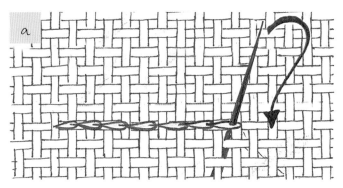

SPLIT-STITCH EDGE

1 Thread a sharp-pointed embroidery needle with Retors d'Alsace no. 12. Tie a knot in one end.

2 Decide on the width of withdrawn band you require. You can mark this with pins or tacking if you find this helpful.

3 Place the knot close to the point you wish to start stitching. There is no need to work any starting stitches. The thread will be secured as you work over it.

4 Work a row of small, even split stitches across the width of the band. The split stitches sit on top of the fabric thread which runs along the end of the band to be withdrawn. The split stitches therefore split the linen thread. Hence it is essential to use a sharp needle (embroidery or chenille) for this process.

SPLIT-STITCH EDGE CONTINUED

The process shown in diagram a, left, is repeated back and forth across three further fabric threads, below the first, as shown. Each row of split stitch again sits on top of the fabric thread.

These four rows of split stitch help to trap and secure the linen.

On a finer fabric, the split stitch could be worked across every two threads rather than on every thread.

BUTTONHOLE

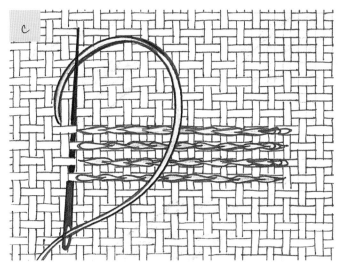

1 Continue to use the same thread for the buttonhole as for the split stitch, if it is in good condition. If not, finish the split stitch thread with a couple of tiny backstitches hidden within the rows of split stitch.

2 Start the new thread for the buttonhole by carrying it behind the band you are about to work.

3 Bring the needle up in the row of holes above the split stitch band, and one thread to the left.

4 Work a buttonhole stitch as shown, which drops down in the row of holes below the split stitch band, and emerges in the row of holes above. The buttonhole therefore encloses four fabric threads.

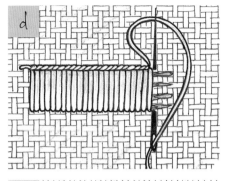

BUTTONHOLE STITCH CONTINUED

Continue to work buttonhole stitch across the band, enclosing the four horizontal fabric threads.

Do not simply work a buttonhole stitch into each hole in the fabric however; work some buttonhole stitches which split the vertical linen threads. This is essential to form a dense band and will further secure the ground fabric to enable you to cut threads away safely. You do not have to work into every hole and every thread; simply work a dense, even buttonhole across the width of the row.

COMPLETING THE ROW OF BUTTONHOLE STITCH

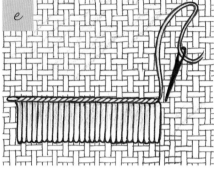

At the end of the row of buttonhole, take the needle down one hole to the right of the end of the split stitch band. The buttonhole stitching thread emerges at the end of the band and then slides back under the band to secure it. Then cut away the excess.

Work a buttonhole bar at the opposing end of the band of fabric to be withdrawn. The buttonhole will face the opposite direction to the existing band, with the knotted head facing towards the band to be withdrawn.

Take great care to ensure that the two buttonhole bands are worked across the same vertical linen threads, so that they line up exactly.

WITHDRAWING THE THREADS

The threads will be withdrawn from the reverse of the work where it is easier to cut them cleanly away against the buttonhole bands. It is also best to have the ground fabric loose while removing threads.

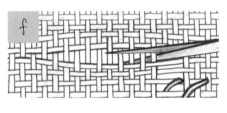

At a distance away from the buttonhole band, use a blunt tapestry needle to push the horizontal linen threads apart, exposing the vertical threads to be withdrawn more clearly.

Using very sharp scissors and great care, cut across the vertical fabric threads which are to be removed.

COMPLETING THE BUTTONHOLE BAND

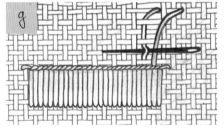

Use the tapestry needle to carefully and gradually unpick a fabric thread back to the buttonhole band barrier.

As you reach the band, pull gently on the fabric thread while snipping it cleanly away, flush against the buttonhole, ideally using curved-tip scissors.

Repeat this process with each fabric thread in turn. Note that the last vertical thread enclosed by the buttonhole, on both the left and right edges, should not be cut and remains intact. This gives greater support to the band at the edges.

Tip
You may find it helpful to work lines of tacking thread along the two edges of the band, to ensure that the two bands of buttonhole line up exactly.

HEM STITCHING

Hem stitching is used as a decorative and strong means of securing a rolled hem on a fabric.

Hem stitch is also used to secure and neaten the edges of drawn fabric bands, preventing the fabric threads running alongside the band from sliding inwards. It also pulls the exposed band threads together into tighter 'clusters'. These clusters are stronger than individual fabric threads. This also creates more space between the groups of threads, resulting in greater visual definition. Hem-stitched bands therefore create the perfect base onto which further pattern stitches can be worked. The following samples are worked on an evenweave linen with 12 threads/cm (30 threads/in).

SIMPLE SLANTED HEM STITCH

When using hem stitches to create the clusters for a drawn thread band, it is important to consider how many threads will be drawn into each cluster. If too many threads are drawn together, this may distort the edges of the band. It will also limit the patterns which can be worked onto the clusters, as broadly spaced clusters are difficult to draw together.

In finer fabrics, more threads can be clustered into each stitch than in coarser fabrics. Threads may need to be grouped into even numbers for certain patterns. Ultimately, the band should be planned and a sample worked, to allow for the cluster sizes to be tested and to ensure that they are appropriate for the pattern.

The ground fabric should be taut when working hem stitches.

Simple hem stitch is worked from left to right along the edge of the withdrawn band.

Needle: All hem stitching is worked using a blunt-tipped tapestry needle which will pass between, rather than through, the linen threads.

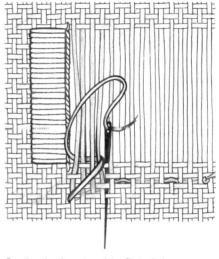

Starting the thread, and the first stitch.

STARTING THE THREAD

1 Use a knot on the surface a short distance from the point at which the hem stitching will begin (see yellow thread in diagram, above right).

2 Work two running stitches, each over one thread of the ground fabric as the diagram, above right, shows. These stitches will disappear into the fabric.

WORKING THE STITCH

1 Bring the needle up at the left-hand end of the band, and four fabric threads down from the edge.

2 Take a diagonal stitch up and across two by four fabric threads. *Note that the diagram shows four by four threads but two by four is more appropriate for 12 threads/cm (30 threads/in) linen and for working the following patterns.*

3 Loop the thread behind and then around in front of the cluster of two fabric threads.

4 Pull the wrapping stitch tight.

5 Return the needle vertically down behind four linen threads, ready to work the next stitch.

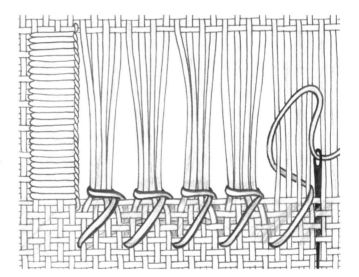

CONTINUING THE STITCH

The stitch continues across the width of the band, grouping the exposed fabric threads into clusters of two. Each hem stitch must be pulled tight to ensure that the fabric threads are clustered effectively and securely.

WORKING THE OPPOSITE EDGE

The opposite edge is worked in the same way. It is often best to turn the work around so that you can comfortably work from the left to right again.

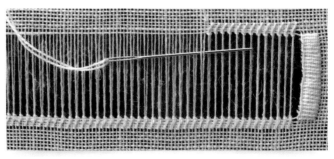

DECORATIVE PATTERNS

Innumerable patterns can be worked over a prepared drawn and hem-stitched band. These can be simple and bold, or highly intricate and detailed. The choice and effectiveness of patterns depend on:

- **The weight and count of the ground fabric** Stiff fabrics with a low thread count will suit only simple patterns as there will be insufficient 'give' in the fabric threads to manipulate into anything more complex;

- **The number of fabric threads clustered by the hem stitches** Complex patterns often require smaller numbers of threads per cluster, so that the clusters have more movement and are easier to manipulate;

- **The width of the withdrawn band** Complex patterns usually require a wide band, again so that the fabric threads have more 'give'.

Patterns are usually created using one or more of the following techniques:

- **Knotting:** to pull threads together or apart;
- **Interlacing:** to manipulate fabric threads into pattern forms;
- **Needleweaving:** to recreate solid areas.

The ground fabric should be taut for working all pattern stitches.

KNOTTING

THREAD Retors d'Alsace No. 8 (or perlé cotton No. 8)

STARTING A THREAD

1 Pass the thread through the reverse of the buttonhole band.

2 Bring the needle up at the centre of the buttonhole emerging through the fabric within the buttonhole band, not just the knotted head of the buttonhole (see point A).

3 Take the needle down again at the same point (see point B) thereby forming a loop of thread.

4 Bring the needle up through the loop and pull tight. This locks the thread securely around the buttonhole edge.

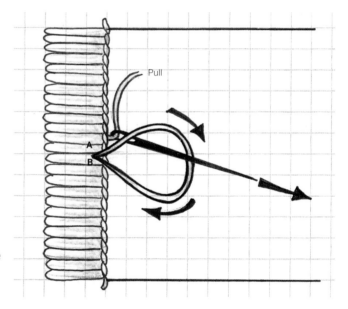

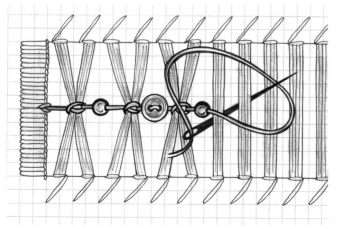

WORKING THE 'CORAL KNOT'

The diagram on the left shows how to work a coral knot to draw together two clusters of threads.

1 The working thread lies along the centre of the drawn band, flowing to the right.

2 A loop of thread is formed to the left of the centre.

3 The needle passes beneath the two clusters of fabric threads, emerging out through the working loop.

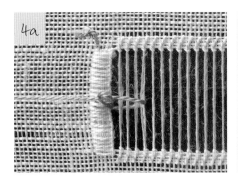

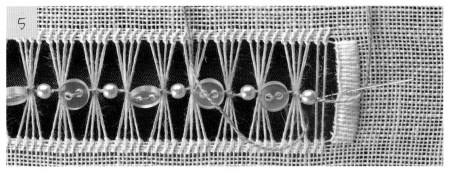

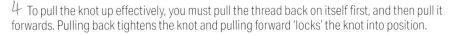

85

4 To pull the knot up effectively, you must pull the thread back on itself first, and then pull it forwards. Pulling back tightens the knot and pulling forward 'locks' the knot into position.

5 At the end of the band, the working thread can be finished by working a coral knot around the edge of the buttonhole band (in a similar way to starting the thread).

Unless you have counted the number of fabric threads to form clusters to fit a pattern exactly, you may find that you have to create a half block of the pattern at the end of the row. Secure the working thread by passing to the reverse of the buttonhole band and darning back and forth through the reverse of the stitches.

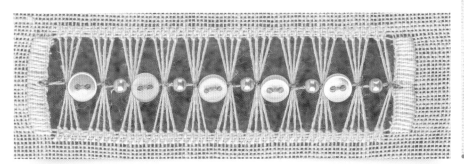

The completed band.

INTERLACING

Use Retors d'Alsace no. 8 (or perlé cotton no. 8).

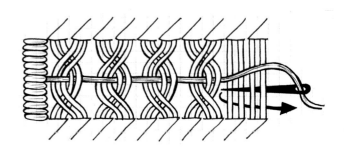

1 Start the thread in the buttonhole band, as previously described, using a coral knot to anchor it at the centre (see page 84). The clusters are grouped into even numbers of twos or fours. The working thread passes to the right through the centre of the band.

2 The needle passes back to the left, slipping under the first two clusters in the group and over the second two.

3 The needle now passes to the right beneath the four clusters. The working thread is pulled tight to the right, forcing the right-hand group back over the left.

4 The taut working thread traps the twist formed.

5 At the end of the band, the working thread can be finished by working a coral knot around the edge of the buttonhole band.

Different patterns can be produced by varying the numbers of clusters twisted together.

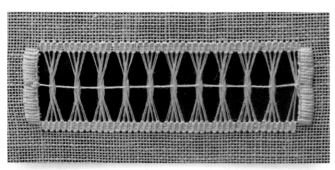

The completed sample with four clusters grouped together.

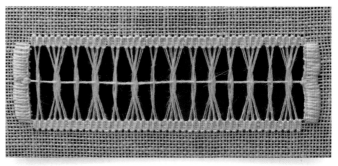

A variation of the pattern alternating four grouped clusters with two grouped clusters.

Tips

The working thread should be tight along the length of the band but should not distort the line of the buttonhole bands excessively.

It also works well to use a fine ribbon through the centre. The ribbon should be secured to the reverse of the buttonhole bands at each end, using firm oversewing with a fine thread.

DRAWN THREAD FILLING STITCHES

These can be worked within a square or rectangle, as shown here, but can also be worked within curved design motifs in fine whitework pieces (see *Small Birds May Fly High* design, pages 128–187). Fabric threads can be removed in a pattern vertically or horizontally only, to form stripes, or in both directions to form a web-like lattice. To prepare for working samples of these stitches:

1 Plot the design area using pins or tacking, calculating the number of fabric threads to produce an even pattern repeat.

2 Secure the four perimeter edges using rows of split stitch covered with closely worked buttonhole stitch, in the same manner as for the simple bands (see pages 81–82).

3 Slacken the tension on the ground fabric and turn the work to the reverse. At the centre of the section of threads to be removed, lift the first thread using the tip of a tapestry needle and snip.

4 Gradually unpick the thread back to the buttonhole edge. Pull gently while clipping away flush with the edge, using curved-tip scissors. Continue to remove each fabric thread required in the same manner, working across the design shape to produce the desired pattern.

5 Re-tension the ground fabric, taking a little more care due to the weakening effect of removing many threads.

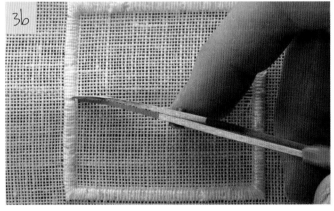

Tip

When working a drawn thread filling within a square/ rectangle, it is more visually pleasing to have an open band running alongside each buttonhole edge, rather than a solid section of the design.

AYRSHIRE-STYLE VERTICAL DRAWN THREAD FILLINGS

This is a beautiful, delicate form of drawn thread work which appears often in finer examples of nineteenth-century Ayrshire whitework. It is most commonly worked in a vertical direction, helping to draw the eye up through a design. It can however also be worked horizontally.

As a small pattern, it fits well into confined areas within a design. The technique has various options for embellishment (see overleaf), creating many possible pattern combinations.

Binding: Retors d'Alsace no. 12, tapestry needle no. 24

Patterns: Retors D'Alsace no. 12 for feather stitch and raised chain, Retors d'Alsace No. 8 for satin triangles and blocks.

CREATING THE STRUCTURE

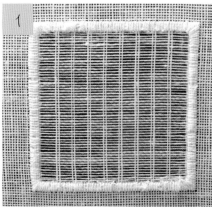

> ## Tips
> Try variations of this pattern to create different effects, such as draw six, leave two, draw two, leave two, draw six, leave two, and so on.

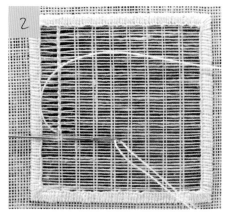

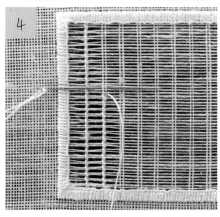

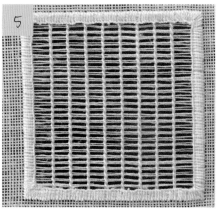

1 Work on the reverse of the loose fabric. Starting along the left-hand edge of the shape, withdraw vertical threads in a regular pattern of draw four, leave two, draw four, leave two. Tighten the fabric.

2 Each remaining band of two vertical threads is now oversewn (working each stitch diagonally over two by two threads), binding the threads together to make them stronger and visually more defined. This also clusters together the remaining horizontal threads into twos, in the same manner as hem stitching. The clusters and the spaces between are also more defined, in readiness for working pattern rows. The thread for working the oversewing is secured by darning into the reverse of the buttonhole outline. The needle then emerges at the point required, passing out as if from beneath the head of the buttonhole edge.

3 At the bottom of the row of oversewing, tuck the needle firmly into the solid edge, beneath the buttonhole stitching.

4 Work a tiny hidden locking stab stitch by bringing the needle up and down between the buttonhole stitches, to fully secure the row. Move to the next row to be worked and work a further hidden stab stitch into the buttonhole band at the base of the row. Oversew back up the row in the same fashion, aligning the diagonal slant of the stitch with that of the first row (you can work each row in the opposite direction if preferred).

5 Oversew each band in the same manner.

Fill the remaining open bands with the patterns of your choice. You can choose to work a pattern in alternate bands rather than in every band, as this highlights the patterns more effectively (see pages 89–90).

WORKING THE FILLING PATTERNS

These are usually worked in alternate rows of the ground structure so that they can be seen more clearly.

Secure the working thread for each row of pattern in the reverse of the buttonhole band. Allow the needle to emerge from beneath the buttonhole band to start the pattern. Use thread long enough to allow you to work along the full length of the band without running out.

> ### Note
> Drawn thread fillings are often best worked using a sharp-tipped chenille or embroidery needle, as you will need to pierce the fabric at the perimeter edge.

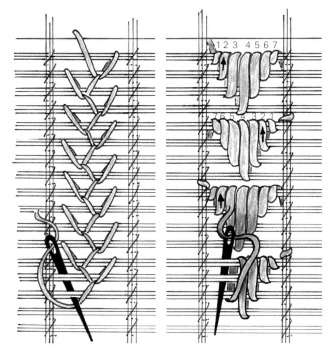

Feather stitch.   Satin triangles.

FEATHER STITCH (WORKED USING RETORS D'ALSACE NO. 12)

1 Bring the needle up at the top left-hand side of the band. Form a loop of thread to the right and pass the needle down beneath the first two clusters of the band, to emerge up through the loop. Ease into place snugly around the bars until the stitch appears settled and steady. Avoid pulling the stitch so tight that the bars become distorted and the stitch less visible.

2 Now throw a loop to the left. Take the needle down behind one cluster from the previous feather stitch group and one new cluster. Emerge through the working loop. Ease the stitch into place as before.

3 Return to work a stitch to the right and then the left again, before continuing in this zigzag formation down the length of the band. At the base, secure the thread by tucking into the buttonhole band beneath its rim. Finish the thread by darning into the reverse of the buttonhole.

TRIANGULAR SATIN (WORKED USING RETORS D'ALSACE NO. 8)

1 The diagram above shows the working of the fourth triangle in the row. Bring the needle up at the right-hand side of the band. The needle passes down underneath the first cluster and is then pulled back up towards the top of the band, forming a wrapping stitch.

2 The next wrapping stitch to the left picks up the second cluster as well in the same way.

3 A third wrapping stitch picks up three clusters.

4 A fourth picks up four clusters. This creates the peak of the triangle.

5 The fifth stitch returns to wrapping three clusters, the sixth, two, and the seventh, one, completing the left half of the triangle. To move to the next triangle, the thread travels to the left of the wrapped bar, at a point level with the base of the worked triangle. It slips over this bar to lock the first triangle, putting the thread in position to work the next satin triangle towards the right.

6 The tension of the wrapping stitches should be settled rather than tight: as too much tension will distort the bars and make the triangles less defined. The locking stitches worked over the wrapped bars should be firmly tensioned to ensure they are less visible. Continue to work triangles back and forth until the band is complete. Secure the thread in the buttonhole edge as before.

See the photograph overleaf for the finished effect.

RAISED CHAIN (WORKED USING RETORS D'ALSACE NO. 12)

1 Bring the needle up at the centre of the band. The thread passes down over two clusters before passing back up beneath these two clusters to the left of the centre.

2 Form a loop of thread to the right and pass the needle down beneath the two clusters to the right of centre, emerging up through the loop to form a chain stitch. Ease the stitch up quite firmly, without pulling too tight. The two clusters will ease together to form a bow-like shape.

3 Repeat along the band.

SATIN BLOCKS (WORKED USING RETORS D'ALSACE NO. 8)

1 Bring the needle up at the left side of the band and pass it beneath three clusters. The thread is passed back up over the three clusters to form a wrapping stitch before passing under the same group again.

2 Wrapping stitches continue in this manner over to the right-hand side, forming a block of satin stitch.

3 The tension of the wrapping stitches should be a little tighter than for the satin triangles but a rectangular shape to the block should be retained rather than pulling too tight.

4 Moving to the next block uses the same process as described for the satin triangles, working a locking stitch over the bound bar. Continue to work blocks back and forth along the length of the band.

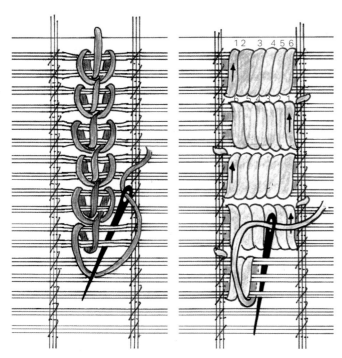

Raised chain.

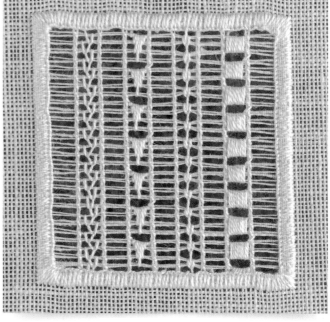

Satin blocks.

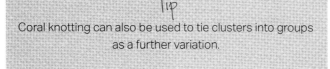

Tip

Coral knotting can also be used to tie clusters into groups as a further variation.

VOIDED TECHNIQUES

At the opposite end of the whitework spectrum to sculptured techniques, voided techniques provide some of the most dramatic and therefore visually pleasing effects to be achieved in white-on-white embroidery.

Strong stitches are used to pull open larger holes, with definite shapes, in the ground fabric. Even larger design shapes can be outlined and secured with strong, decorative stitchery which can also be padded and raised. The fabric within these outlines can then be cut and removed, creating large open decorative voids. Decorative stitching can also be worked across the voids to restore some density, and to add further texture and the web-like quality of lace.

This is a bold form of work, creating dramatic rents – and therefore great depth – in the fabric, particularly when juxtaposed by weighty or padded stitchery. Voided design areas must be balanced carefully throughout a design, since their stark effect is usually more impactful than surface work. These holes draw the viewer's eye more deeply into a design, and through to the world beyond the fabric.

CHOICE OF FABRIC

Traditionally: Cottons and linens with a dense weave.

In practice: Any fabric with sufficient density to facilitate working stitching which is strong enough to support large holes. Cutwork can be effectively worked on silk organza, wool flannel and even on some papers.

CHOICE OF THREADS

Traditionally: Fine strong threads such as stranded cotton, perlé cotton, coton à Broder.

In practice: Any, fine, strong thread such as stranded cotton, perlé cotton, lace threads, Retors d'Alsace, Coton à Broder.

TINY PUNCHED EYELETS

Eyelets are holes in the ground fabric with a shape defined by a bound edge. Small eyelets are made simply by punching a hole in the ground fabric using a stiletto, before the edge is bound. The threads of the ground fabric are pushed apart rather than being broken. These eyelets are very strong, even though their size is limited in diameter.

Eyelets provide pinpoints of light within a design, revealing tiny glimpses of whatever is placed behind the work. Using eyelets throughout a design (in whitework or indeed any other form of embroidery) can have the effect of turning on fairy lights in a darkened room, adding life and sparkle.

The thread used for the sample is Floche à Broder (although one strand of stranded cotton is excellent for a finer finish); the needle is an embroidery size 10.

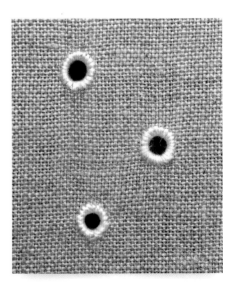

The completed eyelets.

Draw a tiny circle no greater than 5–6mm (³⁄₁₆–¼in) diameter using a circle template and fine pale grey marker pen. The outline should be smaller than the required size of the eyelet, as the eyelet will become slightly bigger when worked.

Rather than casting on, place a knot on the surface of the work, close to the eyelet.

1 Bring the thread up on the design line and work small, evenly spaced running stitches (approximately 1mm or ¹⁄₁₆in) around the edge. The spaces between the stitches should be the same size as the stitches themselves.

2 Work around the eyelet again in the same direction, filling in the spaces with double running stitches to form a continuous line. Bring the working thread up outside the running stitch at the base of the eyelet.

3 Push and twist a stiletto firmly into the circle formed, until the fabric pushes out fully to meet the running stitch, leaving a clean hole.

4 Bind the edge by bringing the needle up in the fabric, just outside the running stitch, and dropping it down into the hole. As the needle drops, pull the thread firmly back away from the eyelet, beneath the work. This helps to pull the fabric open and trap fabric fibres into the bound edge. Avoid pulling on the fabric around the eyelet, and keep the stitches an even length and tension. Also avoid making the bound edge too narrow: not only will this produce a weak eyelet, but it is also the contrast of the solid edge against the open hole which provides the most visually pleasing effect. Keep using the stiletto to open and polish the hole throughout the binding process.

5 If the eyelet is set within, or next to, a solid design area, the thread can be secured within this area in the normal fashion. If the eyelet is isolated, it must be finished using the 'double loop technique' as follows: stop binding the eyelet edge two stitches short of the join. Bring the thread to the surface as if you were about to work the next binding stitch. Place a stiletto (or similar) as shown and work the binding stitch over this.

92

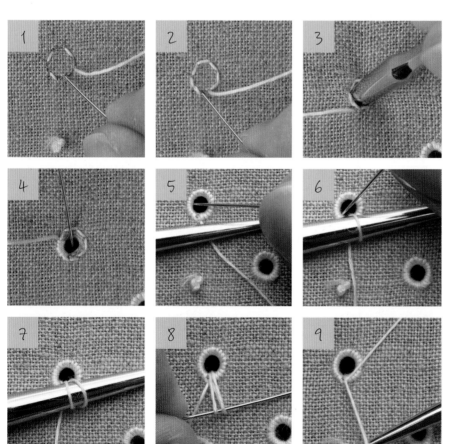

6 The needle emerges on the outer edge to work the next binding stitch, again working over the stiletto.

7 The needle emerges again on the outer edge as if to work a third stitch. Take care not to pierce the thread of the stitches sitting over the stiletto as you do this.

8 Carefully remove the stiletto and pass the needle and thread back through the two loops. Do not pull the thread tight at this stage. Ensure that the loops lie in the correct order and do not slip over each other.

9 Insert the tip of the stiletto into the second of the two loops made (on the left in the eyelet shown below). Raise the stiletto, pulling the loop upwards, to tighten the first loop snugly into the edge of the eyelet. Pull the stiletto firmly to tighten the stitch, retaining the tension on the stiletto.

10 Take the tail of working thread and pull, retaining tension on the loop throughout, using the stiletto. If you relax tension on the stiletto, the first stitch, which has already been tightened, may work loose. At the last minute, remove the stiletto and pull up the tiny amount of remaining slack in the working thread. Pull firmly on the thread in the same direction as it travelled through the loops (do not fold it back on itself) and wiggle it from side to side until it is as tight as possible.

11 Pull on the working thread while clipping it cleanly away using curved-tip scissors. Finally, place the stiletto back in the hole and twist to give a final crisp and polished finish.

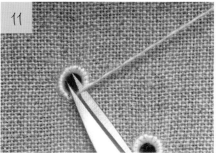

Tip
Avoid over-cramming the binding stitches together – this can produce an uneven edge. Remember that the diameter of the circle on the outer edge, where the needle rises, is larger than on the inner edge, where the needle descends. If you cram the stitches together on the outer edge, they will fall over each other as they drop into the eyelet.

93

LARGER EYELETS

Larger eyelets can be created by cutting the fabric within the perimeter of the running stitch edge. These larger eyelets can vary in shape – circular, triangular, square, asymmetric; they are crisp and defined and their effect, bold, stark and dramatic.

The thread used for this sample is, again, Floche à Broder (one strand of stranded cotton is excellent for a finer finish); the sample is worked with a number 10 embroidery needle.

1 Draw a circle 1–1.2cm (⅜–½in) diameter using a circle template and fine pale grey marker pen. Secure the thread using a simple knot, as for the tiny eyelets.

2 Bring the thread up on the design line and work small evenly spaced running stitches (approximately 1mm or 1/16in long), around the perimeter. The spaces between the stitches should be about the same size as the stitches themselves.

3 Work around the eyelet again, filling the spaces, to make double running stitch. On completion, bring the needle up on the outer edge of the running stitch at the base of the eyelet.

4 Insert a stiletto in the centre to make a small hole. Then use sharp scissors to snip from the hole out towards the running stitch edge, creating evenly-sized flaps. Cut as many as required to allow these to fold back smoothly around the edge (six in this example).

5 Use the stiletto to push the flaps of fabric back neatly to the reverse, producing a hole with a clean edge. Press each fold back with your finger to firm the crease.

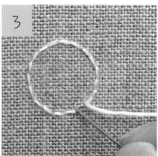
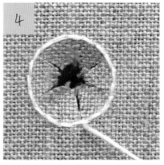

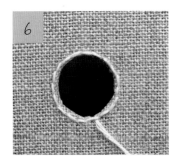
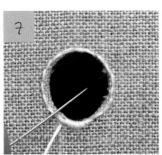

Tip

If you are working much larger eyelets or working on a delicate fabric, you may wish to work a second row of double running stitch next to the first – two rows will provide extra strength and a little more padding.

6 Now bind the edge, bringing the needle up in the fabric, outside the running stitch, and dropping it down into the hole.

7 Lay each stitch carefully in place and try to maintain a consistent depth, to ensure a smooth, crisp edge. Do not pull as tightly on these stitches as when working a tiny eyelet: due to the weakening of the fabric from the cutting process, a gentle tension should be employed. Avoid making the edge of the eyelet too thin – these large voids require a slightly deeper edge (1mm/¹⁄₁₆in minimum) to restore their strength.

8 Finish the thread as for the tiny eyelets (see pages 92–93), and roll the stiletto around the interior of the eyelet to smooth and burnish. Finally, turn to the reverse of the work and trim away closely the excess flaps of linen using curved-tip scissors.

SHADED CUT EYELETS

Shaded eyelets have a bound edge, which 'shades' from wide to narrow. The contrast of the heavy, padded areas of the bound edge against the large hole created is quite dramatic. Teardrop shapes are traditional for these eyelets, but the method can be adapted to many different shapes, as shown right.

The thread used for the surface and padding is Floche à Broder (one strand of stranded cotton is excellent for a finer finish, combined with Floche for the padding), worked with a size 10 embroidery needle. The templates for all four shapes shown on the right can be found on page 189.

1 Trace the teardrop eyelet pattern shape onto the fabric. Secure the thread as for the round eyelets (see page 93).

2 Work around the outer edge with small, evenly spaced running stitches.

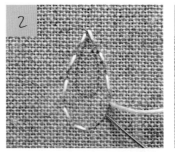

3 Fill the spaces in between with more running stitches to create double running stitches.

4 Travel the thread from the base of the teardrop, back up to the tip, by working a few tiny stitches within what will be the padded area of the eyelet. Work a neat, even running stitch around the smaller, inner teardrop shape. (This does not need to be double running stitch.)

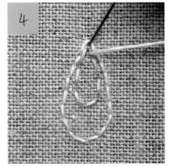

5 Fill the eyelet border with padding (shown in blue for clarity) using concentric rows of long running stitches, worked back and forth around the curved shape. Make the stitches as long as possible on the front, for impact, and as tiny as possible on the reverse, for a flat back. Long split stitch can also be used for padding. Run the first row around the perimeter of the inner teardrop, then work outwards.

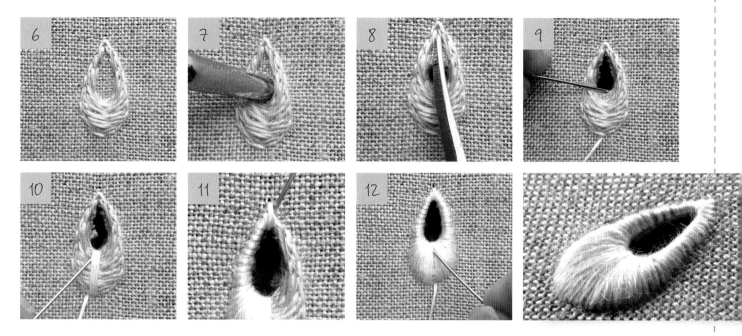

6 Add a further layer of padding on top to give greater weight to the broad base of the eyelet. Work in the same way as the first layer, finishing slightly inside the perimeter edge to produce a domed effect. Here, the second layer is shown in a green thread for clarity.

7 Insert a stiletto into the round part of the inner teardrop.

8 Use scissors to cut up to the point, making two fabric flaps. Use the stiletto to push the flaps back and press between your fingers to firm the crease.

9 Start to bind the edge of the eyelet. Bring the needle up on the outer edge of the eyelet at its widest point. The needle then drops down into the central hole.

10 Begin to work around the edge of the eyelet in this way. Place each stitch carefully so that it lies neatly and does not overlap its neighbour. Avoid pulling the stitches too hard – these eyelets are quite delicate. The outer perimeter of the teardrop shape is longer than that of the inner teardrop void: wedge stitches ensure that

the outer edge remains solid without clogging the central hole and causing the binding stitches to overlap. The needle emerges as usual on the outside edge and works a three-quarter-length stitch, worked down into the padding stitches and tucked towards and beneath the previous satin stitch. These stitches can be worked at any point within the wide section of the edge, to turn the angle of the stitch more rapidly.

11 The binding continues around the left-hand side, gradually becoming thinner. When working these narrow sections, avoid pulling the working thread too tightly, thus causing the central hole to gape. The tip of the shape can be strengthened, and the point sharpened, by working three-point stitches, slightly longer than the rest, to form a tiny 'triangle'.

12 Continue binding down the right-hand side, adding wedge stitches as necessary. You will require more of these in this second half. Finish with a wedge stitch, which settles the two halves of binding neatly together and prevents them overlapping.

Tip
If you would like to achieve greater definition on a large padded eyelet, a split stitch can be used around the perimeter edge in place of the double running.

BEADING

Beading is technically a larger version of ladder stitch (see pages 77–78) which allows much bolder holes to be created, and taper in size. It is an extremely strong technique as no fabrics threads are broken. It is therefore very effective for creating dramatic swathes of openwork within a design.

Thread: Floche à Broder

Needle: Embroidery 10

The template for the sample, shown right, can be found on page 188.

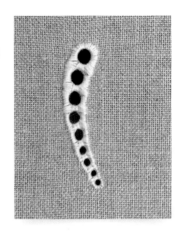

1 Trace the design shape onto the fabric. Work a running stitch around the perimeter edge, then fill the spaces to make this double running stitch.

2 Firmly insert a stiletto to make the first hole within the running stitch outline, at the broadest part of the shape. The hole will push out to meet the running stitch outline.

3 Bring the needle up at the bottom-left corner of the first eyelet hole, on the outside of the split stitch, and down into the hole. Note that the stitch will be a little broader and slightly angled at this point.

4 Continue to bind around the top of the eyelet; the needle should always emerge on the outside edge and drop down into the hole. Pull the thread firmly back away from the hole to ease the fabric open further as you work each stitch. The stitches become shallower as they travel around the top edge of the eyelet. As the stitches travel down the right-hand side of the eyelet, they begin to widen and become angled again. At this point, stitch a straight stitch (a bar) across to the far side of the design shape, to the outside of the running stitch edge.

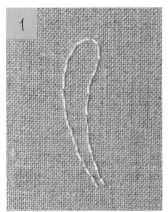

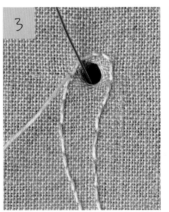
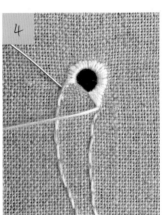

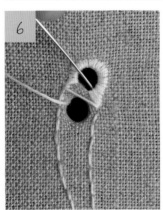

5 Reinsert the stiletto just below the bar, to define the width of the bar. Avoid making it too thin, which will weaken the beading; too broad, and it can appear heavy and clumsy. It should ideally be the same thickness as the bound perimeter edge.

6 Remove the stiletto and bring the needle up in the new hole before dropping it down into the first hole. This stitch begins to bind the bar of fabric. Work three or four further binding stitches, and pull these tight.

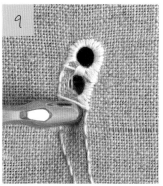
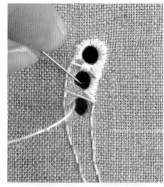

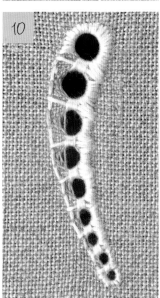
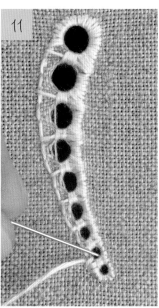
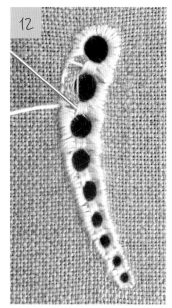

7 Bring the needle back up on the right-hand edge, outside the running stitch and down into the new hole.

8 Bind along the right-hand edge of this hole. The stitches will initially be angled and a little longer, they become straight and short, and then increase in length and angle again. At this point, the second bar is worked.

9 Make the third hole and bind the bar in the same manner. On completion, bring the needle back up on the right again to bind the next section of the edge.

10 Continue to bind and create holes and bars down the full length of the right-hand side.

11 On reaching the bottom, bind around the base edge before starting to bind along the left-hand edge.

12 Continue to bring the needle up on the left-hand side and down into the holes. No further binding is applied to the bars. The stitch angles echo those on the right.

Tip

Some embroiderers do not like to see the slight gaps which form between the stitches where the bar meets the edge. These gaps tend to be more prominent at the larger end of the design shape, and are emphasized here by the coloured fabric but are reasonably invisible in white-on-white. If you do not wish to see these, however, you may tuck some tiny wedge stitches into the spaces, as shown in the image for step 12.

LACE SPIDER'S WHEEL FILLING IN ROUND EYELETS

This is a simple web-like filling, which can be used to add further interest to even the tiniest eyelets. It can also be used to fill the larger holes worked in beading.

Use Coton à Broder no. 25, or cotton lace threads for smaller eyelets; adjust the thread size used in proportion with the size of the eyelet.

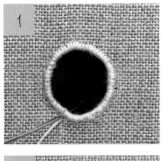

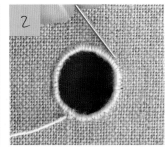

1 Secure the working thread by working two tiny stitches tucked in between the binding stitches, at the bottom-left corner of the eyelet. Bring the needle up on the outside edge of the eyelet.

2 Throw a bar across the eyelet to the upper right-hand corner.

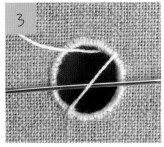

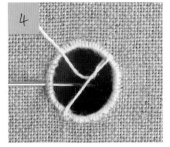

3 Bring the needle up in the hole and pass it around the laid bar to form a twist. Pull towards the centre of the eyelet to tighten.

4 Pass the thread over to the centre-left.

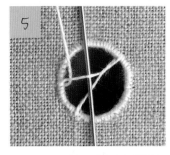

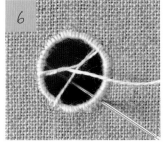

5 Pass the needle and thread around the bar to form a twist. Pull towards the centre to tighten.

6 Pass the thread out to the lower-right and twist back to centre in the same way. Tighten towards the centre.

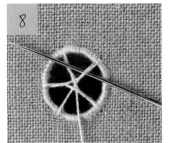

7 Repeat with a final bar to the top-left. Pull tight to the centre.

8 Begin to weave around the centre anti-clockwise, weaving over and under the uneven number of spokes. Ease the weaving stitches tight into the centre.

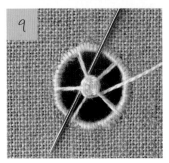

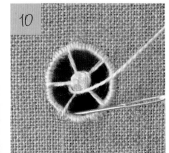

9 Continue weaving until a neat, firm centre is produced. Finish weaving at the top-right corner. After weaving over the bar, the thread travels behind the centre circle to emerge as shown.

10 Pass the thread over the untwisted bar and to the reverse of the work, putting a final twist onto the plain bar. The thread should be secured by catching into the edge of the eyelet on the reverse of the work.

A TYPICAL ROUND AYRSHIRE NEEDLELACE FILLING

Lace fillings appear in many forms of historical whitework but some of the most famed, for their intricacy and beauty, appear in nineteenth-century Ayrshire work. These are worked using fine cotton lace threads and are principally based on detached 'twisted buttonhole stitch'. They provide an airy, delicate laciness to designs and reduce the starkness of larger holes, while restoring strength to bigger eyelets.

It takes practice to perfect the technique and to achieve a perfect tension: I highly recommend that you practise within a larger eyelet, using heavier threads, before moving to finer lace threads.

The filling shown here is typical of Ayrshire work and produces a beautiful effect; innumerable variations of the patterns can be achieved simply by changing the spacing and number of stitches in each row. This sample is worked using perlé cotton no. 8, and a number 24 chenille needle. The template can be found on page 189.

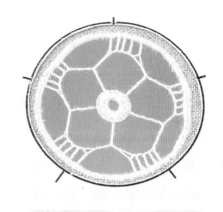

BEFORE YOU BEGIN

1 Draw a circle on your ground fabric using a template: this sample uses a 3cm- (1¼in-) diameter circle. Work a cut eyelet (see pages 93–94); it is advisable to work adjacent rows of double running stitch as a preparation for an eyelet of this size.

2 Take a long length of thread for working your filling – approximately 75cm (29½in). Cast on your thread by burying two tiny stab stitches into the bound edge of your eyelet.

3 Photocopy the template provided on page 189, which shows the markings required to divide the circle into five equal portions. This template can be enlarged or reduced to give a size appropriate to other eyelets. Cut out and remove the central circle.

4 Place the template over the prepared eyelet and use tacking thread to stitch the corners in position.

WORKING THE NEEDLELACE FILLING

1 Bring the needle up on the outer edge of the eyelet at X beside the first mark on your template.

2 Take the needle down on the outer edge of the eyelet again at point Y, about 1mm (1⁄16in) away from point X. Draw the needle down through the fabric just enough to allow it to re-emerge, eye first in the eyelet hole, as shown in step 3. Do not pull the rest of the working thread down through the fabric at this stage. This remains as a large loop on the upper surface.

3 Bring the eye of the needle immediately up inside the eyelet hole. The needle eye must be ahead of the working thread in a clockwise direction. Hold the tip of the needle with your other hand beneath the frame to steady it. The needle is now in the correct position to work the first twisted buttonhole stitch.

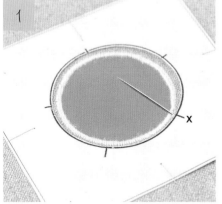

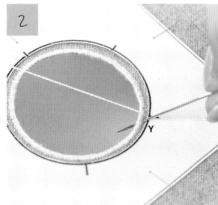

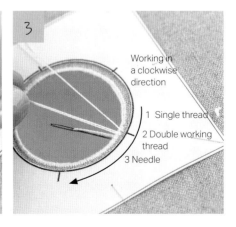

Working in a clockwise direction

1 Single thread
2 Double working thread
3 Needle

4 Twist the working thread twice around the eye of the needle in an anti-clockwise direction.

5 Grab the needle eye, trapping the twists on the needle, and pull towards the centre of the eyelet.

6 Use your needle (or a stiletto) within the resultant loop to tension and settle the twisted buttonhole formed as you pull it into place. Pull until the twisted stitch sits firm and neat, protruding out from the bound edge. Avoid pulling too tight, which would cause the stitch to buckle and seem to disappear.

This first process makes **two stitches: one untwisted and one twisted**. The untwisted stitch will appear to curl over the twisted stitch and can be therefore difficult to see, but if a needle is placed between the two, both will be visible.

7 Take the needle down over the edge of the eyelet in readiness to work the next twisted buttonhole, keeping the spacing between the stitches consistent.

8 Twist the working thread twice around the needle as before, drawing the needle out through the twists towards the centre of the eyelet. Tension carefully as before.

9 Add two further twisted buttonholes in this group to make five in total (remember the first of these remains untwisted). Carry the thread to the next mark on the template, to work the first twisted buttonhole of the new group.

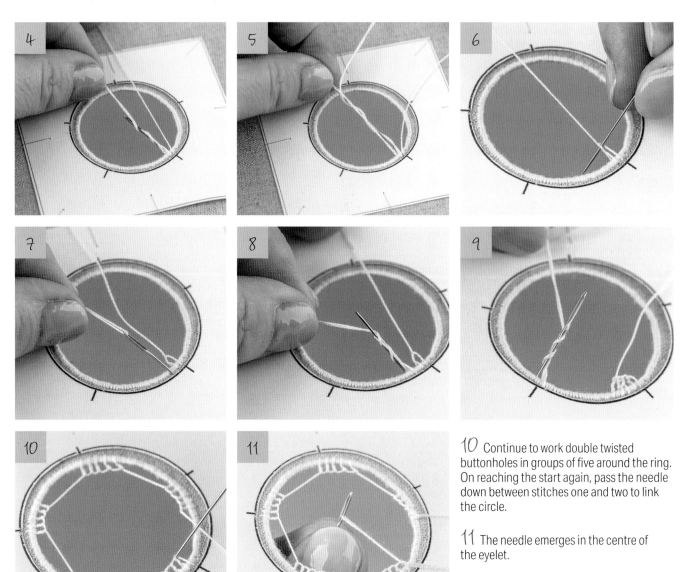

10 Continue to work double twisted buttonholes in groups of five around the ring. On reaching the start again, pass the needle down between stitches one and two to link the circle.

11 The needle emerges in the centre of the eyelet.

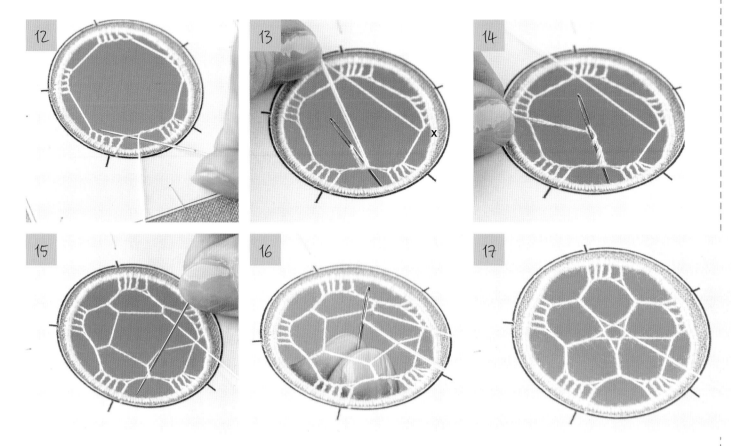

12 Pass the needle down once between every pair of twisted buttonholes round the circle, each time emerging eye first in the large centre hole. This puts a simple wrapped twist between each pair of buttonholes.

Note: Twist twice along the spaces between the groups of five buttonholes. Pull each wrap tight as you work it, in the direction of the circle, *not* towards the centre. This process defines the pattern of twisted buttonhole stitches and strengthens the row, pulling it in towards the centre.

13 On completing the row of twists, work *one twist only*, into the last large space before the starting stitch. Your thread will then sit at the centre of this long bar (point X). From here, begin the second row of twisted buttonholes. Take the needle down into the next large space, as shown. Bring the eye of the needle straight up in the large centre hole. The needle eye must be ahead of the working thread in a clockwise direction.

14 Twist the working thread twice around the needle. Pull the needle through towards the centre of the eyelet. Ease the new double twisted buttonhole into place firmly. You have now made two stitches, one untwisted and one untwisted, just as you did at the start of the first row.

15 Work a further three more double twisted buttonholes on this row, one into each large space on the previous row. Pull each tight by pulling towards the centre of the eyelet again. On reaching the start, drop the needle down into the space between the untwisted starting stitch and first twisted buttonhole.

16 Bring the needle up again immediately in the centre, eye first.

17 Work a further wrap or twist into every space between the remaining twisted buttonholes of the row. Pull each twist tight as you work by pulling round with the direction of the circle. As you pull up these twists, the centre of the filling will begin to close inwards, applying tension across the filling as a whole. This will produce the six-pointed star shape shown. Do not pull so tight that the centre closes completely.

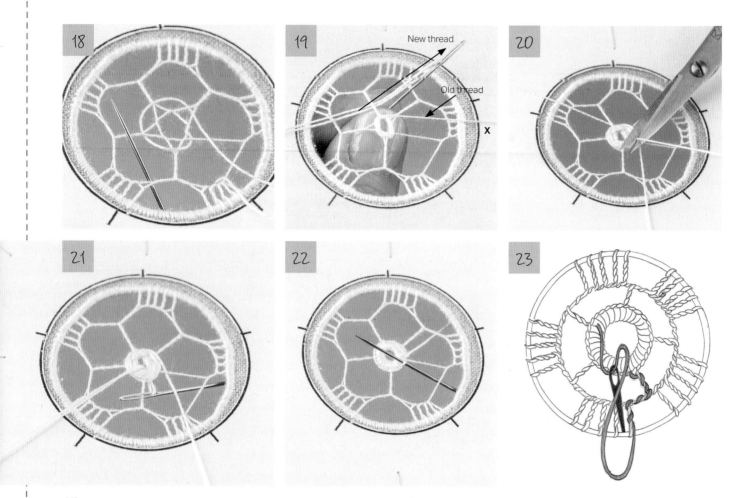

18 Use the needle, eye first, to weave over and under the five spokes created, to pad out the centre. Weave approximately 15 times round; always finish at the same point at which you started. This will pull the centre in a little tighter and put a little more tension on the overall filling, which should now feel taut across the space. Do not pull so tight that the central hole closes completely.

19 Padding the centre is a good opportunity to discard your thread if it is becoming short or worn and start a new one. Simply pass the thread out to the right-hand side and catch it into the surrounding fabric, leaving it hanging. See point X in the photograph. Take a new length of thread and use a knot to secure this temporarily into the fabric to the left of the eyelet. Bring the thread across to the centre of the filling and continue to weave from the point at which you left off.

20 Continue to wrap around the centre for at least eight wraps. You can then safely cut away the tail of the old thread and the starting tail of the new thread.

21 Again starting next to the untwisted stitch of the previous row, cover the padded ring with tight, neat buttonhole stitches, working clockwise. There is no need to work a certain number of buttonhole stitches between each spoke – just work a dense ring.

22 On reaching the starting point, pass the needle up through the looped head of the first tight buttonhole stitch, thereby linking the ring.

23 Now return the thread to the outer edge of the eyelet by twisting around the so-far-untwisted sections of work. This should give an even tension across the filling.

The thread finishes on the reverse of the work where the thread can be secured by working a couple of tiny overcasting stitches into the reverse of the eyelet edge.

NET DARNING

A significant whitework technique, used to add a delicate lace-like texture within large, voided areas of designs, is darning patterns onto pre-made net – known as net darning. Originally, the nets were made in fine cotton, and some cotton nets are still available today but tend to be heavier than the early tulles. Patterns can certainly be worked onto these nets but these appear to visually change the structure of the net, as the thread used for the darning is likely to be similar in weight to that from which the net itself is made.

The following samples are worked on nylon 'conservation net', which is very fine, with a beautifully translucent quality. The darned patterns, therefore, appear crisp and clean, and almost as if suspended in space, supported but visually undisturbed by the fabric structure.

Almost all stitches are counted and follow the grid of the net, forming rhythmic, regular patterns in vertical, horizontal or diagonal lines. However, organic patterns are also possible by darning freely drawn patterns into the structure.

There are huge numbers of patterns but the simplest are usually the most visually effective. The following provides a range of patterns with distinctly different character and texture, so forming a useful palette for inclusion within a design. Many other patterns can be invented simply by experimenting with the net structure.

WORKING A PANEL OF NET DARNING

The net should be placed into a shallow hand-held hoop for work. It should be eased smooth, but not tight, since a little give in the fabric is helpful and over-taut net can tear. Both rings of the hoop should be bound with cotton tape to ensure that the net does not catch on the wood.

Study the net carefully to find its straight grain. This is illustrated in the diagram on the right, which shows the straight line of hexagons running through the net, parallel to the cut edge. This is the straight grain.

If you study the edges of your squarely cut piece of net, you will clearly be able to see a straight row of hexagons along two edges, whereas the other two edges will have a zigzag appearance. The two edges with the straight rows of hexagons denote the direction of the straight grain.

Some patterns are worked along the straight grain, others perpendicular to it and others on a diagonal line across the net. Selection of a pattern to suit a design may depend on the direction it is worked on the net and the linear effect this creates. Many further designs can be created by combining patterns together in alternating rows, and by changing the space left between rows.

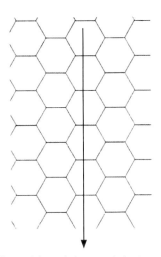

The straight grain in a panel of net.

CASTING ON THREADS

When starting a pattern, the thread is secured to the structure of the net using two tiny buttonhole stitches, each worked around the same bar of the net, as shown on the right. These knots should be pulled tight. This method is very secure, allowing the tail of excess thread to be cut close to the knot without risk of the knot working undone. Within a design, this knot would usually be hidden around the perimeter of a design shape.

Finish threads in the same way using two tight buttonhole stitches worked around a single bar of the net.

TURNING AT THE ENDS OF ROWS

The stitches shown here demonstrate how to turn at the ends of rows. Again, within a design, this turning point would often be hidden within the perimeter of a design so a neat turn is not always essential.

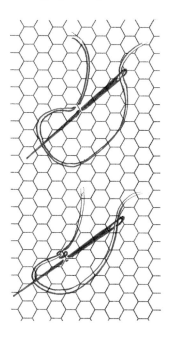

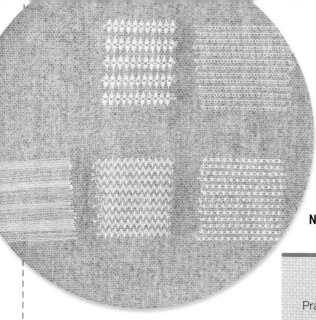

YOU WILL NEED:

Threads Patterns are generally worked using cotton lace threads. Ideally the thread selected should be slightly thicker than the structure of the net but it is effective to experiment with different thread weights, perhaps alternating between thread weights between rows. The threads selected must be smooth and strong: fibrous threads can catch during work and patterns would appear less precise.

These samples are worked using 60/2 cotton lace thread.

Needles Blunt-tipped tapestry needles are essential for net darning.

Tips

Practise patterns on coarse, large-cell net before trying to use finer nets. It is difficult to learn a stitch and work on a small scale at the same time.

Stitches benefit hugely from finding a rhythm of working – hence, practice is essential. Achieving a rhythm will result in the best tension.

The ideal tension for net patterns is achieved when the stitches settle snugly into the structure of the net, without distorting the cell structure. Stitches should not be too loose or else the pattern will not appear crisp and threads could easily be caught, causing damage. Placing your finger beneath the net as you work, pushing gently up into the net and sliding the working needle/thread over the finger, can help to maintain tension and avoid over-tightening stitches.

Work over a plain piece of dark-coloured cardboard to help you see the structure of the net.

BASIC DARNING IN ROWS

Work with the straight grain of the net running horizontally; alternatively, the net can be turned 90°, allowing the rows to flow vertically.

Cast on the thread and then weave over and under the vertical bars of the net, following the straight row of hexagons.

Turn and weave back along the same row of hexagons, weaving over where you wove under previously and so on. Move to the next row and repeat. See diagram, below right.

In this sample, some rows are worked as shown in the diagram, others working just one row of darning within each row of hexagons, creating less density.

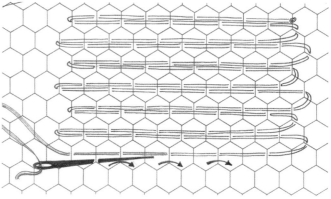

Basic darning in rows.

UPRIGHT LOOP STITCH

This stitch is worked with the straight grain of the net running horizontally. Alternatively, turn the net 90°, to allow the rows to flow vertically.

Cast on the thread as described on page 103. Each loop is produced by weaving over and under the six bars surrounding an individual hexagon, creating a perfectly round form. Leaving a space of one hexagon between each loop, the pattern continues.

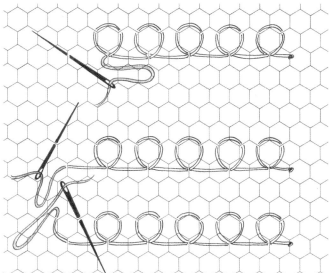

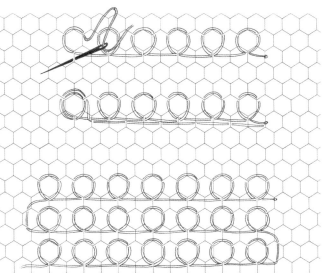

Above, two methods for turning at the ends of rows.

FREELY WORKED LOOPED STITCH

This is a freely worked version of upright loop stitch, which creates a lovely, dainty, frothy effect.

The loops are worked randomly to either side of the centre spine and with varied spacing between them. The space is also varied between the rows.

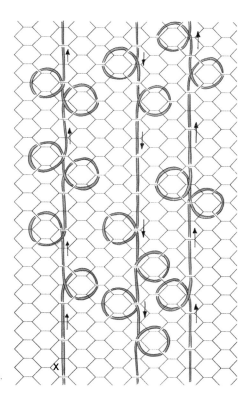

Freely worked loop stitch.

WINGED LOOP STITCH

This delicate stitch is worked along the straight grain and in two parts, working the first row from right to left, creating looped 'wings' along the top, followed by working the mirror image of the stitch from left to right, adding the corresponding 'wings' along the bottom.

Varying the space left between the rows can produce very different effects. Try combining with alternating rows of plain darning for an attractive linear effect.

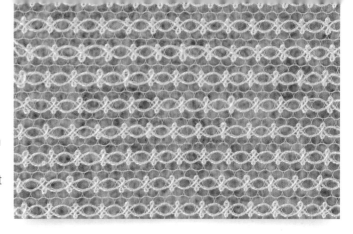

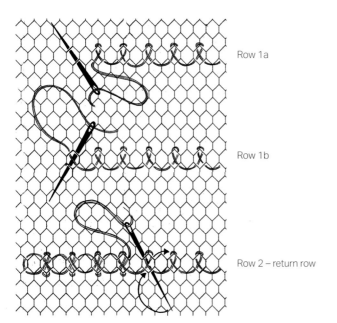

Row 1a

Row 1b

Row 2 – return row

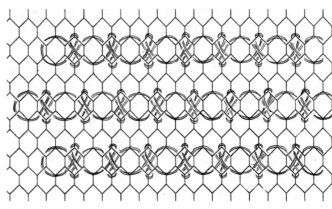

This diagram shows the correct spacing between the rows.

SUNRISE STITCH

Sunrise stitch is worked with the straight grain of the net running horizontally. This creates a pretty suggestion of starburst eyelets.

The stitch is formed by wrapping stitches around a central hexagon and is worked as two rows, the second row being a mirror image of the first. However, it is also effective to work repeating rows of the upper or lower half of the stitch only.

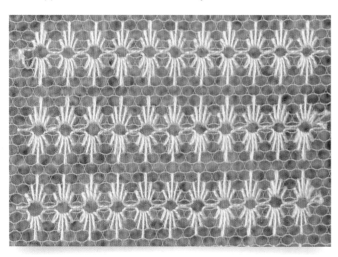

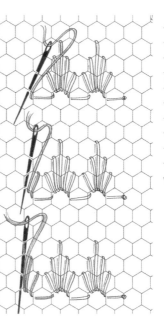

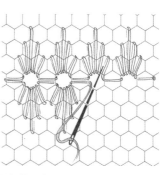

Working the return row.

Working the first row from right to left.

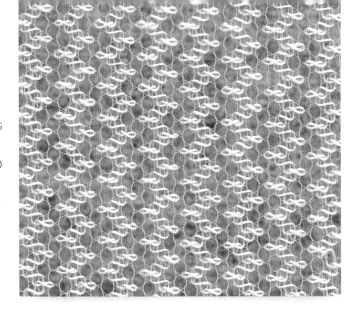

FIGURE-OF-EIGHT STITCH

This intricate stitch creates a beautiful zigzag silhouette. It looks very complex but is actually much easier to work than it appears. It is worked along the straight grain.

Worked in two parts, the figure-of-eight loops are worked from top to bottom, adding a wave pattern to travel back from bottom to top. Try working the wave stage using a slightly heavier weight of thread.

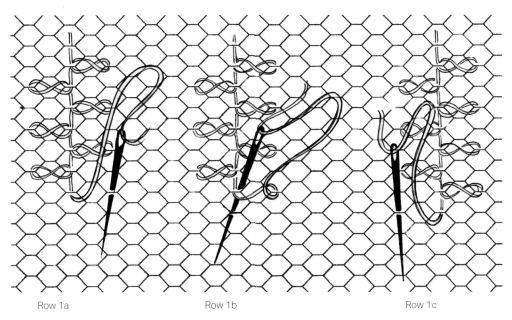

Row 1a   Row 1b   Row 1c

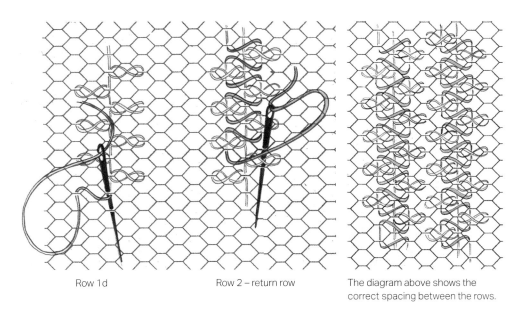

Row 1d   Row 2 – return row   The diagram above shows the
                                                    correct spacing between the rows.

Scabiosa

8cm (3¹⁄₁₆in) diameter

This design is based on the highly textured and almost architectural form of the scabious flower. It contrasts delicate shadow work petals against bold and highly sculptured satin petals. These are set against the textural interest of padded French knots to simulate the flower centre, with the addition of tiny pearls for added lustre and interest. The flower is given a greater sense of depth with the contrasting voided backdrop of open ladder stitch, cutwork and pulled eyelets.

The design is also inspired by the structure of buttons in my own button collection. I love these tiny treasures of design, which cry out to be interpreted in whitework with their sculptured forms and engraved surfaces set against stark holes.

This is a superb design to work to gain a thorough understanding of the full spectrum of the whitework tonal scale and how these techniques can be brought together to create a design with great depth and textural interest.

TRANSFERRING THE DESIGN

Follow the instructions on pages 20 and 34 to transfer the design on page 189 to the silk organza base fabric using the shallow hoop. Transfer the fabric to the deep-edged hoop, ready for stitching.

YOU WILL NEED:

- 25 × 25cm (13¾ × 13¾in) silk organza
- 25 × 25cm (13¾ × 13¾in) 'Bisso' linen, or similar, very fine and sheer linen
- Retors d'Alsace size no. 8 in B5200, bright white (or perlé cotton no. 8)
- Retors d'Alsace size no. 12 in B5200, bright white (or perlé cotton no. 12)
- Stranded cotton in B5200, bright white
- Floche à Broder in B5200, bright white
- Cotton lace thread size 50/2
- 2.5mm white glass pearls × 26
- Circle of stiff acid-free mount board 7.2cm (2¾in) diameter, approximately 1.5–2mm (¹⁄₁₆in) thick
- 16 × 9cm (6¼ × 3½in) of cotton padding or felt (max. 2mm/¹⁄₁₆in thickness)
- 15 × 15cm (6 × 6in) natural coloured fine linen fabric (or a similar, contrasting colour linen or cotton)
- 'Nymo' beading thread (or other strong thread)
- Sandpaper
- Good-quality PVA or EVA glue and glue brush
- Shallow-edged 15cm (6in) diameter embroidery hoop
- Deep-edged 15cm (6in) embroidery hoop, with both rings bound
- Stand to support the hoop
- Sharp, curved-tip embroidery scissors
- Ball-tipped lace scissors
- Stiletto
- Fine awl
- No. 10 and no. 8 embroidery needles
- No. 24 chenille needles
- 0.05mm permanent black drawing pen
- Template – see page 189

Tip
If you find using a pen difficult for transferring the design to the fabric, use a very fine propelling pencil with an H lead, which will not discolour the threads.

Opposite
The finished button.

DOUBLE BACKSTITCH LEAVES

See pages 66–68 for instructions on working double backstitch. Each design shape should be worked using a new length of stranded cotton.

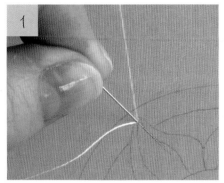
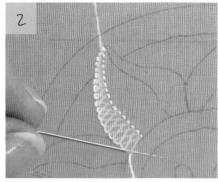

1 One half of each petal is worked in double backstitch, starting at the tip, and working towards the base. Start the thread with a knot placed well away from the design and using two tiny backstitches, work along the design line as described on page 66.

2 As the design shape curls, gradually increase the size of the stitch on the outer edge to keep the two edges in line with each other.

3 On reaching the base of each petal shape, finish off the working thread by working two tiny backstitches along the circular design outline which will be covered by the edge of the 'beading'. Once all the double backstitch petal halves are complete, carefully snip away each starting knot and tail of thread.

LAYERING YOUR FABRICS

Carefully take your silk organza out of your embroidery hoop. Loosen the screw with your screwdriver first so that you do not strain the fabric. Take your piece of fine linen and place the silk organza over the top, aligning the straight grain of both fabrics carefully. The herringbone stitches will be trapped between the two layers and the backstitch edges therefore visible on the top.

Place the two layers together into your embroidery hoop and ease tight carefully until both are smooth and taut. Take care not to distort the design. Lock the ring frame tension by tightening the screw again.

The organza and linen are layered together.

BEADING

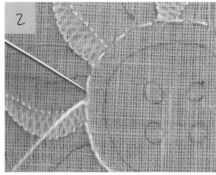
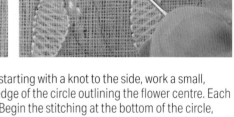

1 Using a length of Retors d'Alsace 12 and starting with a knot to the side, work a small, neat, even running stitch around the outer edge of the circle outlining the flower centre. Each stitch will be about 1.5mm (1⁄16in) in length. Begin the stitching at the bottom of the circle, and close to one of the as-yet unworked satin stitch petals, as the join will be least obvious at this point.

2 Work around again, filling in the spaces between the running stitches, making this double running stitch. Bring the thread up on the outside of the circle, ready to begin the wrapping stage.

3 Using a new thread, repeat the double running stitch around the inner circle. Finish off this thread on completion by working two tiny backstitches within the flower centre, where they will be covered by French knots.

110

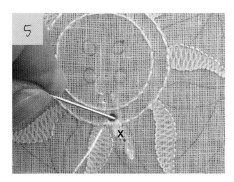
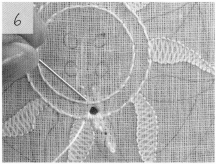
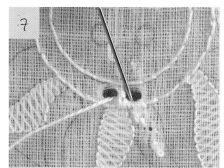
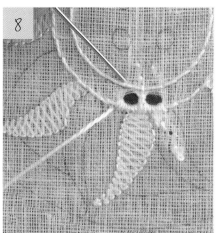
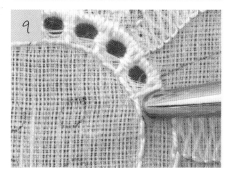

4 Make the first hole with a stiletto between the two rows of running stitch, at the base of the circle. The fabric will push out to meet the rows of running stitch.

5 Starting at X, bind the lower edge of the hole from right to left. Always bring the needle up on the outside edge and take it down into the hole. The stitches will be forced to fall into the angles shown.

6 Pass the working thread over to the opposite edge, forming a bar between the eyelets.

7 Make the next hole to the left before binding the bar, bringing the needle up in the second hole and back down in the first. You will need to work about three binding stitches.

8 Begin to bind the lower edge of the next eyelet hole before creating the next bar, in the same way as before.

9 Repeat steps 7 to 8 around the outer edge of the circle, keeping the holes and bars as evenly sized as possible. On nearing the last quarter of the circle, you may like to portion out the spacing for the remaining eyelet holes using your stiletto, to be sure these are distributed evenly.

10 Once you reach the beginning again, secure the thread. This can be done inside one of the adjoining petals to be worked in satin stitch. Then, taking a new thread, bind the inner edge in the same manner. Inner threads can be secured and finished within the centre of the flower, where they will be covered by French knots.

Tip
If you run out of thread while working around the circle, finish and start the threads within the satin stitch half of a petal, where the small securing stitches will be covered.

The finished effect.

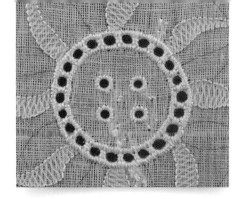

INNER EYELETS

Work the four inner eyelets, following the method previously described (see pages 91–92).

Finish the threads within the main body of the flower centre where they will be covered by French knots (see page 37).

FILLING THE CENTRE WITH PADDED FRENCH KNOTS AND PEARLS

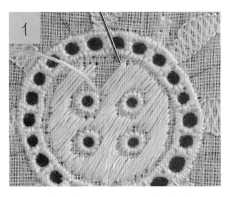

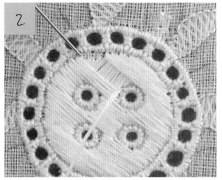

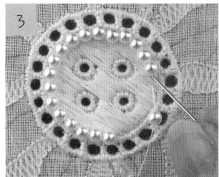

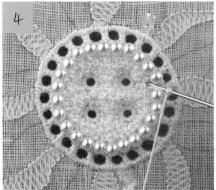

Tip
Work a locking stab stitch into the
padding between backstitching
every bead, to ensure that each
bead is firmly secured
and will not move.

1 Using a length of Floche à Broder, work densely packed padding stitches back and forth across between the eyelets. Take care not to cross the back of the work with a long stitch. Do not extend the padding right out to meet the beaded circle or eyelet edges.

2 Work a second layer of padding in the opposite direction. Again, ensure the stitches are worked back and forth. The stitches will now touch the eyelet edges and beading.

3 Using a length of your lace thread, and a fine needle, stitch a ring of pearl beads around the outer edge of the flower centre, just inside the beading. Each should be stitched as a backstitch, angling the needle back toward the previous bead. This ensures that the beads sit snugly against each other. Each backstitch should equal the width of the bead in length to ensure the beads sit well. If the stitch is shorter, the beads will wobble.

4 The remaining space is now filled using French knots (see page 37) and Retors d'Alsace, no. 12. Start by working a ring of single twist knots around the perimeter of each eyelet. Then fill the rest with knots using two twists on each for greater height. This combination gives an effective sense of contouring.

SLANTED SATIN STITCH PETALS

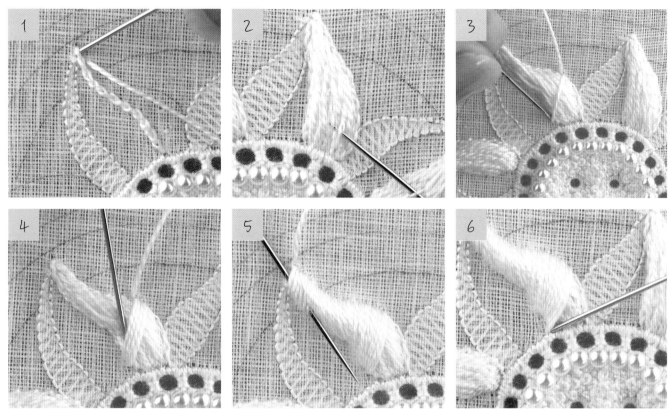

1 The remaining half of each flower petal is worked in padded, slanted satin stitch (see pages 50–52). Each shape is first outlined with a small, neat split stitch, using Retors d'Alsace no. 8. Sharpen the tip of each petal shape by tucking the needle under the existing split stitch as you start to work the second edge.

2 The shapes are then filled with two layers of long split stitch padding (see page 53), again using Retors d'Alsace no. 8. You may also like to add a third layer of surface whipped padding for additional height.

3 The slanted satin stitch begins at the widest point. Stitching then follows the satin stitch rule (see page 47) as you progress towards the top point.

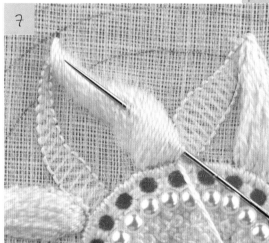

4 Add wedge stitches to turn the angle as required to maintain 45°.

5 Finish at the tip by extending the point a little beyond the split stitch before passing the needle back beneath the padding and satin and trimming away the excess.

6 Work the base using the guidance provided previously on working triangular satin corners. (See page 61.)

7 Finish at the tip by passing the thread back beneath the padding.

LADDER STITCH OUTLINE

The outline around the flower is now worked using ladder stitch (see pages 77–78).

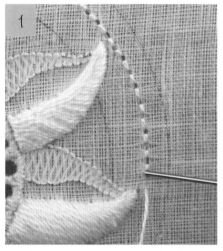

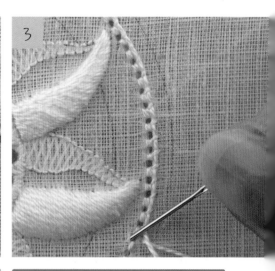

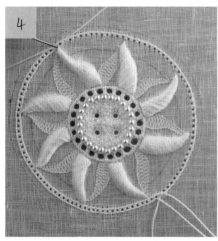
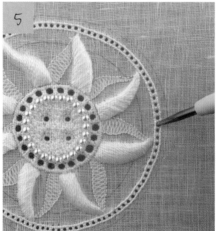

> **Tip**
> If any of the satin petals have extended out over this design line, you may like to plunge the laid thread to one side of the petal and allow it to re-emerge on the far side, therefore appearing to cross behind the petal.

1 Start close to the tip of a satin petal and towards the lower edge of the design. Using Retors d'Alsace no. 12, work small, neat even backstitches around the shape. Pull all stitches tightly to ensure holes are created and avoid making them too small.

2 Use an awl to open all the holes further. On completion of the backstitch, secure the thread by passing through the reverse of the satin petal.

3 Take a length of Retors d'Alsace no. 8 which is long enough to travel around the circle, plus extra to allow tails to be left at both ends. Start close to the tip of another satin stitch petal and again towards the lower edge of the design. Using Retors d'Alsace no. 12 in the needle, work the outer perimeter edge using the ladder stitch technique, couching the laid thread and whipping the bars. Pull tight throughout. On completion, secure the stitching thread into the reverse of the satin stitch.

4 Repeat this process for the inner edge of the ladder, again using Retors d'Alsace no. 8 for the laid thread, secured using no. 12.

5 On completion, the laid threads must be threaded and passed to the reverse of the work where they are secured in the same manner as the stitching threads, by darning into the reverse of a satin petal. Use an awl to open all the holes further, to show the ladder stitch at its best.

FILLING BETWEEN PETALS WITH CUTWORK AND/OR FREE EYELETS

Both of the following methods provide attractive options for filling the spaces between the petals. You may like to select one method or to alternate them as the sample shows. The cutwork is a great deal more time-consuming and fiddly but gives a lovely dramatic contrast to the sculptured petals. The eyelets are more delicate but are beautifully simple to work and therefore provide a pleasing alternative.

CUTWORK

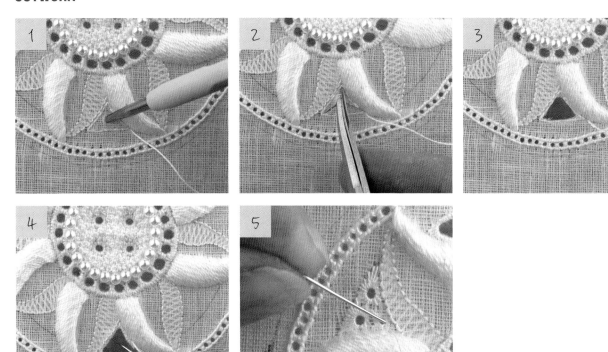

1 Starting at one corner (close to a satin stitch petal), using a single strand of stranded cotton, work a double running stitch around the perimeter of the triangle. A narrow margin (just the width of a no. 10 needle) should be left between the double running stitch and the existing embroidery. Use an awl to open the centre of the space.

2 Use sharp scissors to snip out into the three corners, cutting up to but not through the running stitch.

3 Carefully fold back the flaps of organza/linen and finger press to firm the folds.

4 Begin to carefully bind the edge of the triangle with tiny, neat and densely packed oversewing stitches, with the needle always emerging on the outer edge and descending into the hole. Take particular care as you bind the edge running alongside the shadow work petals. Since these are convex curves, it is easy to distort them. On completion, turn to the reverse of the work and secure the thread in the back of the satin stitch. Clip away any flaps of visible fabric around the perimeter of the cutwork on the reverse, using curved-tip scissors. Repeat for every alternating triangle.

5 The remaining spaces can now be filled with freely worked eyelets using a length of 50/2 lace thread and following the instructions on pages 70–71. Fit three to four eyelets into each space, varying the sizes.

MAKING UP THE COMPLETED BUTTON

1 Take your embroidery out of the hoop (there is no need to press it). The excess linen around the design will now be cut away, cutting up to the ladder stitch outline and leaving the organza intact to surround the embroidery. Start by trimming back the linen to a border of 1cm (⅜in) depth. Snip this border into manageable flaps. Use ball-tipped lace scissors here: slide the ball tip between the organza and linen, to avoid piercing the organza. These are useful for making the first cuts as you begin to release the excess linen, and for trimming away the flaps up to the ladder stitch. Try to pull the linen firmly back away from the edge of the ladder stitch as you trim each flap away with great care. Once trimmed, brush a fingernail in both directions around the ladder stitch edge, then trim again to remove using curved scissors.

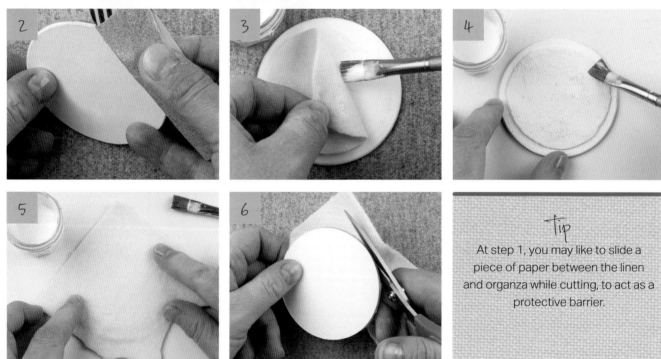

Tip
At step 1, you may like to slide a piece of paper between the linen and organza while cutting, to act as a protective barrier.

2 Use sandpaper to sand the upper edges of the pre-cut card circle to smooth and produce a taper.

3 Cut a piece of your cotton padding to sit slightly smaller than the full circle shape – approximately 5mm (³⁄₁₆in). Stick in place with the glue.

4 Cover the padded surface of the circle with a layer of glue.

5 Lay the remaining piece of cotton padding over this and press down firmly.

6 Trim away the excess padding neatly to the edge of the card.

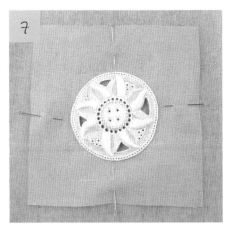

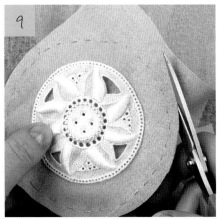

7 Place the embroidered design (right side uppermost) centrally over the top of your piece of natural beige linen. Pin the layers together.

8 Lay the circular card centrally over the reverse of the embroidery, centred behind the design. Draw a line around the card circle if required, so that you do not need to hold it in position. Starting with a knot, work a running stitch gathering thread about 8mm (⁵⁄₁₆in) away from the edge of the card shape, using a long length of Nymo thread. Again, you can draw a line to follow with the running stitch as this will not be seen later. Leave the tail of excess thread hanging.

9 Cut out the design, about 4–5mm (³⁄₁₆in) outside the running stitch.

10 Place your padded card form centrally behind the embroidery, with the padded dome facing the natural linen. Pin the design to the edge of the card, starting at the north, south, east and west positions and then adding more pins in between. Keep the design pulled taut, and central.

11 Pull up the gathering thread tightly until the design sits neatly across the front. Check the position of the embroidery on the front and adjust as necessary. Secure the stitching thread with a few oversewing stitches. Now work lacing stitches in a rotating fashion back and forth across the reverse of the circle, pulling each firmly. Continue to work until the embroidery sits neat and taut across the front, then finish the thread and remove the pins.

The finished lacing.

EMBELLISHING THE EDGE

Embellish the edge of the button further using buttonhole loops. Turn the work to the reverse and lay centrally over the top of the pattern provided (see page 189).

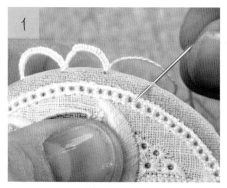

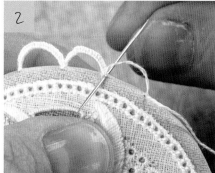

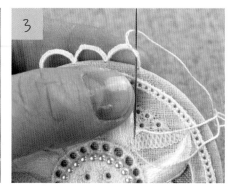

1 Use a fine marker pen to mark the positions of the buttonhole scallops on the reverse of the button. Take a length of Retors d'Alsace no. 12 and secure by oversewing into the reverse of the button, close to one of the marked points. Adjacent to this mark, pass the needle to emerge on the side edge of the button. Pass the needle to the right (or left if you prefer to work in the opposite direction) taking a stitch into the edge of the button, adjacent to the next mark. Ease the thread through until a neat, shallow loop remains.

2 Take the needle back to the left and stitch into the edge of the button at the starting point again. Ease the thread through to produce a loop of an equivalent size to the first.

3 Slip the needle down into the two loops formed, then allow it to emerge through the working loop of thread to form a buttonhole stitch. Slide the stitch around the loop until it sits snugly at the left-hand side. Continue to work dense buttonhole stitches around the loop to the right. On completion, stitch into the edge of the button again to secure.

4 Continue to work buttonhole loops in the same fashion around the perimeter of the button. Secure old and start new threads by oversewing into the reverse.

On completion, you may wish to present the finished button in a picture frame, set against a backdrop of coloured or fabric-covered card, perhaps combined with some real buttons.

The button can also be finished as a brooch if preferred by applying a circle of baize or felt to the reverse, or perhaps a circle of card covered in a contrasting fabric, with an added brooch pin.

VARIATION PIECES

The Honeysuckle Pin Wheel and Hydrangea Needlecase are two further designs which combine techniques from the fine whitework spectrum. These are superb pieces to work to allow you to practise your skills before embarking on a larger fine whitework project.

The honeysuckle design (shown below, left) is mounted over an oval of card with an equivalent, fabric-covered oval on the reverse. It is designed to store decorative pins, which are inserted around the perimeter.

The hydrangea design (shown below, right) is also mounted over a card oval and attached to a second fabric-covered card oval, with needlebook pages inside, using wool flannel.

All of the stitches used to work these designs are shown in the stitch guide within this book. The templates, requirements and order of work details can be found by visiting the Bookmarked Hub (www.bookmarkedhub.com).

FURTHER INSPIRATION

The following gallery displays a range of varied fine whitework pieces produced by my students for your inspiration. These illustrate the eclectic sources of design which can be interpreted so effectively in this medium. They also display the graphic clarity which can be achieved through careful use and balance of the whitework tonal scale, creating designs which are visually bold at first glance and yet minutely detailed on close inspection.

Heart, inspired by the work of Lady Evelyn Stewart Murray
13 × 15cm (5⅛ × 6in)

Lianne Hart

This elegant design shows fine whitework at its best with the simple, elegant design brought to life with richly padded satin stitch contrasted against exquisitely delicate net, drawn and pulled patterns, achieving a great sense of depth.

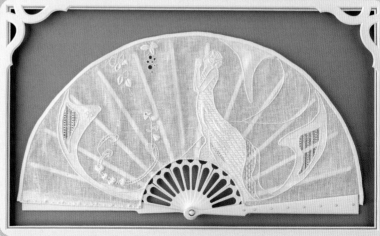

Art Nouveau Fan
41 × 22cm (16⅛ × 8¹¹⁄₁₆in) – fan;
56 × 39cm (22¹⁄₁₆ × 15⅜in) – mounted
Dorothy Sargent

Woodland Toadstools
36 × 25cm (14³⁄₁₆ × 9¹³⁄₁₆in)
Ursula Hodson

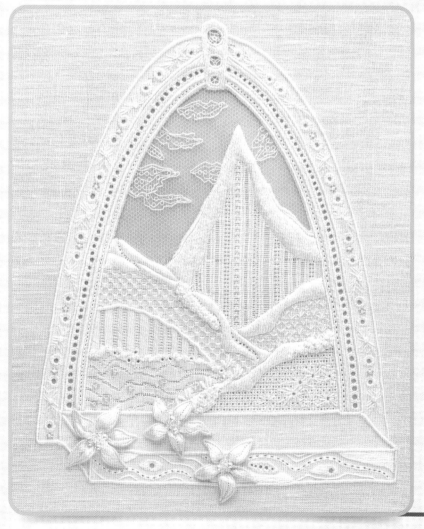

Designs can also be 'drawn' onto net using freely worked running stitch. Here the clouds are edged with a heavier thread and filled with freely worked loop stitch using a finer thread.

Alpine Scene
14 × 17cm (5½ × 6¾in)
Sarah Higham

I Saw Three Ships

22 × 27cm (8¾ × 10½in)

Gail Beer

A complex scene is simplified into flowing design forms, which create a great sense of movement and energy and fully exploit the depth of the whitework tonal scale.

Art Nouveau Portrait

15 × 15cm (6 × 6in)
Sara Rickards

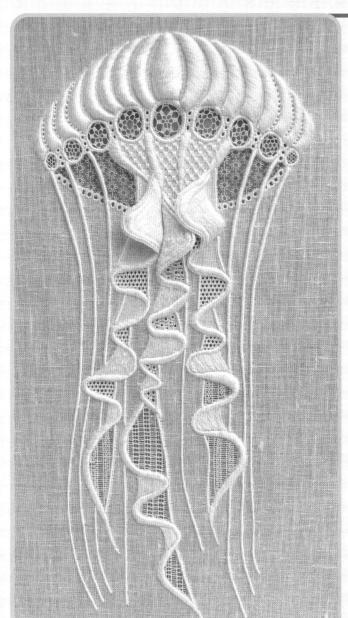

Fine Whitework Jellyfish

19.5 × 29.5cm (7¾ × 11⅝in) – mounted
Lucy Margolius

This design illustrates how a complex natural form can be simplified to essential elegant lines, which read clearly in white-on-white, enhanced by the bold padded and raised forms set against delicate net and Ayrshire needlelace fillings.

View from the Beach: Clevedon Pier

14 × 21cm (5½ × 8¼in) – embroidery; 18.5 × 26cm (7¼ × 10¼in) – mounted
Deborah Wilding

This design is greatly enhanced by the wired forms, which draw the eye out from the design, contrasting the great depth created by the large expanse of net with the hand-painted backdrop.

Art Nouveau Portrait
24 × 27cm (9½ × 10⅝in)
Florence Collingwood

Most whitework pieces benefit from a plain fabric placed behind; however, this piece shows how effective a patterned fabric can be when carefully selected to complement a design.

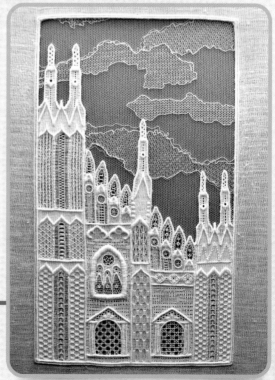

Duomo di Milano
18 × 22cm (7¹⁄₁₆ × 8¹¹⁄₁₆in)
Luisella Strona

London Skyline

20.5 × 15.5cm (8¹⁄₁₆ × 6⅛in)

Masako H. Newton

This beautiful design depicting the London skyline exemplifies the clever stylization of a complex scene to be suitable for whitework, with a careful balance of solid and open areas and the appropriate use of contrasting whitework patterns to define the various architectural forms. The net darning is simply worked but to great effect to show the structure of the famed 'Gherkin' building, and the Ayrshire filling works so well to depict the face of 'Big Ben'.

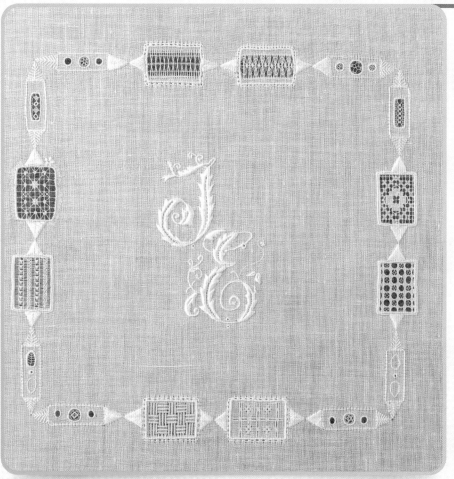

Sampler

24 × 24cm (9½ × 9½in)

Janet Every

This sampler was inspired by the work of Lady Evelyn Stewart Murray who collated a large collection of historic pieces of whitework, studying them to discover their techniques and stitches. Janet studied antique pieces and book illustrations, bringing together her own record of surface embroidery, drawn thread, pulled thread and needlelace techniques within an attractively arranged sampler surrounding her initials.

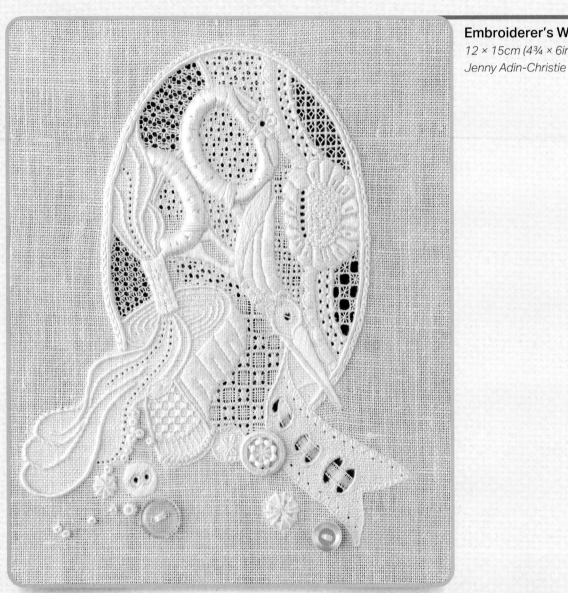

Embroiderer's Work Basket
12 × 15cm (4¾ × 6in)
Jenny Adin-Christie

Lake Louise

14 × 17cm (5½ × 6¾in)

Mary Potter

Here, the fine net sky is used to bold effect without darning patterns, and with the addition of the hand-painted moon. The water uses the simple process of withdrawing threads and randomly shifting those remaining to produce an undulating effect and darker tone.

Whitework Collar

27 × 17cm (10⅝ × 6¾in)

Rachel Doyle

A gorgeous piece showing the contemporary use of fine whitework in a unique garment.

Small Birds May Fly High

22.5 × 26.5cm (8⅞ × 10½in)

This piece was designed during the first UK lockdown of the 2020 Covid pandemic. So much of the life we were used to had been curtailed and we were limited to one precious hour outside each day. It felt so sudden, so shocking and so claustrophobic at first. Then gradually the healing power of nature began to creep into our souls. The skies were empty of planes, the roads were quiet, the air pollution eased, sights and sounds long forgotten began to creep back to our consciousness; silence, stillness, birdsong, insects. This design provides a window into this world, drawing the viewer in. The wren symbol is very important to me. I was always known as 'Jenny Wren' as a little girl; and the original motto of the Royal School of Needlework was 'Small Birds May Fly High'. The motto spoke of the RSN's early mission to provide training in embroidery as a means for young women who had fallen on hard times to learn a respectable skill by which they could earn their own living.

YOU WILL NEED:

Slate frame, with webbing measuring minimum 30cm (12in) or maximum 38cm (15in)

Stand or clamp (to support the slate frame)

15cm (6in) diameter shallow edged, hand-held embroidery hoop

15cm (6in) embroidery hoop with a deep edge, in a stand

Pale grey fine-liner pen

Curved-tip scissors

Lobe-tipped lace scissors

Stiletto

Fine awl

Paper scissors

Low-tack sticky tape

Lightbox, or equivalent

Tape measure

Thimble

Fabric scissors

Very fine pins

Pair of tweezers

FABRICS

30 × 30cm (12 × 12in) linen batiste, or a coarser linen (ideally with thread count of between 25 and 21 threads/cm or 65 and 55 threads/in)

Note: If you opt for coarser fabric, a different weight of thread should be used – this will be stated in brackets following the thread recommendation for the fine fabric – i.e. (coarse L50)

Three further pieces of the same linen, each measuring 20 × 20cm (7⅞ × 7⅞in)

Fine nylon conservation-grade net, 30 × 30cm (12 × 12in)

White, finely woven silk organza 25 × 25cm (9¾ × 9¾in)

Piece of pelmet Vilene, 5 × 5cm (2 × 2in)

THREADS

The letters/numbers included in brackets show the notation used for each thread throughout the instructions.

Two skeins of stranded cotton (**ST**) in bright white (the original design is worked using DMC B5200). Use as a single strand, in 50cm (20in) lengths, unless otherwise stated

One reel each of the following 100% cotton lace threads (from finest to heaviest):

- Size 80/2 (**L80**)
- Size 60/2 (**L60**)
- Size 50/2 (**L50**)
- Size 36/2 (**L36**)

Those used in the design are 'Fil au Chinois', produced by Toulemonde. Use in 50cm (20in) lengths unless otherwise stated.

One hank of DMC Cotton Floche à Broder in bright white B5200, used in half-skein lengths of approximately 68cm (26¾in) (**F**)

One reel of pale blue or green polyester tacking thread (**TACK**); one reel of red polyester tacking thread (**TACK**)

At least 50cm (20in) of no. 50 crochet cotton in bright white

NEEDLES

Embroidery/crewel no. 10 and no. 12

Tapestry no. 28

Chenille no. 20 and no. 24

OTHER MATERIALS AND TOOLS

Thin sheet of coloured (ideally blue) soft plastic (such as a file divider), at least 13 × 8cm (5⅛ × 3⅛in)

Size 8 demi-round beads in translucent or white × 7 (minimum), or an equivalent doughnut-shaped glass bead with an approximate diameter of 3mm and a large hole

2mm white glass seed pearls × 9

0.2mm diameter ivory or white coloured craft wire, 3 × 15cm (6in) pieces

Plain dark-coloured cardboard

Small screwdriver

A note on Floche à Broder

Floche will be used singly in some areas but also used double for speed and effectiveness of padding. When double Floche is used, the thread will be passed singly through the needle, doubled over and the two tails tied together. The needle is therefore trapped at the centre of the loop of thread.

Small Birds May Fly High

DRAWING ON THE DESIGN

1 Frame up your plain linen on the slate frame using the method described on pages 22–24. Ease drum-tight. Take two or three photocopies of the outline design provided on page 190.

2 Work bisecting horizontal and vertical tacking lines. Then, working over a lightbox, align, apply and trace the design using a 0.1mm pale grey fine-liner pen, following the instructions on pages 33–36.

WORKING THE NET INSERTION

In this design, the sky will be worked in darned net insertion. When the design is complete and the linen cut away to reveal the net, this negative space, with its delicate transparent filling, will create a great sense of depth, drawing the viewer into the scene.

PREPARING THE TEMPORARY PLASTIC FILM

First, a piece of thin, flexible plastic is applied to the linen over the reverse of the design area which will contain the net insertion. When the linen is cut away to reveal the net at the end of the project, this plastic film acts as a barrier, allowing the linen to be cut away confidently without piercing the net. The plastic can then be removed.

A blue plastic file divider is ideal as the plastic needs to be soft, and easy to pierce with a needle. The strong colour assists with clarity when cutting the linen later on.

The lettering

The *Small Birds May Fly High* lettering is an optional part of this design, so you do not need to draw it on at this stage. It can be added at the end of the project (see pages 171–173) if you do wish to include it.

If you wish to add the lettering at this stage, you will need to tack a straight line (following the grain of the linen) before tracing on the design. This line should run along the bottom edge of the lettering to ensure that it lies straight.

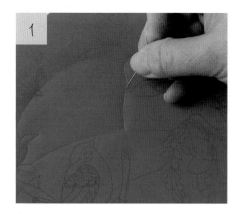

1 Place your outline design on a flat work surface. Lay the plastic sheet over your design. Using a no. 24 chenille needle, score the plastic around the perimeter edge of the sky area, following the contours of the honeysuckle flowers which overlap this area.

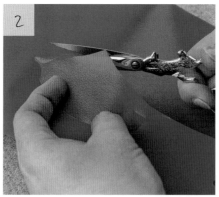

2 Using paper scissors, cut out the plastic design shape, approximately 5mm (³⁄₁₆in) within the scored line.

The image shows the final, trimmed plastic shape, inside the design outline.

APPLYING THE FILM TO THE LINEN

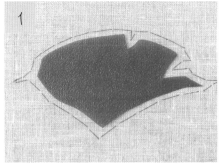

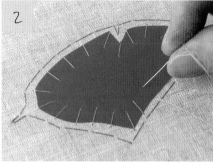

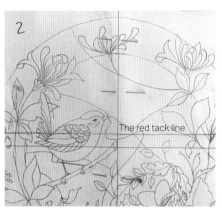

The plastic film when viewed from the front of the fabric.

1 Working on your prepared linen, use coloured tacking thread and a no. 10 embroidery needle to work running stitch around the perimeter of the design area which will contain the net. This temporary stitching will allow you to locate the position of the design area on the reverse at the next step.

2 Turn over your frame to the reverse and place the plastic centrally within the tacked design area. Using pale coloured tacking thread, stitch the plastic in position using large oversewing stitches. Start the thread with a knot on the front of the work (to avoid it becoming trapped between linen and net). For each stitch, the needle emerges in the linen at the edge of the plastic and descends into the plastic to hold it flat. On completion, secure the thread with a couple of oversewing stitches on the spot.

PREPARING THE NET

1 The straight grain of the net should run horizontally across the sky area so that the net darning patterns will flow with the direction of the grain, suggesting cloud formations. Take a length of red tacking thread: starting with a knot, use a no. 28 tapestry needle to work a line of running stitch through the centre of the net, following the straight grain.

2 Now place a copy of your outline design flat on your work surface. Lay your net over the top with the horizontal tack line running east to west. Align the tacking line parallel with the horizontal centre design line and position it approximately 1cm (⅜in) above this. Pin your net to the paper pattern as shown.

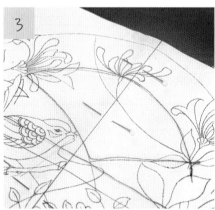

The red tack line

3 Again, using red tacking thread and a fine tapestry needle, map out the outline of the sky area on the net using running stitch. Start and finish the thread with a couple of oversewing stitches on the spot rather than a knot. The blunt needle will slide over the surface of the paper pattern rather than piercing it. Ignore the overlapping honeysuckle flowers at this stage. On completion, remove the pins and release to release the net.

4 Ensure that the screw on your 20cm (7⅞in) diameter, shallow-edged embroidery hoop is not too tight. Place the larger top hoop down on the work surface. Place the tacked net over the hoop with the sky design area centred and the right side uppermost. Gently push the smaller bottom hoop down into the top hoop to tension the net. Gently ease the net a little tighter if required, though avoid distorting the design shape – take great care when pulling the net as it is such a delicate fabric. Tighten the screw of the hoop with a screwdriver.

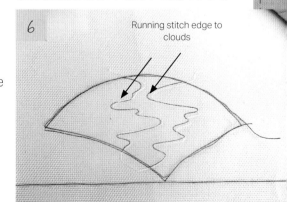

5 Place the taut net flat over the top of the template for the cloud shapes (see page 191).

6 Use a length of L80 in a no. 28 tapestry needle to work a small running stitch to mark out the shapes of the clouds on the net. Start this thread using a couple of oversewing stitches on the spot, approximately 1cm (⅜in) outside the perimeter of the sky area. Work running stitch around the curved design line on the left, extending beyond the sky perimeter a little, then double back on yourself to work the right-hand design line. Finish 1cm (⅜in) beyond the design shape, using oversewing stitches. This thread will be removed on completion of the net darning, so accuracy is not important.

Running stitch edge to clouds

WORKING THE NET DARNING PATTERNS

BEFORE YOU BEGIN

1 Release the screw of your embroidery hoop and remove the prepared net.

2 Place the smaller lower hoop down on the work surface. Place the net centrally on top of the hoop with the right side uppermost. Place the larger hoop on top, thereby tensioning the net.

3 Ease taut gently and evenly, to avoid distorting the design shapes. Tighten the screw fully to lock in the tension, though there is no need for the net to be drum-tight.

For this design, you can mix five complementary net darning stitches, all of which run with the straight grain of the net to suggest cloud-like patterns: winged loop stitch, figure-of-eight, sunrise stitch, upright loop stitch and darning stitch (see pages 105–107). Combine the stitches within the parameters of the marked cloud shapes. The original design was worked in L80, but you may like to combine L80 with L50 for further textural interest.

The net darning should be extended by 5–8mm (³⁄₁₆–⁵⁄₁₆in) beyond the outer red tacked design shape on all sides, to be sure that the full patterns will be seen throughout the entirety of the sky once complete.

1 Start the net darning at the widest point of the design shape: it is easier to achieve a good flow and good tension when working longer rows.

2 Cut a length of L80 to approximately 40cm (15³⁄₄in). Cast on by working two tight buttonhole knots, each around a single bar of the net, approximately 5–8mm (³⁄₁₆–⁵⁄₁₆in) beyond the tacked design line.

3 Work the pattern along the straight grain of the net, over the tack line, into the design area.

4 Continue darning until you meet the cloud design line, before turning back on yourself to work back to the outer edge again. The stitch diagrams provided on pages 105–107 show suggested ways of turning back, either completing the second half of a stitch pattern on the return row, or working a second adjacent row. Continue to work further rows of darning in the same manner. The spacing between the rows can be varied to achieve different effects.

Tip

Practise the net patterns on a spare piece of net until you are confident, prior to working the real piece as this technique is very difficult to unpick. You may like to trial them on a coarser cotton net prior to working on the very fine conservation net, as this will help you to see and understand the stitches before moving onto a finer net.

Tips

Use your finger beneath the work to ease the net upwards to help with sliding the needle under into the structure of the taut fabric.

Stretch each new length of thread from the reel between your two hands and 'tweak' the taut thread before use – this can help to reduce tangling.

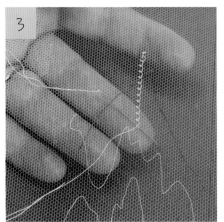

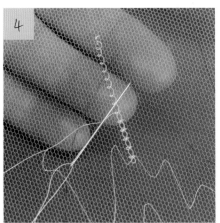

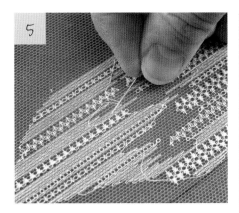

5 Once the cloud areas are filled with net darning patterns, carefully remove the tacking for the cloud edges, and the red tacking marking the design shape. Do not remove the horizontal tack line yet. Use a tapestry needle as shown above to lift a loop of the lace thread. Snip carefully, then gently and gradually unpick the thread back to the edges and remove. If you have caught the thread at any point with your needle, you may need to snip it again to release it. Take great care not to cut the net.

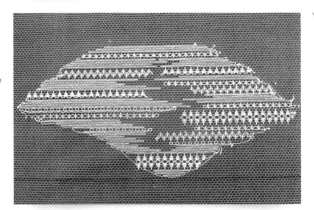

Your net panel is complete.

133

APPLYING THE NET TO THE DESIGN

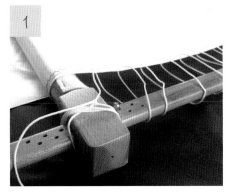

1 Before applying the net, the tension of your linen must be slackened. It is essential when applying one fabric to another that they are both at the same tension, to avoid possible distortion. Begin by slackening the string of your slate frame to loosen the fabric widthways, then move the pegs inwards two to three notches, to slacken the depth.

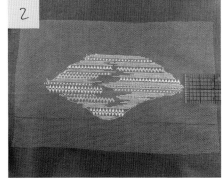

2 Take your net out of the hoop and use an iron on a *cool* setting to press the creased edges. Lay the net right-side uppermost on your piece of coloured cardboard. Use fabric scissors to trim the edges of the net back to a rectangle which sits 2.5cm (1in) larger than the outer extremities of the darned design.

3 Turn your slate frame over to the reverse side. If the pegs drop out, replace them in the same hole positions on the reverse of the frame to keep the rollers from slipping, but do not apply tension to the fabric. Work with your frame supported on trestles or over a clean, solid work surface – you may wish to place dark-coloured cardboard beneath, to help you to see the work more clearly.

4 Turn over your panel of net darning so that the right side is facing the reverse of the linen. Place the net centrally over the sky design area highlighted by the prepared tacking and the applied blue plastic. Ensure that the net darning pattern extends evenly beyond the tacked design shape around its perimeter.

5 Pin the net firmly in place on either side of the design area. Then pin the edges in place as shown, with the points facing inwards. Start with a pin at the centre of each side and work out to the corners, pinning about every 2cm (13⁄16in). Ensure that the net remains smooth and flat against the linen.

6 Carefully remove the red tacking marking the straight grain of your net. Using a length of pale coloured tacking thread, work a row of basting stitches, starting through the centre of the net (see first diagram below). Start with a knot placed on the front of the work in

the linen, just above the centre top of the net. Work diagonal basting stitches, each about 1cm (3⁄8in) in length down the centre of the net panel until you reach the linen at the bottom. Finish with two or three oversewing stitches in the linen. Take care when working the basting not to pull the stitches up tight as this could distort the net. Add further vertical rows of basting, centrally within the remaining net, to the left and right of the centre row.

7 Add another row of basting through the horizontal centre, perpendicular to the existing rows, following the second diagram below. Secure the edge of the net with a herringbone stitch around the perimeter, starting from one corner, with a stitch depth of approximately 1cm (3⁄8in). The stitches must wrap over the edge of the net to allow you to pull the net tight. Remove the pins as you work.

On completion, re-tighten your slate frame carefully, as previously described. The net will pull tight together with the linen. Take care to tension the slate frame evenly on both sides. Check the tension of the net on the reverse and ease the slate frame tighter if required.

Return to the front of the work and carefully unpick the tacking around the edge of the sky and the original, central vertical and horizontal lines used when transferring the design.

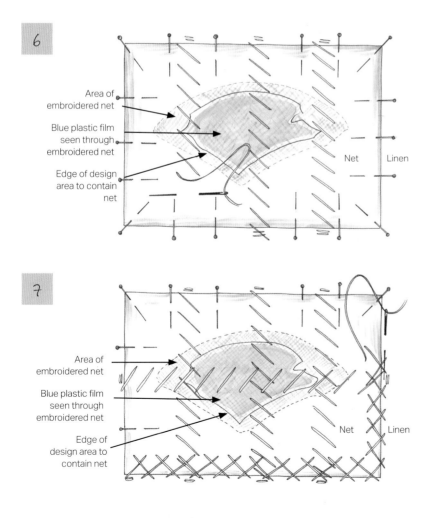

6

Area of embroidered net

Blue plastic film seen through embroidered net

Edge of design area to contain net

Net   Linen

7

Area of embroidered net

Blue plastic film seen through embroidered net

Edge of design area to contain net

Net   Linen

WORKING THE EGGS

Pulled thread work is ideal for the tiny eggs in the nest. The stitches give a lacy texture without creating any particular sense of direction, suggesting the mottled patterns of bird eggs.

The double running stitch border is required only where the design line divides a pulled work area from an area of plain fabric. If the pulled work sits against an area of satin stitch, or other solid stitching, there is no need for a double running edge, as the edge will be defined later. This small firm stitch serves as a barrier to prevent the 'pull' of the pulled work stitches extending beyond the design shapes, into the surrounding fabric.

Work double running stitch around the upper perimeter edges of the three eggs as shown (first following the stitches marked in blue and then doubling back with the red). Use L60 thread and a sharp needle. There is no need to work running stitch along the bottom edges as they lie next to heavily worked shapes.

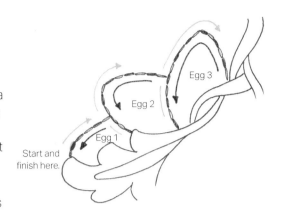

FILLING THE EGGS

EGG 1

Fill the first egg with double wave stitch (see page 75), worked in a vertical direction, with each row worked over a width of four linen threads. Cast on your thread using the WKT within the double running stitch outline.

The eggs can be worked with a no. 28 tapestry needle (on coarse linen, use no. 26), using L60 thread (or L50 on the coarser linen).

1 Start the first row across the widest part of the shape, then work out to the edges. Adjust the stitch at the ends of the rows, to fit the curved edges of the egg shape as best as possible, ensuring a continuous appearance to the stitch texture within.

2 At the end of each row, work a tiny stab stitch onto the outline to lock the 'pull' of that row in place. Begin each new row in the same manner with a stitch on the outline.

3 If you need to travel from one point to another to work a new row of stitch, use tiny stab stitches worked along the outer design line so that you do not have to cross behind the pulled work.

EGG 2

Fill this egg with diagonal drawn filling stitch (see page 74); work the larger stitches over four linen threads and the smaller over two.

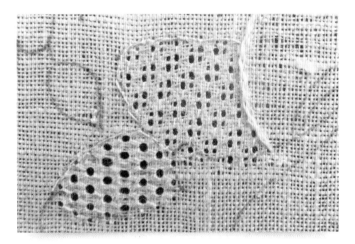

Egg 1 (left), worked in double-wave stitches.

Egg 2 (right), worked in diagonal drawn stitch.

Note

The recommended stitch size for the pulled stitches is stated in the text: feel free to adapt this to work the stitches larger if you wish.

Tip

Practise the pulled thread stitches on the side of your fabric before working the final design: this will help you achieve a rhythm to your stitching, which will produce better overall tension.

Egg 3

Work this egg using freely worked eyelets (see pages 70–71) to give a softer feel. Due to the satin stitch-like nature of the edges of these eyelets, you can work a row of split stitch along the left-hand edge of the egg to give a firmer barrier. The eyelets are worked over this edge creating a slight padding and a crisp finish.

Begin by working the edge in split stitch using one ST, on top of the double running stitch. Using L50, fill the left-hand half of the egg with freely worked eyelets. Make these sufficiently dense to cover the split stitch at the left and spread them out a little more towards the right.

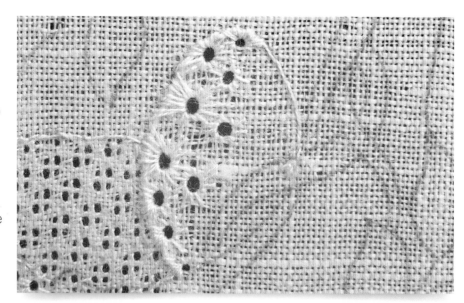

OUTLINING THE EGGS

Use a no. 10 embroidery or crewel needle, with ST.

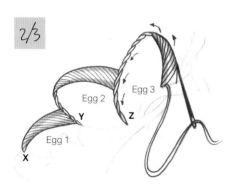

1 Work a row of split stitch along the outer edge of egg 1, in preparation for satin stitch.

2 Starting at X, work slanted satin stitch from the tip of the egg and down the upper edge, allowing the stitches to widen as you work. This tapered stitching helps to give the egg more sense of perspective. Use the tips on pages 47– 49 to help you to work effective slanted satin stitch. Use wedge stitches as required to alter the stitch direction.

3 For egg 2, starting at Y, work reverse stem stitch along the left-hand edge of the egg, gradually moving into slanted satin stitch at the tip and allowing this to broaden down the right-hand side as for egg 1. Repeat for egg 3, starting at Z.

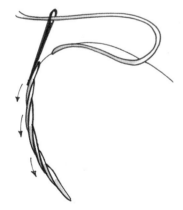

Detail of reverse stem stitch.

The outlined eggs.

THE FURROWED FIELD

THE FRAMEWORK

Using a no. 12 embroidery/crewel needle with L60 thread, work double running stitch around the perimeter edge of the field, to contain the 'pull' of the stitches within.

PULLED THREAD WORK

Use a no. 28 tapestry needle (or coarse no. 26) and L60 thread (coarse L50). The field is filled using horizontal rows of a freely worked version of reeded stitch (see below) to give a sense of the movement of the land, and furrowed earth. This stitch combines alternating sections of double backstitch with bands of vertical satin stitch. Work these blocks of stitch in varying depths and lengths to create a soft, naturalistic effect.

Start your first row at the approximate centre of the field and on the right-hand side, casting on your thread using the WKT within the double running stitch outline. Work your first row of reeded stitch towards the left. Alternate between double backstitch and satin stitch, altering the sizes and depths of the blocks as you wish.

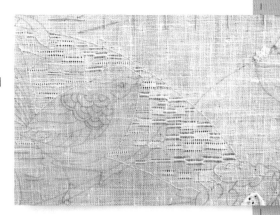

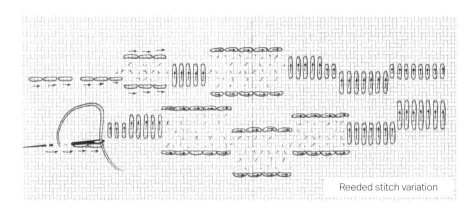

Reeded stitch variation

In the original design, the maximum width of the double backstitch sections is over six linen threads and the minimum over three; and the satin stitch, six and two. The aim is to create greater density and prominence of stitch towards the right-hand edge of the field, thereby highlighting this edge and drawing the eye towards the centre of the design. The stitches should therefore be at their broadest, and the blocks at their longest, towards this edge. They can begin to recede as they move towards the left.

Fade the reeded stitch out into a row of simple counted backstitch as you near the left-hand edge of the design shape to create a sense of the stitch fading gradually away.

The length of your rows will vary; for most you will reach, or almost reach, a design line at the left end. Finish the row here by working a couple of tiny stab stitches on top of the double running stitch. Then turn around and work a row back to the right, or start with a new thread for each row and work all from right to left.

If you wish to complete a row in the middle of the design shape, you can finish the thread by turning to the reverse and carefully darning through the back of the double backstitch and satin stitch blocks for a short distance. Change to a no. 12 embroidery needle to do this. The rows crossing behind the wren do not need to line up exactly on either side.

137

THE EDGE OF THE DISTANT FIELD

The distant field will eventually be filled with drawn thread work, wherein some fabric threads will be removed to form a lace-like web. The sky area above the hillock will be filled with net once the linen is removed. It is therefore crucial that the top edge of the hillock is worked with very strong stitching to sustain all this strain.

Densely worked French knots (see page 37) provide an excellent edge, suggesting texture and foliage on the horizon line, but also forming a strong barrier. Use a no. 10 embroidery needle and ST.

1 Work a row of dense, neat split stitch along the design line along the top of the hillock. Follow this with a second row worked above, and right up against, the first.

2 Starting at the centre of the design line, work dense French knots over the top of the two rows of split stitch. These should form a smooth edge on the field side of the line, and undulating tree-like forms against the sky.

3 Vary the size of the knots adding one, two or three twists to create greater texture. Use the heavier knots towards the bottom edge and the smaller knots towards the top to create a sense of perspective.

4 The knots must be at least two deep across the top of the field and should ideally be deeper than this at most points, to ensure sufficient strength. There should be no spaces between the knots.

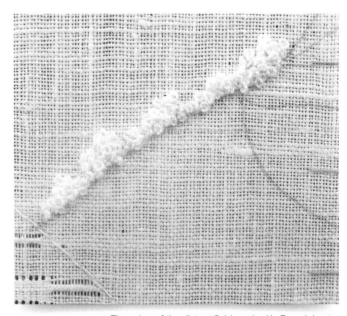

The edge of the distant field, worked in French knots.

CREATING THE CIRCULAR BORDER

Use ladder stitch (see pages 77–78) to create a delicate open border: the tiny string of holes will frame the design and draw attention to the centre, contrasting effectively with the overlapping padded shapes.

The position of ladder stitch on the border

Please note that this diagram also indicates the order of work for each of the leaves, explained over pages 140–142.

BACKSTITCH PREPARATION

Use a no. 10 embroidery/crewel needle with ST thread. The diagram on the opposite page illustrates the position of the ladder stitch border, intertwined between the honeysuckle flowers and leaves.

1 Beginning at A, work backstitches 1–1.5mm (¹⁄₁₆in) long along the design line. At the first yellow dot (on leaf Z), finish the backstitch by working two tiny backstitches along the leaf design line.

2 Carry the thread across behind the leaf and work two tiny backstitches on the upper edge of the leaf to re-secure the thread.

3 Work the next section of backstitch; finish the thread on the design line again, then cross the leaf and re-secure, ready for the next section.

4 The yellow dots show where to secure the working thread fully at the edge of the larger leaves. The working threads crossing behind these leaves will then be safe to trim away on completion of the ladder stitch. If left, they may show through the open fillings.

5 As you meet all other smaller design shapes around the border, simply carry the backstitch thread behind these without securing it.

6 On completion, insert a fine awl into each of the holes in the ladder to open these up further.

EDGING THE LADDER STITCH

1 Starting again at A (see opposite), take two strands of stranded cotton which are sufficiently long to travel around the entire perimeter of the border with excess of about 6cm (2⅜in) at each end for finishing. Lay these along the right-hand edge of the prepared backstitch line, leaving a 6cm (2⅜in) tail. Secure a new stitching thread at A (WKT).

2 Work the ladder stitch using the ladder stitch variation technique (see page 78): couch the laid threads densely in between adding a further backstitch wrap to each bar. Close binding is essential as the ladder stitch forms the border around the net sky, and needs to provide sufficient strength to allow the linen to be cut away eventually.

3 Pull the stitches tight to achieve good holes. Keep tension on the laid thread to ensure that it lies smooth and taut.

4 On reaching the first yellow dot (see opposite), plunge the laid threads down on the design line using a no. 24 chenille needle and bring them back to the surface at the next yellow dot before continuing to work the ladder. These threads will be cut away later but do not require further securing as they are tightly bound in place. However, the same securing process as described for the backstitch thread (above) must be used again here for the working thread at each yellow dot.

5 On completion of the inner edge of the ladder, push your awl into each hole again to increase the precision. Thread the double couching thread tails into a needle (no. 24 chenille) and finish along the perimeter of the neighbouring leaf shape with two tiny backstitches. Repeat for the tails at the start.

6 Repeat the same edging process for the outer edge. There is no need to bind the couching thread densely, apart from just

before reaching each yellow dot, binding closely at each of these points for five or six stitches. Otherwise, you can work in the manner of ordinary ladder stitch. The close binding at the yellow dots will allow the cording threads to be safely cut away from the reverse of the leaves later on.

7 On completion of the ladder, use the awl in every hole again to give a final polish. Finish the remaining tails of cording thread in the same way. Trim away any remaining threads on the reverse which are still crossing the leaf design shapes.

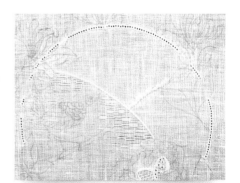

USING BEADING TO EXTEND THE LADDER STITCH BORDER

The image on the right and the diagram opposite show how section B extends down from the tip of the ladder stitch border, and, due to its greater width, is worked in beading.

1 When edging the beading, a double running stitch is used along the edges marked in orange, whereas it is effective to move into split stitch along the sections marked in red. The split stitch gives a little more padding and therefore emphasis to the edges for this bolder section of beading.

2 Work the beading (see pages 96–97) from the broad end upwards using your stiletto to make the larger holes, and then moving into the use of a finer awl as the shape narrows.

WORKING THE COUNTED SATIN STITCH LEAF FILLINGS

The diagram above shows the leaves to be filled with counted satin patterns, which create lovely contrasting textures and rich density. You can fill these leaves with any combination of satin patterns; the following describes those used in my original design.

LEAF A: THREADED HONEYCOMB STITCH (SEE PAGE 40)

Use needle no. 28 tapestry (coarse no. 26) with ST threaded with L50.

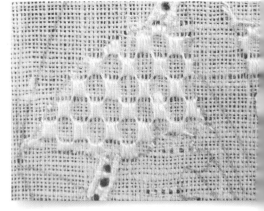

Leaf A, filled with threaded honeycomb stitch.

1 Starting across the broadest part of the leaf shape, secure your length of stranded cotton on the design line (WKT). Work across the shape in a diagonal row of blocks of four vertical stitches, each worked over five threads of the linen (you can vary this size in accordance with your own design).

2 Adjust the shape of your blocks to fit the curved design line as you reach the opposite edge.

3 Work a single stab stitch on the design line before working back across the shape with the following row of blocks.

Try to keep sufficient thread to complete a full row of blocks. If you run out of thread in the middle of a row, you can secure by darning into the reverse of the existing blocks. You can start the new thread by laying the starting tail behind the new section to be worked.

4 Fill the shape with rows of blocks. Then use L50 to work the horizontal zigzag threading of the blocks to compete the pattern.

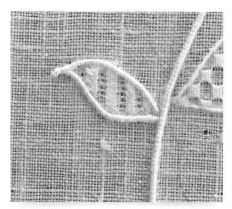

LEAF B (TWO LEAVES): DIAGONAL SATIN WITH BACKSTITCH

Use a no. 28 tapestry needle (coarse no. 26) with ST for satin/L60 for backstitch (coarse L50).

For each of the two leaves:

1 Using ST and starting across the broadest part of the leaf shape, work a vertical row of counted diagonal satin stitch, each stitch worked over four by four linen threads.

2 Continue to fill the leaf with rows of the same, with the slant of all stitches falling in the same direction. Leave two free linen threads between the satin rows.

3 Use L60 to work a row of backstitch centrally between each of the rows of satin, each backstitch being worked over two linen threads. Pull the backstitches tight to achieve an attractive open effect.

LEAF C: DIAGONAL BANDS OF VERTICAL SATIN WITH BACKSTITCH

Use a no. 28 tapestry needle (coarse no. 26) with ST thread for satin/L60 for backstitch (coarse L50).

1 Using ST and starting across the broadest part of the leaf shape on the right-hand side, work a diagonal row of vertical satin stitches. Work each stitch over seven linen threads and keep the row travelling in a south-west direction. Stop when you reach the centre vein.

2 Continue to work the satin from the vein out into the second half of the leaf in a north-west direction to form a 'V' shape.

3 Leave six linen threads between each of the following rows of satin. Only the centre row will form this true 'V' shape at the vein. Due to the curved line of the vein, the following rows will not meet perfectly at the centre.

4 On completion of the satin, use L60 to work a diagonal row of backstitch centrally between each of the rows of satin; work each backstitch over two by two linen threads. Pull the backstitches tight to achieve an attractive open effect.

LEAVES D (TWO LEAVES): DIAGONAL BANDS OF BACKSTITCH

Use a no. 28 tapestry needle (coarse no. 26) with L60 thread (coarse L50).

For each leaf:

1 Starting at the widest part of the leaf, work a horizontal row of backstitch (each stitch worked over two threads of the linen) working from the right-hand outer edge of the leaf to the centre vein. Pull the backstitch to create lace-like holes.

2 On reaching the vein, continue to work backstitch vertically upwards until you reach the outer edge of the leaf, forming a right-angled row of backstitch to suggest diagonal leaf veins. Secure the thread with a locking stab stitch on the outer perimeter design line.

3 Leave six linen threads to the left of the existing row of backstitch. Work another row from the outer edge towards the centre vein.

4 On reaching the centre vein again, work out to the right with a horizontal row. Focus on leaving six linen threads between this and the previous row as, due to the curve of the centre vein, your vertical and horizontal rows will not all meet at a perfect right angle at the centre.

5 Continue to fill the leaf with horizontal and vertical rows of backstitch, each six linen threads apart. Repeat for the second leaf, adjusting the direction of the backstitch veins accordingly.

OUTLINING THE LEAVES USING TRAILING AND REVERSE STEM STITCH

Use a no. 10 embroidery/crewel needle with ST thread. See: trailing, pages 41–47, and reverse stem, page 136.

1 LEAF A: Outline using reverse stem stitch using one ST, creating a sharp point at the tip.

2 LEAVES B, C and D: Outline using trailing. The diagram shown on page 140 indicates the number of strands of stranded cotton for the trailing core thread for each section.

3 Trailing begins at the centre of each leaf edge and tapers towards the base and tip. Remove one or two strands at regular intervals to achieve the change in core thread numbers.

4 The two trailed edges on each leaf are plunged separately at the base of the leaf and blended at the tip to produce sharp points. Reduce the number of strands as the core threads from both edges are blended together (see page 145).

5 Finally, work the centre veins in leaf C and in the two leaves D using reverse stem stitch and ST.

Note

The number of core threads suggested for trailing is a guide only. Adjust these numbers as you wish, to make the trailing heavier or lighter.

WORKING THE EDGE OF THE FURROWED FIELD

It is important that the edge of the field is worked with strong stitching as it runs adjacent to the net sky, where the linen will be completely cut away later on.

Here, we use 'sketched satin stitch', which gives a nice texture contrast and draws the eye across the field, into the distance. Use a no. 10 embroidery/crewel needle with ST thread.

1 First, work a row of split stitch along the upper edge of the field. Keep the stitches small, tight and smooth. Do not worry about crossing behind the overlapping section of honeysuckle: this will be covered in solid stitching later.

2 Work a second row of split stitch above and tight against the first: this double row gives strength to the edge as satin stitch itself will not provide sufficient strength to cut the linen away.

3 Starting at the left-hand tip of the design line, work slanted satin stitch, slanting the stitches towards the top-left. The needle should always emerge in the pulled thread field and descend over the split stitch edge.

4 Vary the stitch lengths to give a soft, sketchy look, but maintain density between the stitches to give a smooth edge to the field. Any protruding stitches will cause difficulty when you come to remove the linen later. The depth of the stitches from the edge of the field, should be quite shallow – 1–2mm (1⁄16in) to begin with but this should increase to 3–4mm (1⁄8–3⁄16in) as you work along the field edge, to create a greater sense of perspective. The stitch lengths will be about 2–4mm (1⁄16–3⁄16in) to start with, increasing to 6–7mm (1⁄4in) at the lower end.

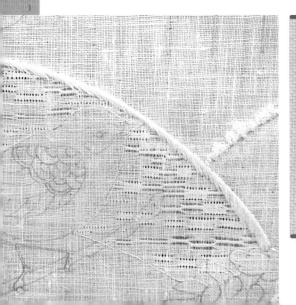

Tip

Be sure to maintain a steep angle and a fluid flow to the stitches. Remember the rules for working effective slanted satin stitch: leaving a gap as the needle emerges and using the FNA (Fundamental Needle Angle) as it descends over the split stitch (see page 48).

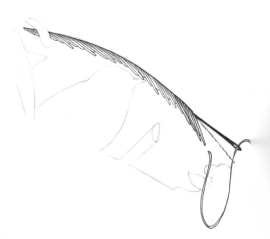

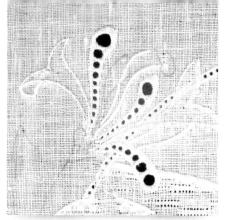

HONEYSUCKLE FLOWERS

The honeysuckle flowers include lots of similar, long, thin petal shapes, which could easily become confused and cluttered. Therefore, using a variety of strongly contrasting stitches gives clarity and depth to the flowerheads.

Use a no. 10 embroidery/crewel needle for embroidery, no. 24 chenille for padding; use ST thread for embroidery and F for padding, used singly. The following diagram clarifies where each technique should be worked:

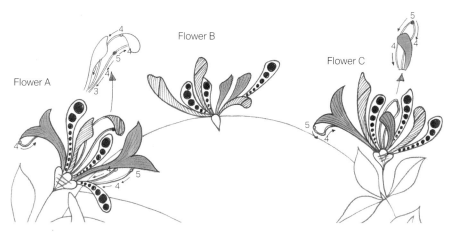

Key

Shapes with black dots = beading;

Shapes in peach = padded natural shading;

Shapes in blue = high relief padded satin stitch;

Blue lines = trailing.

BEADING

For each section of beading:

1 When casting on your thread for beading (WKT), remember that much of the design shape will be open, so work your stitches along the edge of the shape.

2 Referring to pages 96–97, and starting at the narrow end of the shape, work a small (1mm/¹⁄₁₆in) even running stitch around the outer perimeter of the design shape until halfway up the shape. Then, change to split stitch to work around the top half of the shape, changing back to a running stitch for the last half to the base. Then work back, filling the gaps in the running stitch to make double running stitch (see diagram).

3 Carry your thread to the top of the design shape by working a couple of small stab stitches at the edge. Insert a stiletto centrally at the broad tip of the design shape before binding around the perimeter of the first eyelet hole. Proceed to work the first bridging stitch across the design shape before making the second eyelet hole and binding the bar.

4 Continue to work beading down the length of the design shape, the holes gradually becoming smaller towards the base. On reaching the base, complete the wrapping of the remaining edge. Finish the beading by turning the stiletto in each hole to give a final polish. Finish the thread by darning through the stitching on the reverse.

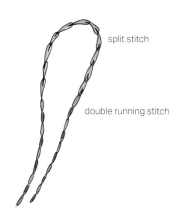

split stitch

double running stitch

Use turning 'wedge' stitches as you bind the edge of the beading, where the tip of the design shape is pointed rather than rounded. These will ensure a densely bound edge without clogging the eyelet hole.

If you notice any fluffy fibres around your eyelet holes, do not be concerned: these will settle when you wash the piece at the end. However, you should never use worn and fluffy threads.

TRAILING

1 Referring again to the diagram on page 143, work all the relevant design edges using tapered trailing, starting at the positions shown and using the number of stranded cotton core threads specified. The yellow dots refer to trailing starting from the end of a line, anchoring the core threads using a knot. The red dots refer to starting trailing midway along a line, tapering in both directions.

2 Where another design shape crosses the trailing, plunge the core thread down beneath this overlap, allowing it to re-emerge on the other side. The section of core thread lying beneath the work does not have to be removed as it will be covered by heavy stitching (see diagram, right, using flower A as an example).

3 Plunge and finish the trailing at the base of each section and trim off the core threads neatly on the reverse (as described on page 42).

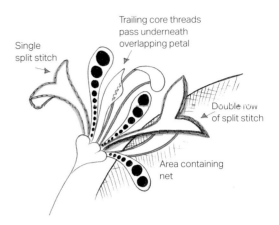

Single split stitch

Trailing core threads pass underneath overlapping petal

Double row of split stitch

Area containing net

PADDED NATURAL SHADING (SEE ORANGE SECTIONS ON THE DIAGRAMS, PAGE 143 AND BELOW)

1 Work a row of small, neat split stitch around the perimeter of each remaining design shape.

2 Add a second row of split stitch to the inside of the first row on the flower petal shown in the diagram (flower A, above right). This shape overlaps the net sky so requires extra strength.

3 The design shapes are now padded using satin stitch padding, working two layers in the two small compact shapes and three layers in the larger 'fishtail' shapes.

4 Work a new row of split stitch over the top of the existing one around the perimeter of each design shape, to give a crisper, firmer edge.

5 Fill the shapes using natural shading, starting from the tip and working to the base, following the guidance on pages 62–64. Use the FNA to ensure that the edges of the shapes are smooth and flowing.

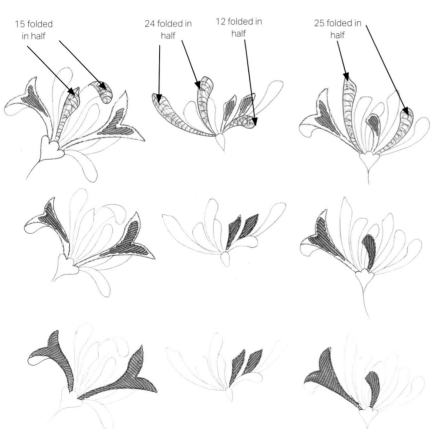

15 folded in half

24 folded in half

12 folded in half

25 folded in half

First layer of padding for natural shading (coloured orange), high-relief padding for satin (coloured blue) and highlighting how many strands of F to use for padding, which are doubled when folded in half.

Second layer of padding for natural shading.

Third layer of padding.

HIGH-RELIEF PADDED SATIN STITCH

The remaining design shapes (see pale blue shapes in the diagrams on pages 143 and 144) are worked in satin stitch, padded with laid threads to create extreme height, as an effective contrast against the beading and low-relief techniques.

1 Work a small, neat split stitch around the perimeter of each shape. The diagram opposite shows the total number of strands of Floche à Broder needed to pad each shape. When folded in half at the broad tip of each shape, these numbers will be doubled. Ensure that your threads are long enough to travel down the full length of the shape when doubled over, with plenty of extra length to make handling easier.

2 Following the guidelines on pages 50–52, work the padding within each design shape, tapering the padding threads as you work, and adapting your cutting to the feel of your own work.

3 Following the diagrams on the right, adjust the folded threads to fit the design shape where the tip is little more pointed (this applies to flowers A and C). The core threads are initially secured at the centre tip of the design shape with a locking stab stitch. Further stitches are used to draw some of the padding threads in the left-hand half out into the pointed tip. Use several stitches like this to ease out the padding evenly before binding over the top as normal.

4 On completion of the padding, work a further row of fine split stitch around the perimeter, on top of the existing split stitch, to provide a firmer edge and smooth any areas which may have been damaged by the padding process.

5 Work slanted satin stitch over the top of the padding, starting from the widest point of each shape with a stitch at a 45° angle to the flow of the work. Maintain the angle throughout the shape using wedge stitches as necessary to turn the direction. The diagram on page 143 shows the suggested angle of work for each design section with the red marked stitch suggesting where to begin.

6 Blend the satin stitch over the tip of the existing trailing in flower A to create the sense of the petal turning.

3

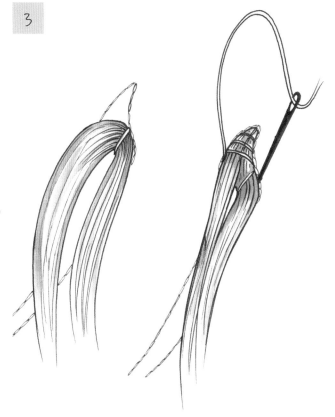

6

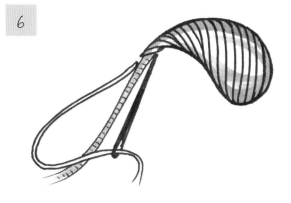

HONEYSUCKLE RECEPTACLES

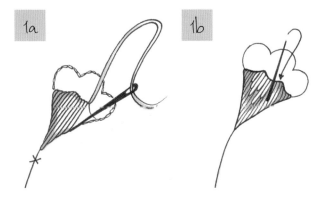 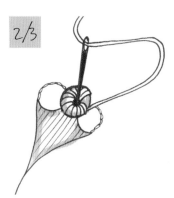 

1 Using a no. 10 needle and ST, work a split stitch around the perimeter of the tri-lobed design shape. Fill the shape with satin stitch starting at the centre and working towards the point. Use the FNA to smooth the edges. Do not fill the tops of the three lobes. Work a few shading stitches through the longest of these to ensure they are thoroughly secured.

2 To create each lobe, apply one no. 8 demi-round bead. Place the bead in position. Secure by working three stitches from the outer edge down into the centre.

3 Push a fine awl into the centre to open the fabric in the middle of the bead. Then satin stitch the bead in place, as you would work an eyelet, working stitches solidly around the perimeter. The needle should always emerge on the outside and descend into the centre. Repeat for each lobe and flower. Note that the central honeysuckle flower requires only one bead.

> ### Tip
> Avoid packing in too many stitches, which may otherwise clog the centre hole excessively. Use your awl again at the end to open the centre a little.

THE WREN'S TAIL

The tail is worked in a combination of alternating bands of three-sided stitch and natural shading, overlaid with fly stitch. The open three-sided stitch provides a feather-like quality and is contrasted and highlighted by the dense shading. Fly stitch is superb for feathers; it creates a sense of life and direction in the main part of the tail.

THREE-SIDED STITCH (SEE PAGE 79)

Use a no. 10 embroidery/crewel needle and L50 thread. For each section:

1 Starting at the tip of the tail, work three-sided stitch along the length of the design shape. Note that there is no design line across the top of the shape, as this would be difficult to cover with this stitch. On completion, use your fine awl to open all the holes.

> ### Note
> The tail is solidly embroidered so there is no benefit to having a second layer of linen present; as it would be much harder to achieve good holes within the three-sided stitch and the linen would have to be trimmed away later around the perimeter of the tail, leaving unnecessary bulk.
>
> Although much of the wren is worked on a double layer of linen to give emphasis to this key feature, I advise that you work the tail in advance on a single layer of linen.

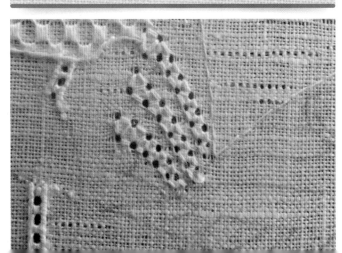

NARROW SECTIONS OF NATURAL SHADING BETWEEN THE BANDS OF THREE-SIDED STITCH

Use a no. 10 embroidery/crewel needle with ST thread.

For each section, work a split stitch across the top end and along the sides of the design shape, then fill the shape with natural shading. The first few stitches are worked up over the split stitch edge. The following stitches are worked through these and towards the bottom of the shape. Take care not to force in too many stitches, which can creep over the three-sided stitch holes.

The diagram shows how – although the shading stitches are worked towards the bottom of the shape, emerging through existing stitches – it can be helpful at the edges to work in the opposite direction, gliding the needle up along the edge using the FNA. This ensures smooth edges and can help push the shading inwards, to prevent it falling over the three-sided stitch.

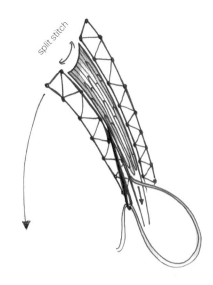

LARGE SECTION OF THE TAIL IN NATURAL SHADING AND FLY STITCH

Use a no. 10 embroidery/crewel needle with ST (for natural shading) and L50 (for fly stitch).

1 Work a split stitch around the perimeter of the design shape. Fill the shape with natural shading, starting at the tip and working towards the base.

2 Starting at the top of the tail, work open fly stitches over the solidly stitched surface (see right). It looks effective to vary the spacing a little to create a feather-like pattern.

3 Use the awl to open all holes of the three-sided stitch again on completion.

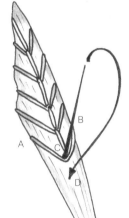

THE EDGE OF THE FOREGROUND FIELD

Use a no. 10 embroidery/crewel needle with ST thread. Refer to the template for the full embroidery on page 190.

1 Take a core thread of six strands of stranded cotton. The core thread will emerge at the right-hand tip of the design line using the knot technique (see page 41).

2 Work trailing along the design line towards the left (see pages 41–42). On reaching the wren, plunge the core thread, allowing it to re-emerge on the far side of the bird to work the rest of the trailing. Taper to five strands mid-way along this last section and plunge and finish at the tip of the line. Trim off the core threads neatly, including snipping away those crossing behind the wren.

3 Finally, work a neat, even row of backstitch above the trailing stitches approximately 1mm (1⁄16in) in length. Pull the backstitches a little so that the holes between them can be seen. On completion, you may like to open up these holes a little more using your fine awl.

The foreground field will be worked by drawing out or removing some of the linen threads. A barrier of two rows of stitch along this design line is recommended to provide the security required for this process. Trailing with a backstitch alongside is effective, providing contrast, texture and a sense of shadow.

THE BRANCH

Use no. 10 embroidery/crewel needles for embroidery, no. 24 chenille for padding, no. 22 chenille for crochet thread; use ST for embroidery; F for padding used double; no. 5 crochet cotton and L50 for basketweave bars.

The branch is worked in couched basketweave over padding. This technique produces the rich density and high-relief effect of padded satin stitch, with a richer texture. It also forms a regular pattern with ridges and hollows, which simulate the effect of a bark-covered branch.

1 First, create the tip of the branch by working a split stitch outline around the end of it (ST). Work trailing stitches over this, using the split stitch as a base, rather than adding a core thread (ST).

2 Fill the end of the branch using backstitch seeding (see page 52). Start by working a row around the edge and then work in concentric circles to the centre. The backstitches on each row do not need to align. The backstitches should be approximately 1mm (¹⁄₁₆in) long (ST).

3 Outline the branch itself in split stitch, including across the end of the outer tip (ST). Then densely fill the branch with two layers of long split stitch padding using F (see page 53).

4 Take your length of crochet cotton and thread into your no. 22 chenille needle. Tie a knot in the end and take the thread down through the fabric in one of the leaves of the bird's nest. Carry the thread across the reverse of the design and emerge approximately 1mm (¹⁄₁₆in) down from the tip of the padded branch. Take a stitch of crochet thread over the padded branch, perpendicular to the branch itself. Leave a space which equals the thickness of the crochet cotton, then take a second stitch across the branch in the same direction. The crochet thread crosses behind the branch, and the stitches are worked in a wrapping motion around the branch. Continue to work stitches of crochet cotton in the same manner along the length of the branch, keeping them straight and with consistent gaps between them. Do not work a bar right at the very bottom of the branch. On reaching the base, bring the remaining tail of crochet thread up temporarily in a remaining leaf to be finished off later.

5 Take two 50cm (20in) length strands of stranded cotton. Separate them and then fold them in half. Using L50, secure the fold in the stranded cotton at the centre base of the branch by stab stitching over it. Smooth the four strands and lay them down the length of the branch. Bring the needle up at the centre between bars one and two and take a couching stitch over the four strands. This stitch should fit the width of the four strands, rather than crushing them into a tight bundle. Pull the stitch down firmly so that the strands of cotton are pulled down into the gap and taut over the surface of the first bar. Diagram 5b shows the correct angle of the needle as it emerges and descends, allowing room for the couched threads to sit comfortably between.

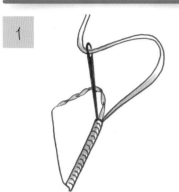

x

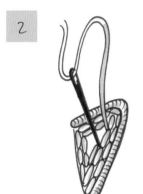

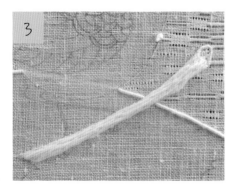

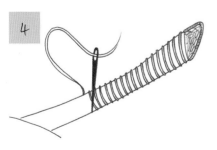

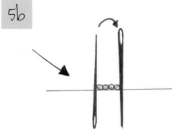

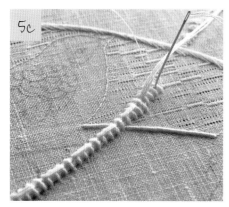

6 Work a tight, locking stab stitch within the padding of the branch to prevent the couching stitch working loose. Smooth and lay the strands of cotton over the branch again. This time, leave two bars before taking the next couching stitch over the strands and locking as before. Lay the strands again, this time leaving one bar before couching and locking. Work along the branch in a pattern of two bars, one bar, two bars, one bar, until you reach the far end. Secure the working thread with an extra couple of locking stab stitches worked into the padding at the end – use a thimble here if necessary.

7 Thread two of the strands of cotton into a no. 24 chenille needle and pass them to the reverse of the work. Re-emerge to the left in readiness to work the next band of basketweave down the branch. Repeat for the remaining two strands, bringing them up next to the first to re-form the group of four. Then couch them back down the branch. This time, the pattern moves up by one bar, which will eventually produce a spiral-like pattern across the branch.

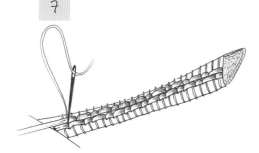

8 Keep the four strands of cotton lying as smoothly as possible next to each other and ensure an even, firm tension on the couching stitches, to ensure a glossy finished effect with a crisp basketweave pattern. On reaching the base of the branch, plunge the stranded cotton threads as before, returning them to the surface, at the left-hand side, to work a further row up the branch.

9 Continue the rows of couching back and forth along the branch, maintaining the pattern, as far as required to cover the padding bars completely. Since the edge of the branch is curved, you may only be able to couch partial rows along the edge to fill the shape. It is also acceptable to couch only two strands if there is not sufficient room for all four.

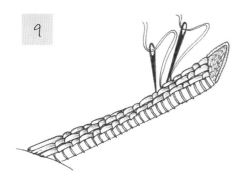

On completion, the remaining strands are plunged to the reverse of the work, staggering them to fit the design shape, and are secured by working a couple of oversewing stitches into the reverse of the work.

10 On completion of the left-hand side, repeat the process on the right. Start with a new set of two strands of cotton, folded in half, at the bottom end of the branch, and couch these up the length of the design, following the established spiral pattern.

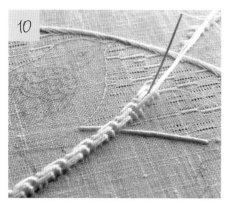

11 Work rows back and forth until the entire branch is covered: stagger the edge rows as required. (The original design uses four complete rows across the width of the branch, supplemented by staggered rows.) Finish the threads on the reverse as before.

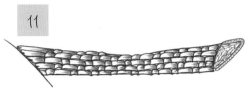

12 On completion, turn to the reverse of the work and release and secure the two tails of crochet thread by oversewing them to the back of the stitching for about 5mm (³⁄₁₆in).

The finished branch.

WORKING THE WREN'S BEAK

The wren's beak is also worked on the single layer of linen, as for the wren's tail, as it would be cumbersome to trim back a second layer of linen back around the tiny delicate beak later. Use a no. 10 embroidery/crewel needle with ST.

1 Work a split stitch around the outer perimeter of the beak. Fill the beak with satin stitch starting at the centre and working towards the tip of the beak before filling out to the sides.

2 Support the satin stitch by working a few natural shading stitches through the longest sections, to tie down the satin and ensure a beautiful, smooth effect.

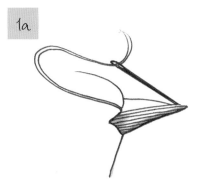

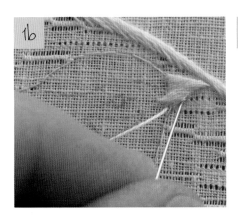

WORKING THE HONEYSUCKLE STEM

The stem is worked using trailing to give a crisp, bold finish to this design line, which frames the left half of the piece. Note that the design line varies from a basic curve, which gives a more organic look, suited to a plant stem. It is also very difficult to work a perfect, accurate curve in trailing. Adding divided and waved forms within the stem distracts the eye, and gives a stronger and more pleasing line overall. Use a no. 10 embroidery/crewel needle with ST thread.

1 The diagram, right, shows the suggested number of strands of core thread to be used, and starting positions (see circled numbers). The trailing tapers from these to the right and left. Use the tapering numbers and positions as a guide. The red dots denote where two pieces of trailing will blend to become one: remove several threads as they join to prevent bulk. The yellow dots mark where the core threads must be plunged beneath the overlapping leaves. The core thread can be left sitting behind these leaves as it will be covered by solid stitching later on. At the green dot, the trailing separates into two for a short distance to create interest, before recombining at the second red dot: no further threads need removing at this point. Trim away the core thread behind the existing beading where it crosses behind.

2 The remaining core threads will be finished by plunging at the tips of the design lines in the usual fashion.

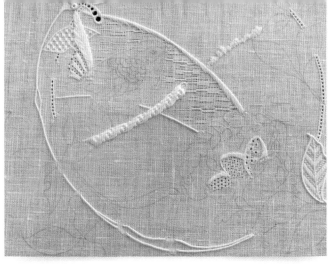

The completed stem.

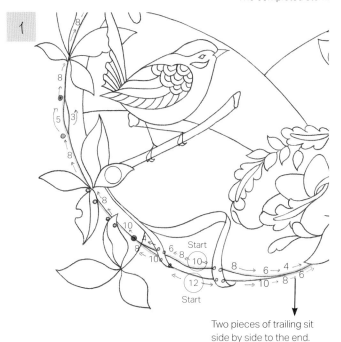

Two pieces of trailing sit side by side to the end.

WORKING THE THREE-SIDED STITCH LEAF VEINS

The diagram on the right shows the three leaves to be worked with a vein in three-sided stitch (see page 79). The lacy pulled-work technique is combined with bolder satin stitch (see overleaf). Use a no. 10 embroidery/crewel needle with ST.

1 First, work three-sided stitch down the centre of leaf E where the stitches will sit just inside the design lines which mark the vein. Pull the stitches tight and use an awl to open the holes. Avoid working on the design lines as these may show through the stitching.

2 Leaves F and G do not have marked veins, as three-sided stitch will not cover these lines effectively. You can judge the position of the row by eye; alternatively, use running stitch and L80 to tack out the position of the shapes to be filled with three-sided stitch. These delicate tack stitches can be left in place and worked over with stranded cotton to hide them.

These three leaves are spread carefully across the design to create a sense of balance.

PADDED SATIN STITCH SECTIONS OF THE THREE LEAVES

The edges of the leaves are worked using padded, slanted satin stitch and sketched satin stitch. The diagram on page 151 defines where each stitch is used and the direction in which the satin will flow.

Use a no. 10 embroidery/crewel needle with ST thread for embroidery and F for padding (used double).

LEAF E

1 Using ST, work a row of split stitch around the outer edge of the leaf. Using 2F, fill each half of the leaf with five layers of satin stitch padding, working as directed in the diagram, below. Each layer of padding gradually increases in size. Work all stitches in a back and forth motion rather than crossing the reverse of the work. The final layer of padding must sit tight against the split stitch outline and close against the three-sided stitch vein. Add a further row of split stitch around the perimeter edge, over the existing row.

LEAF F

1 Using ST, split stitch around the left-hand edge of the leaf and around the perimeter of the padded satin shape. Starting at the tip of the leaf, work sketched satin stitch down the left-hand edge, varying the lengths of the satin stitches to give a softer internal line. Gradually increase the size of the stitch as you move into the fuller part of the leaf. Use wedge stitches as required to turn the direction.

2 Outline the padded satin shape with split stitch (ST). Using 2F, fill the shape with five layers of satin stitch padding using the directions suggested in the diagram below. Do not allow the padding to invade the overlapping leaf at the base of the shape. Add a further row of split stitch around the perimeter edge.

2 Refer to the instruction for working satin stitch from a leaf tip (see pages 61–62). Starting at the tip of the leaf, work satin with a straight stitch at the point. Extend the stitch beyond the split stitch slightly to create a sharp tip. Using wedge stitches, begin to turn the angle as you work to the right side of the leaf, to achieve a 45° line.

3 Maintain this line of stitch to the base of the leaf. The needle should always emerge next to the vein and descend on the outer edge, over the split stitch. Use the FNA to smooth the edges. Repeat in the left half of the leaf.

3 Refer to the instructions on pages 50–52 for working slanted satin stitch in a simple shape. Starting at the widest point of the shape, work slanted satin stitch to the tip of the leaf, maintaining a 45° angle.

4 Return to work from the widest point back to the bottom of the shape, finishing along the flat edge of the overlapping leaf. Again, avoid invading this overlapping shape – leave its design line clear for working its edge in trailing.

LEAF G

Leaf G is worked in the same manner as leaf F. Work the right-hand side with split stitch and then sketched satin. Work the left in padded satin stitch, this time with four layers of padding as shown.

EDGING LEAVES H AND J

Work the edges of these leaves using trailing. Start at the approximate centre of each edge of the leaf and use the number of core threads suggested in the diagram on the right. Use a no. 10 embroidery/crewel needle with ST thread.

1 For leaf H, taper the trailing to the base of the leaf. Cut away two strands at regular intervals until you reach the number specified. Plunge and finish at the base.

2 Taper towards the tip of the leaf in the same fashion. At the tip, the two lines of trailing will be blended to form a sharp point before plunging. The diagram shows the final number of threads which should remain at the tip.

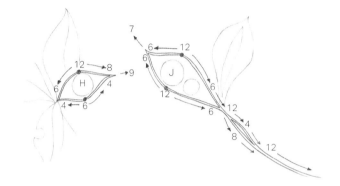

3 The tip of leaf J is created in the same way: blend the two lines of trailing to form a sharp point. At the base, however, blend together the two lines of trailing to form a stem. Allow them to separate again for a short section to add interest, before blending back together, as the diagram shows, then working to the tip of the design line where the trailing will be plunged and secured.

WORKING THE LARGE EYELETS IN LEAVES H AND J

Refer to pages 93–94. Use a no. 10 embroidery/crewel needle with ST.

1 Work a row of double running stitch around the perimeter, sitting on the design line. To increase the strength of these eyelets, add a further row of double running stitch to the inside of the first, sitting tight up against it.

2 Open the eyelets using the stiletto, and cut out to the running stitch creating approximately five flaps of fabric. Fold under and bind the edge.

The working thread can be finished by working two tiny backstitches within the body of the leaf since this will be covered by solid stitching.

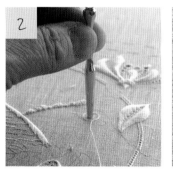

The smaller eyelet in leaf H can be worked with a single row of double running stitch and can be opened using a stiletto alone. Finish the thread within the leaf.

FILLING THE EYELETS

Refer to the instructions on working a lace spider's wheel filling (page 98) and a typical Ayrshire needlelace filling (pages 99–102). Use a no. 10 or no. 12 embroidery/crewel needle, with thread L60; use tacking thread to secure the template for the large eyelets.

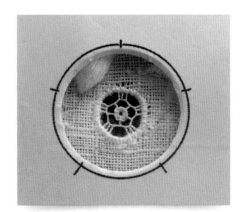

FOR THE SMALL EYELET

1 Cast on and finish the threads for this filling using the WKT within the main body of the leaf. Fill the small eyelet in leaf E with a spider's wheel filling.

FOR EACH OF THE LARGE EYELETS

1 Photocopy the template provided on page 189 for working an Ayrshire filling with five equal sections. Cut out the paper within the circle. Place this pattern over your prepared eyelet and secure in place with tacking stitches worked at the four corners (use tacking thread). See right.

2 Work the needlelace filling within the eyelet using the filling design provided. When wrapping the centre, wrap 10 times before covering with buttonhole stitches (see right).

FILLING LEAVES H AND J

The remaining space within these leaves is filled with rows of backstitch seeding using two strands of ST. When removing these strands from the skein, be sure to separate them fully and then lay them back together, to ensure there is no twist between them. Use a no. 24 chenille needle.

1 Cast on the threads as normal (WKT) within the leaf.

2 Work a full row of backstitch around the perimeter of the leaf, inside and parallel to the trailed edge. Backstitches should be no longer than 1mm (1⁄16in) and should be regular. Do not pull them tight: you are looking for a dense texture here, rather than holes.

3 Work dense rows of backstitch back and forth around the leaf, towards the centre. The backstitches in each row will not align with previous rows due to the curve of the leaf, but do maintain a consistent stitch size.

4 The eyelets will prevent you working full circuits of the leaf, so fill the leaf up to the edge of these; keep your rows of backstitch running parallel to the leaf edges.

Tip

Use a laying tool such as an aficot or mellor to assist with guiding and smoothing the two strands of cotton and keeping them at the same tension.

WORKING THE CURLED LEAF SECTIONS K AND L

Use a no. 10 embroidery/crewel needle with ST for embroidery and F for padding (used double).

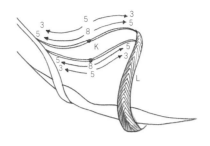

LEAF SECTION K IN TRAILING

Edge the leaf using trailing: start the upper and lower edges from the centre and taper by removing one thread at a time towards the ends. The diagram on the right shows the suggested number of core threads. A second row will be added later.

> ### Tip
> When working trailing along a horizontal line, turn your frame so that the line falls vertically, and work either towards or away from your body. This can be more comfortable than working sideways.

Fishbone stitches can be blended into the tip of the trailing using slanted satin stitches

LEAF SECTION L AND COMPLETING LEAF K

1 First outline the shape using split stitch (ST). Use two strands of Floche à Broder to fill the shape, with two layers of long split stitch padding to create a smooth domed finish. Add a further split stitch outline if desired.

2 Cover the shape using raised fishbone stitch (ST), following the directions on page 65.

The background fabric surrounding leaf K will include some drawn thread work. The existing single row of trailing edging the leaf does not provide a strong barrier to protect the leaf from the drawn thread, which could result in the drawn threads travelling into the leaf itself.

3 Add a second row of trailing outside the first (see diagram above right for number of core threads). This is done after the raised fishbone is complete, to allow you to curl the upper row around the tip of section L, thus enhancing the sense of this long leaf curling over.

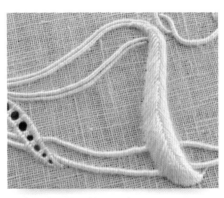

Leaf sections K and L, complete.

WORKING THE LEAVES IN THE NEST

CENTRE VEINS IN LADDER STITCH

Use a no. 10 embroidery/crewel needle with L60 thread. Each leaf will have a vein of delicate ladder stitch worked using L60. The ladder stitch will begin about 1–2mm (1/16in) down from the outer tip of the leaf.

Work the backstitch and then apply a loop of L60 around the upper tip of the backstitch line to to allow you to work the perimeter couching and wrapping process (see diagram, right). Travel your working threads to their required stitch positions by working small stab stitches within the main body of the leaves, as these will be covered by padded satin stitch later.

Finish all working and all laid threads using small stab stitches within the satin area of the leaf.

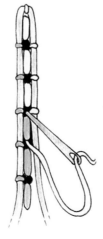

The leaves in the nest.

THE MAIN BODY OF THE LEAVES IN PADDED SATIN STITCH

Work the satin stitch leaves in the order shown in the diagram, right. Note that some leaves overlap others, which is why the order of work is important. Use a no. 10 embroidery/crewel needle with ST for embroidery and F for padding.

For each leaf in turn:

1 Work a split stitch outline. When working an underlapping leaf (leaves 1, 2 and 6, with red outlines), the split stitch outline is worked only around the outer perimeter and not along the section of line adjoining the overlapping leaf. These leaves will be completed with padding and satin stitch before working on the overlapping leaves (with blue outlines). This process avoids a build-up of two sections of split stitch falling along the same line and helps give the impression of the upper leaf sitting in front of the lower.

2 Using a single strand of Floche à Broder, fill each side of the leaf using two to four layers of satin stitch padding, depending on the size of the design shape: adjust as you see fit. All padding stitches should run parallel to the centre vein – the direction will not change with each layer, since the shapes are too tiny. Use long split stitches (see page 53) to extend the padding where the leaves are a little longer or curved.

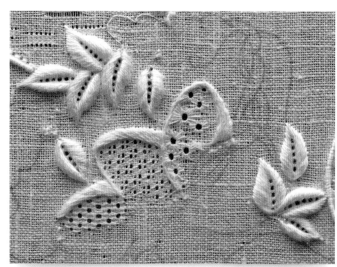

3 Add a second row of split stitch around each leaf if you feel the edges need further definition. Then, starting at the tip, work satin stitch in the same manner as for large leaf E (see page 152).

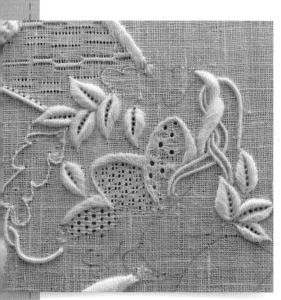

THE BRANCHES WITHIN THE NEST

The diagrams on the right and on the opposite page clarify the order in which to work the tiny trailed branches, and the number of core threads to be used in each.

Use a no. 10 embroidery/crewel needle, and a chenille 24 for plunging, with ST.

1 Section A has two lines of trailing, each starting at the centre over six strands and tapering to four at each end. Plunge and finish at each end as normal.

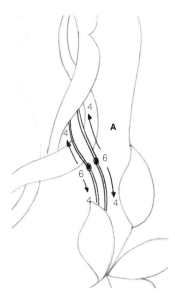

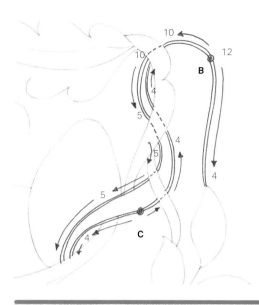

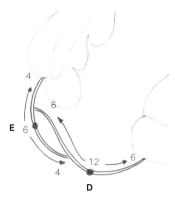

2 Section B starts with 12 strands at the point indicated by the red dot, gradually tapering to four towards the right. Towards the left, the trailing tapers but also plunges and re-emerges several times as it crosses behind overlapping shapes. Plunge and finish at each end.

3 Section C starts with six strands at the point shown, tapering to the left and right and plunging and re-emerging behind the overlapping shapes again.

4 Sections D and E start at the centre and taper to the ends where they are plunged, as shown.

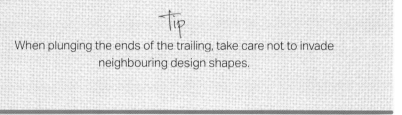

Tip

When plunging the ends of the trailing, take care not to invade neighbouring design shapes.

OAK LEAVES

Use a no. 10 embroidery needle with ST for embroidery and F for padding. For each of the oak leaves:

1 Work beading through the centre, working the double running stitch outline on the two design lines provided (ST).

2 Work a split stitch outline to the leaf (ST).

3 Fill each lobe of the leaf shape with two layers of satin stitch padding using F, following the direction shown in the diagrams on the right. The lower of the three leaves (O) has a longer, narrower section – extend the satin padding stitches into long split stitch here, thus drawing out the padding to fill this section. Work a further outline of split stitch on top of the first for clarity.

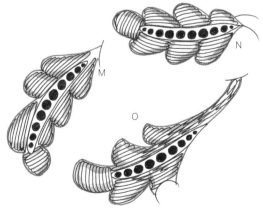

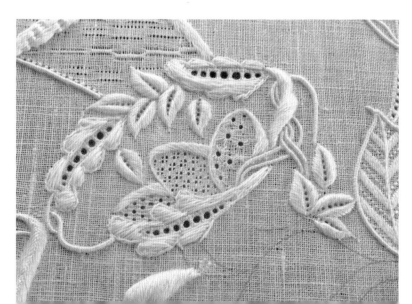

Work satin stitch as follows:

1 Start at the outermost peak of each leaf: the needle emerges at the edge of the beading and descends over the split stitch, with the needle perpendicular to the fabric surface. Repeat for a further stitch either side of the first.

2 Work turning wedge stitches on either side; the needle emerges as if from beneath the existing stitches. As the needle descends over the split stitch outline, use the FNA to shape the edge: angle the needle towards the peak of the rounded tip and the existing stitches, keeping the line of the needle parallel to the split stitch edge.

3 Work around the uppermost lobe of the leaf, adding wedge stitches until a 45° stitch angle is achieved. Maintain this angle to the base of the lobe, using the FNA throughout.

4 Work a locking stab stitch into the padding before moving to the peak of the next lobe. Work a stitch at a 45° angle, the needle emerging next to the beading and descending over the split stitch (see stitches marked in red, below). Continue to work slanted satin stitch down the depth of the lobe, maintaining the 45° angle. Use wedge stitches as required. Secure with a locking stitch into the padding.

5 Work the upper half of the lobe. Following the 'Z' rule (see page 49), this half is worked with the needle emerging outside the split stitch and descending tucked towards the centre vein. Use the FNA throughout. Work each lobe individually in the same manner, then use wedge stitches if required, to blend the lobes together at the base.

6 Repeat steps 4 and 5 for the next set of lobes. For leaf O, the slanted satin continues at the base of the leaf along the narrow design area, maintaining a 45° angle, using wedge stitches as required.

Note
There is no need to work with two needles – these are shown only to clarify the action on each side of the leaf.

Tip
The tips for working curved satin shapes, using the needle at an angle as it emerges from the fabric (see pages 53–56), are useful here to create effective curved tops on the lobes of the oak leaves.

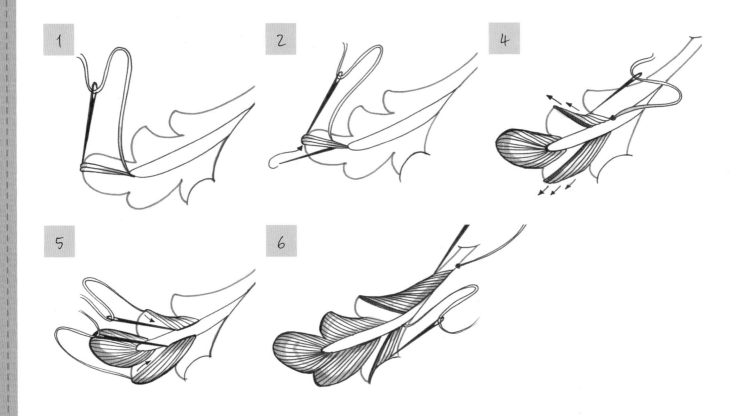

WORKING THE REMAINING SATIN LEAVES IN THE NEST

Use a no. 10 embroidery needle with ST for embroidery and F for padding. Each of the three satin shapes – shapes P, Q and R, shown right – are worked following the angles shown in the diagrams.

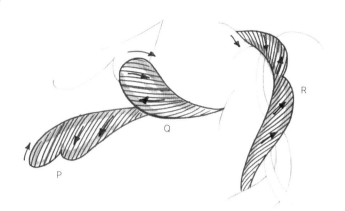

Shape P: Split stitch outline, pad with five layers of satin stitch padding, further split stitch outline, slanted satin starting from the widest point and following the 'Z' rule (see page 49).

Shape Q: As Shape P.

Shape R: Split stitch outline, pad with two layers of long split stitch padding, further split stitch outline, satin following the same method, adding wedge stitches to encourage effective turning.

WORKING LEAF S

This leaf includes eyelets, the holes of which balance out the large amount of beading worked in the oak leaves on the opposite side of the design.

Use a no. 10 embroidery needle; ST for embroidery and F for padding (used double).

1 Work the eyelets as shown right (and following the instructions on pages 91–93), starting with the largest two close to the centre. These eyelets require a double running stitch edge and will open sufficiently using a stiletto alone. It is fine to travel from one eyelet to the next if your thread is sound. If not, use the double loop technique to finish.

2 Work a split stitch around the satin stitch shape. Pad with two layers of long split stitch (2F). Add a further row of split stitch and cover with slanted satin stitch, starting from the widest point and using the 'Z' rule.

ADDING A SECOND LAYER OF LINEN

At this stage, a second layer of linen should be applied to the reverse of the remaining unworked leaves and to the wren's body, increasing the intensity of the whiteness in these areas and creating another layer of interest.

Rather than applying a large piece of linen across the entire design, small pieces can be applied behind clusters of design shapes. Use a small, shallow 15cm (6in) embroidery hoop to hold the fabric taut, along with a no. 10 embroidery needle and stranded cotton.

1 Take your first 20 × 20cm (7⅞ × 7⅞in) piece of linen and place in your shallow embroidery hoop. Ease the fabric taut, keeping the fabric grain as straight as possible. Tighten the screw to lock the tension.

2 Turn your slate frame to the reverse and position the hoop centrally over the first cluster of leaves to be worked (leaves T, U and V), in the bottom right corner of the design *when viewed from the reverse*, with the taut linen pressed against the reverse of the design. Align the straight grain of linen as closely as possible.

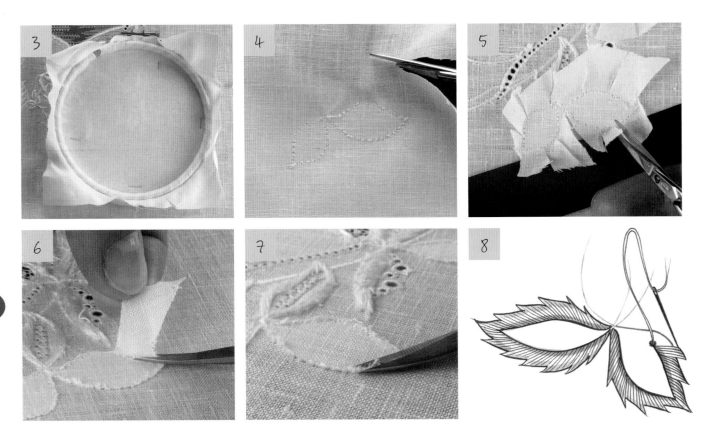

3 Use three to four clean, fine pins to secure the hoop in place by pinning into the linen around the design shapes.

4 Turn the work back to the front. Work a row of split stitch around the perimeter of each leaf in turn. Add a second row of split stitch just inside the first, providing extra strength. Turn back to the reverse of the work, release the screw and remove the hoop. Trim the linen back roughly around each leaf, leaving a border of 1–2cm (⅜–1³⁄₁₆in).

5 Place a strip of coloured cardboard between the excess linen to be trimmed, and the design: cutting over this coloured, solid surface is safer and will give you more confidence. Use lobe-tipped lace scissors here – the ball tip slides between the two layers of fabric as you cut, protecting the precious design beneath. Snip the excess linen into small flaps around the perimeter of the leaves. This makes cutting the fabric away more manageable.

6 Take each flap of linen in turn and pull while using your curved-tip scissors to cut as cleanly as possible against the edge of the leaf.

7 Once all the flaps are trimmed away, use the rounded end of a mellor, or your fingernail, to brush around the perimeter edges of the leaves, flicking upwards, and in both directions. This will lift and loosen any remaining wisps of linen. Use the curved-tip scissors to skim these away cleanly.

8 Return to the front of the work. Work 'spiked' satin stitch around the perimeter edge of each leaf, starting at the tip and working down each side. Each time you wish to create a spike, extend the stitch out beyond the split stitch outline by 1–2mm (¹⁄₁₆in). This creates the tip of the spike. Add further slanted satin stitches, tucked towards this tip, using the FNA; gradually decrease the length until you meet the split stitch outline again. Use wedge stitches to turn the stitch as required. Add as many spikes as you wish. The inner edge of the satin stitch is not solid or worked to the line of a split stitch but try to keep it as smooth as possible as an effective contrast to the spiked edge.

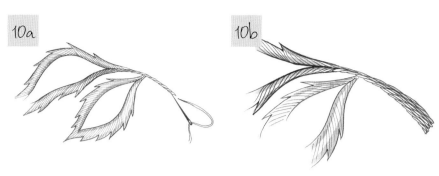

9 Work the stem leading to this cluster of leaves using trailing worked over a core of six threads and starting the core thread at one end using the knot technique (see page 41).

10 Work the second cluster of leaves (leaves W and X, bottom-left of the design *when viewed from the reverse*) in the same manner, using your second piece of linen. When working the central leaf of this spray (leaf W), draw the slanted satin stitch out into stem stitch at the base to create the leaf stem. Add short extra rows at the tip of the stem to create a slightly broader, tapered tip.

The two small remaining unworked leaves (Y and Z) will be worked at the same time as the wren.

ADDING THE SECOND LAYER OF LINEN AND WORKING THE WREN

Use a no. 10 embroidery needle, and stranded cotton thread; use L60 for the eye.

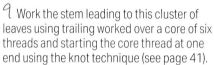

2 rows of split stitch worked side by side

1 row of split stitch

2 rows of split stitch worked side by side with an additional third row on top along the outer edge

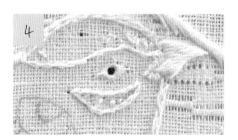

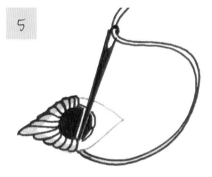

1 Place your final piece of linen centrally behind the design, including the wren and final two leaves (Y and Z).

2 Outline the wren as shown in the diagram above, using two adjacent rows of split stitch (see green lines) around key parts of the body outline, and a single row to define internal lines (blue lines). Work an additional line of split stitch along the edge of the chest/body, on top of the existing line (see red line). This will provide extra emphasis to this leading edge.

3 Work trailing along the back of the wren, starting at the right (see yellow dot) using a core thread of 8ST with a knot. Taper to the left and plunge.

4 Using stranded cotton, work a cluster of single-twist French knots (see page 37) around the base of the beak. These create texture, and also seal the second layer of linen in place around the beak.

5 Use L60 to work the eye as a tiny eyelet. Start with a double running stitch edge and use an awl to open. Extend the stitches at the left and right tips as you bind the eyelet, forming a lozenge shape.

6 Prepare the final two leaves (Y and Z) by outlining using two adjacent rows of split stitch, using ST.

THE WREN'S WING

Use a no. 10 embroidery needle, with ST.

1 Work a row of reverse stem stitch around the outer perimeter of the design shape, starting at X. Add a second row running adjacent to and inside the first.

2 Work each of the bands using densely worked rows of reverse stem, each starting with a row on the left-hand side, continuing to add rows to the right. Start each row from the bottom. These bands create a different texture and give a suggestion of feathers.

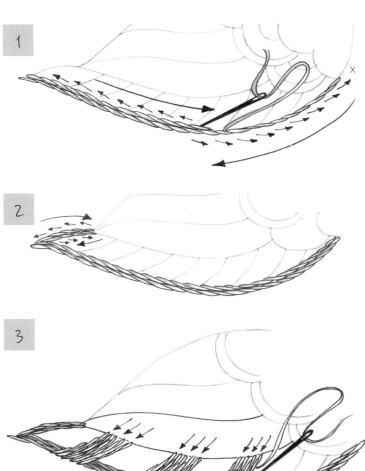

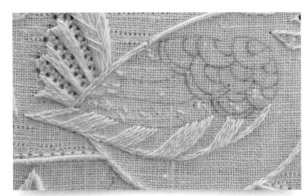

The finished effect.

TRIMMING AWAY THE EXCESS LINEN

Turn to the back, remove the hoop and trim away carefully around the wren and two leaves, as previously described on page 160.

Cutting the excess linen into manageable flaps.

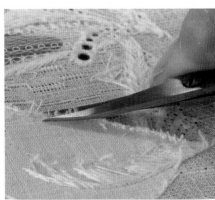

Trimming away the excess linen close to the worked edge.

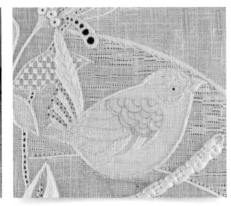

The completed wren with double layer of linen, viewed from the front of the work.

THE WREN'S HEAD AND CHEST

1 Outline the design area at the top of the head in split stitch before filling with natural shading. Start at the point at the back of the head and work the first row of stitches towards this edge (ST).

2 Work through these stitches towards the front of the head. It can help to work stitches at the edges of the shape in the opposite direction to cover the split stitch and smooth the edges.

3 Work further rows of stitches through existing rows until the shape is filled. The angle of stitches gradually changes to create the soft curve of the head. Use the FNA again to smooth the edges as the stitches fall over the final split stitch outline. Work the cheek in the same fashion and direction (ST).

4 Starting at the left-hand side, work sketched satin stitch along the belly and chest of the wren. At the tail end, allow the stitches to form soft spikes as they fall over the split stitch, suggesting fluffy feathers. As you progress under the belly and into the chest, keep the outer edge smooth and crisp using the FNA. Allow the sketched satin to taper and become shallower as it climbs up the chest towards the beak.

5 Extend the internal sketched satin stitches by working through them using shading stitches to give greater depth, a softer texture and a greater sense of the curved body.

The finished effect.

163

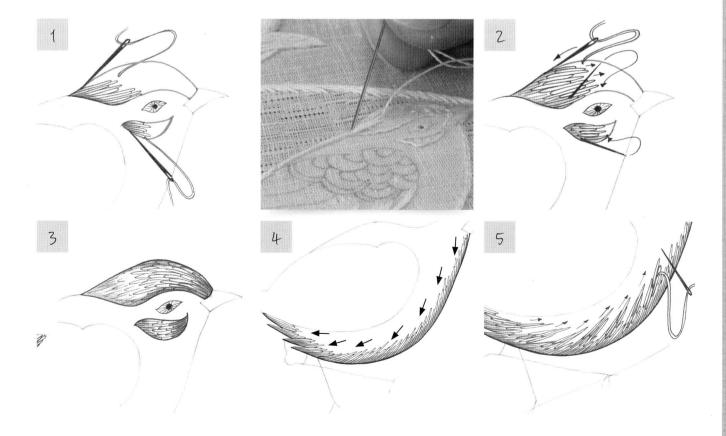

THE UPPER WING

Work a tiny eyelet in the centre of each of the scallops using ST: open each with a fine awl. Work the running stitch preparation as a tiny circle, but work the bound edge to fit to the design shape as shown on the right.

   The lower three scallops of the upper wing are each edged using ladder stitch and L50, working within the narrow design sections marked. The initial backstitch should run through the centre of each strip. Work each section of ladder stitch separately.

Eyelets and scallops on the upper wing.

THE LOWER WING

Starting with the lowest section of the wing, outline the outer edge only using split stitch (see green line).

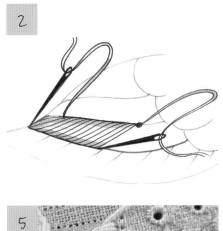

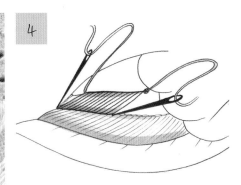

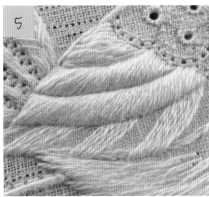

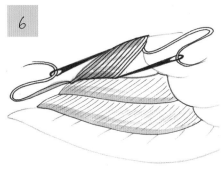

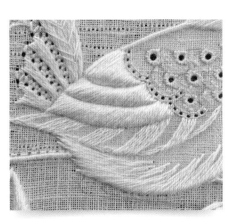

The finished effect.

1 Use 2F to fill the shape with one layer of long split-stitch padding. Work a second row of split stitch over the first.

2 Work slanted satin stitch from the left-hand tip, starting with a stitch at 45°. All stitches will emerge on the top edge of the shape and descend on the bottom edge over the split stitch. On completion, return to cover the last remaining section of padding at the left-hand end.

3 On completion, split-stitch the lower, outer edge of the next design shape (ST). Fill with two layers of long split-stitch padding (2F) and add the extra row of split stitch along the outline (ST).

4 Work the satin in the same fashion (ST). These satin stitches will bite slightly into those of the previous layer, creating the feel of this layer sitting over the first. This is a technique known as 'encroaching satin stitch'.

5 Split stitch all the way around the final shape. Pad with three layers of long split-stitch padding and add the second layer of split stitch.

6 Work satin stitch in the same manner but note the change of direction for the stitches at the left-hand end following the 'Z' rule.

BUTTONHOLE SCALLOPS ON THE WING

The scallops are worked starting from those at the bottom, and working methodically following the order in which they overlap each other. Work the uppermost scallop last. The diagram on the right shows the order in which to work the scallops and the direction of the buttonhole stitches in each.

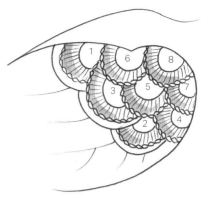

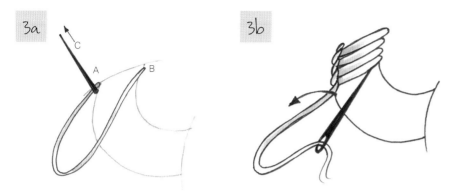

1 For each scallop, outline the outer edge using split stitch with ST.

2 Fill the depth of the scallop with one or two rows of split stitch using F; adjust the number to fit comfortably.

3 Starting from the left, cover the padding using closely worked buttonhole stitch (ST). The diagram, above right (3b), shows how a shorter wedge stitch can be added to assist with turning the angle of the buttonhole stitches.

Tip

When working buttonhole stitch, ply the thread back and forth a little as you ease each stitch into place. This will help to draw the stitch up smooth and tight around the padding and form a neatly purled edge.

165

TRAILED EDGE

Outline the upper half of the wing using trailing, starting with a core of six at the top peak and tapering out to four or five before plunging at each end (ST).

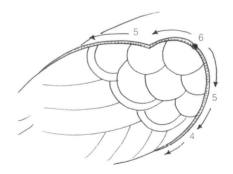

COMPLETING THE TWO REMAINING LEAVES

For each leaf, start at the tip of the leaf and work the perimeter using slanted satin stitch. Maintain a smooth outer edge and a fairly consistent depth of stitch (see page 62).

DRAWN THREAD WORK

There are two areas of drawn thread work within this design.

The **foreground field** is created by simply removing some of the horizontal linen threads within the design area in a random pattern. Those remaining have room to move and are manipulated so that, rather than lying straight across the fabric, they form undulating lines to suggest the texture of a grassy field. The fabric with some threads removed also appears deeper in tone; it contrasts with the double layer and the heavy work within the wren and acts as a foil, drawing attention to the bird.

The **background field** is worked in counted drawn thread work: regular bands of vertical threads are removed before working into these with binding and pattern stitches. This creates an eye-catching, delicate lace-like pattern and texture. Since a significant number of fabric threads are withdrawn, the viewer looks through the work to the world beyond. The darker tone of the background field offsets the bolder elements which overlay it, to create a sense of dimension throughout the design.

PREPARING FOR DRAWN THREAD WORK

To allow the linen threads to be removed effectively, the tension of the slate frame must be reduced.

1 Slacken the lacing on both sides of the frame and then move the pegs in by two to three holes.

2 Turn the work to the reverse. The pegs may drop out so replace them in the same positions on the reverse.

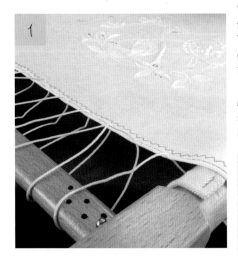

THE FOREGROUND FIELD

1 Starting across the widest part of the foreground field and using a fine (no. 28) tapestry needle, carefully lift a horizontal linen thread at the centre point before snipping it using the tip of a pair of curved-tip scissors.

2 Use the tapestry needle to carefully unpick the linen thread to the left and right until you reach the solid embroidery. This must be done gradually. Do not try to pull the thread back in long sections as this may disrupt the linen beyond the design shape.

3 On reaching the embroidery, pull on the linen thread and clip it away close using curved-tip scissors. Try not to leave a tail of linen at the ends of drawn bands.

4 Continue removing horizontal threads in the same way. You can remove single threads or two adjacent threads, but do not remove three adjacent threads.

5 Leave between two and seven threads intact between removed threads. In this design, the threads are removed more intensively towards the wren to create a shadow around the bird. The spacing between removed threads then increases towards the front of the field to create greater density. Avoid removing too many threads: there must be sufficient density to allow for the working of the wren's legs in trailing later (see page 170).

6 The design area crosses behind the overlapping branch and leaves. Try to link with the same linen threads as you cross to the neighbouring area of the design – laying a clean ruler across can help.

The linen thread may shred or disintegrate as you unpick; this often happens as each thread is quite weak on its own.

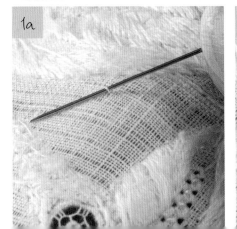

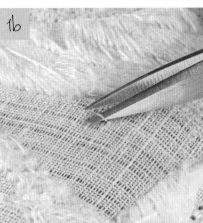

7 Once you have removed a good number of threads, use your tapestry needle to gently move those remaining: push them up and down to create gently undulating lines, moving them as much or as little as you wish. Keep turning the work to the front to be sure you are happy with the effect. Continue to remove further threads if necessary.

It can be difficult to ensure that you are withdrawing exactly the same thread all the way across but this is not important: once the threads are moved, it will be impossible to see any discrepancies.

The finished effect once all the threads have been removed and manipulated.

THE BACKGROUND FIELD

The reverse of this design area will be partially covered in net, which must be removed to give access to the linen and allow the threads to be withdrawn from the reverse of the work.

Use lace scissors to carefully cut into and release the net, then use curved-tip scissors to trim away up to the secure stitching edging the field (see right).

WITHDRAWING THE THREADS

1 Working from the reverse and starting across the widest part of the background field shape, use the fine tapestry needle to carefully lift three or four vertical linen threads at the centre point before snipping.

2 Gradually and carefully unpick the threads back to the top and bottom of the design shape before snipping away as close as possible to the embroidery using curved scissors.

3 Remove further adjacent vertical threads until you have created an open band of six.

4 Leave two vertical linen threads intact before removing a further three. Then leave two intact again.

5 Remove threads following the same pattern throughout the design area: remove six, leave two, remove three, leave two. Continue the pattern to the extremities of the design area. Use a sharp-tipped needle to unpick tiny fibres at the edges.

6 Carry these bands up into the areas above the overlapping stem and leaf. Begin this process through the widest area of the upper isolated design sections: line up the threads removed with those below as best you can.

7 When removing threads in a narrow design shape, lift and snip the threads along one edge of the design, rather than in the centre: this allows the maximum length of thread to be removed across the shape.

8 Check that the areas – rather than individual threads – line up visually, for cohesion; using a clean ruler to guide placement can be helpful. Remove one thread at a time, adjusting which threads you remove to achieve the best effect. Do not be concerned if the bands do not line up exactly.

9 Once you have removed all the required threads, turn back to the front to check whether any solid areas remain.

When you are happy with the end result, tighten the slate frame again: reposition the pegs and tighten the lacing evenly on both sides. Exercise greater caution when tightening than you would in the case of solid fabric. Although it is still strong, the drawn thread work will weaken the piece a little.

Tension the rollers and insert the pegs by hand; avoid exerting any extra pressure (such as by applying a foot to the roller).

The completed effect of drawing the threads, before the frame is re-tightened.

The finished effect of withdrawing the threads.

Tips

Press a piece of low-tack sticky tape over the front and reverse of the drawn thread work to remove any fibres loosened by the removal process. Any remaining 'fluff' will generally fall out as you embellish the drawn thread and will settle further when the work is washed.

If you accidentally snip the wrong linen thread (which happens to everybody), it can easily be replaced using a length of L60 (coarse L50). Remove the remaining sections of the cut linen thread. Using a fine embroidery needle, secure the lace thread at one end of the design by oversewing into the back of the embroidery on the reverse. Darn the thread into the linen across the design shape, following the original pattern of the weave. Tension the thread before securing on the reverse in the same fashion.

BINDING THE VERTICAL BARS

Each pair of remaining linen threads must now be bound. This strengthens them, makes the vertical lines visually stronger and groups the horizontal threads into twos. This opens the design area further and gives precision to the pattern.

Use a no. 12 embroidery/crewel needle and L60 thread (or coarse L50).

1 If any of the remaining vertical threads appear skewed or distorted, use your tapestry needle to manipulate them until they are as straight as possible.

2 Starting at the top of one of the longer vertical bands, secure a length of L60. Use the WKT, burying the securing stitches between the French knots. Bind the vertical bar with diagonal stitches, each worked over two vertical and two horizontal threads.

3 On reaching the bottom, tuck the needle into the base edge of the embroidery. Work a tiny locking stab stitch invisibly into the embroidery. This could be buried next to trailing, or tucked between satin stitches.

4 Move to the next vertical band and proceed to wrap in the same fashion. The direction of the diagonal flow of the stitch should be the same as that in the first row (unless you wish to alternate for effect). Tuck the needle into the embroidery on reaching the top again and work a hidden locking stab stitch between the French knots or into the seeding.

5 Work the remaining rows in the same fashion. Adjust the position and line of these bands as you wrap them, if they require further straightening.

6 Always keep sufficient thread to complete a full row of binding and regularly check the thread condition as the process will wear the thread, potentially causing it to break or to appear less precise.

7 To finish a thread, use two locking stitches worked invisibly into surrounding stitching, or turn to the reverse to work a couple of oversewing stitches.

8 It is possible to carry the wrapping thread across behind the overlapping leaf to continue on the far side, where the seeding will obscure the crossing. Otherwise work the wrapping in these isolated areas separately following the same method.

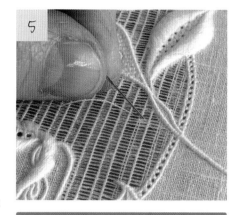

5

Tip

If any remnants of linen fibre show around the perimeter of the design shape, after working a locking stitch at the end of a row of binding, use the thread to work a few tiny oversewing stitches hidden in the edge of the work, to trap and settle the loose fibres.

The completed effect of the bound bands.

169

EMBELLISHING THE DRAWN THREAD WORK WITH PATTERNS

The broader bands of openwork can now be filled using alternating rows of feather stitch and raised chain stitch (see pages 89–90). These create beautifully delicate patterns.

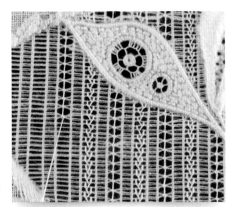

The thread you select for working these patterns should be slightly heavier than that used for oversewing the bands, to create more emphasis: use a no. 12 or 10 embroidery/crewel needle, with thread L50 (coarse L30).

Select a longer band to begin with and secure the working thread by burying invisibly into the surrounding embroidery as before. Work the pattern, treating each gathered pair of linen threads as one. The tension should not be so tight that it distorts the linen ground threads excessively but should be sufficiently tight to lock the stitches into position without excessive movement. Try to maintain an even tension throughout the row.

On reaching the bottom, tuck the needle into the base edge of the surrounding embroidery and secure and finish with two invisible locking stitches (or turn to the reverse to oversew). Each new row will begin with a new thread at the top, working downwards.

At the curved design edges, adjust the stitch as best you can to fit. In the isolated areas, again where possible, the thread can be carried behind the leaf where solid stitching allows. Otherwise work these areas as independent rows.

WREN'S LEGS

Work the wren's legs after completion of the drawn thread work: if worked prior to this, the removal of the background threads will be much more complex as you work around these intricate shapes. Use a no. 10 embroidery/crewel needle with ST.

1 Starting with the horizontal leg, work trailing (starting with a knot) from the left to the right using a 10-strand core thread. On reaching the branch, divide the core thread into six to the left and four to the right. The four threads are trailed for a tiny section – 3–4mm (⅛–³⁄₁₆in) – to the right and plunged, to suggest a toe tucking behind the branch. The six threads are trailed out over the top of the branch to create the foreground toe.

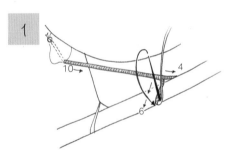

2 Having trailed almost all the way across the branch, pleat the core thread back on itself. Trail over this and the original trailing for 3–4mm (⅛–³⁄₁₆in) to form the heavy tip to the toe. Plunge the remaining core threads.

3 Repeat for the remaining leg using an eight-strand core thread and dividing into five and three at the tip to work the claws. Add a claw at the tip of each foreground toe using two tiny bullion knots (see page 37). Finally, work a few French knots at the top of the foreground leg to blend the narrow trailed leg into the body.

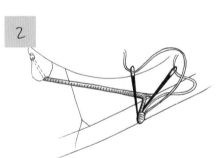

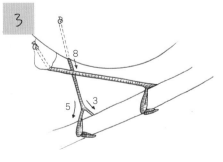

COMPLETING THE NEST

The edges of the nest are softened by adding tiny sprigs of leaves, worked using satin stitch over applied pelmet Vilene shapes. The applied shapes allow this heavy stitching to be worked effectively over drawn thread work, where the stitches would otherwise fall into the holes.

Use a no. 10 embroidery/crewel needle with L60 for appliqué and ST for satin stitch.

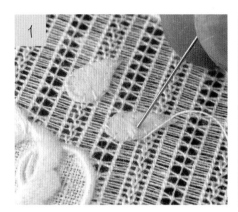  

1 Trace the leaf pattern shapes provided on page 191 onto a piece of pelmet Vilene, using a lightbox (or window) and a fine marker pen. Cut the leaves out. Using the pattern as a guide, position the leaves and pin in place. Use L60 to secure each in place by working tiny stab stitches around the perimeter edge. The needle should always emerge in the ground fabric and descend into the Vilene.

2 Using ST, work each leaf in turn using satin stitch: start at the tip and work from the centre vein outwards (see page 62). The firm edge of the Vilene works in the same way as a split stitch outline.

3 On completion of each satin leaf, work a section of stem from the base of the leaf to meet the nest, using reverse stem stitch.

LETTERING (SEE PAGE 190 FOR TEMPLATE)

Work a tacking thread across the design, following the straight grain, to denote the base line of the lettering, setting this at your chosen depth below the main design. Place the design outline beneath the work, aligning the lettering with the tacked line and centring with the main design. Secure to the reverse with tabs of tape. Trace carefully using a pale grey fine-liner, with the assistance of a lightbox.

Use a no. 12 or 10 embroidery/crewel needle; use ST for split stitch, surface satin stitch, eyelets and trailing, and F for padding in satin stitch (all used single).

1 First work the four small eyelets (ST). Then complete the sections of trailing using the number of stranded cotton core threads specified in the diagram above (see yellow lines). Start with a knot in the core threads, emerging at the tip of the design line to be worked.

2 Outline all the sections of satin stitch in split stitch (ST). The split stitch should sit on the design line: do not allow it to spread beyond the design line as this will make the lettering appear too heavy. The split stitches should be smaller around the tighter, curved sections to ensure a smooth outline.

Each section of satin stitch will be padded using long split stitch (F). The majority of the design shapes will be padded with two layers. However, three can be used in the larger sections of the capital letters to make these a little more prominent. The third layer will simply be a line of long split stitch running through the centre spine of the shape. In the very smallest shapes, you may prefer to simply work one layer of padding.

3 Redefine any split stitch edges with a second row on top, particularly around prominent sections of the lettering. Avoid doing this in very narrow, intricate sections.

Work the satin stitch shapes in turn following the guidance provided in the diagram at the top of the page.

Start each section from its widest point, shown by the red lines. Note that some letters inevitably have several starting points due to their increasing and decreasing thickness.

The arrows show the direction of working the stitches, adhering to the satin stitch and Z rules and their related needle angles. Add wedge stitches as required throughout to maintain and turn the angles smoothly around the curves.

Tips

Avoid travelling working threads between letters as these may show through the work. Start and finish threads within each letter.

Remove the base tacking line as you stitch to be sure that this is not caught in the embroidery.

The peach-coloured areas show where a triangle of satin stitch is worked (see page 61).

The pale blue areas show where a curved end is worked using the needle angles to shape and round the curve (see pages 57– 59).

At certain points, the satin gradually flows into reverse stem stitch to form the narrowest sections, as one letter flows into the next (see stitches marked in green). The arrows again show the preferred direction of working. As the satin moves into stem, the space between the new and previous stitch increases as the needle emerges. It descends, tucked halfway back along the previous stitch. The stitches lengthen and form a narrow line (for example, at the base of the 'i's).

Where letters have two sections which overlap slightly, always work the shape which appears to be 'behind'; first – for example, work the tight, curled section of the 'a' before the upright section, and work the curl of the 'd' before the vertical.

NEEDLELACE FILLING IN LEAF K

Needlelace can be used to fill long narrow shapes, as for round fillings: the fabric is simply cut away within the design shape, cutting up to the pre-worked trailing edge, rather than turning the fabric under. Use a no. 12 embroidery/crewel needle with L60.

1 Use curved-tip scissors to carefully cut away the linen within the leaf shape. Cut cleanly against the trailed edge, without snipping the trailing itself.

2 Turn the work to the reverse and brush a fingernail, mellor (or similar implement) around the perimeter edges of the leaf, in both directions. This will loosen any linen fibres which remain trapped. Flick them upwards away from the trailing. Use curved-tip scissors to carefully trim these away to produce a clean, crisp edge.

3 Secure a long length of L60 (approximately 70cm or 27½in) into the reverse of the fishbone stitching at the right-hand end of the open leaf, by working small oversewing stitches. The thread emerges at the right-hand tip of the open leaf, catching up through the outer edge of the fishbone stitches (see point X). Work a row of evenly spaced, single twisted buttonhole stitches along the upper edge of the open leaf, with just under 1mm (¹⁄₁₆in) between them. Work these in the same way as the round Ayrshire fillings (see pages 99–102), but twist the thread once around the needle this time, rather than twice (this process is detailed overleaf).

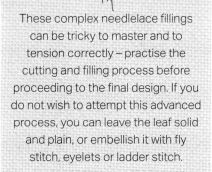

Tip

These complex needlelace fillings can be tricky to master and to tension correctly – practise the cutting and filling process before proceeding to the final design. If you do not wish to attempt this advanced process, you can leave the leaf solid and plain, or embellish it with fly stitch, eyelets or ladder stitch.

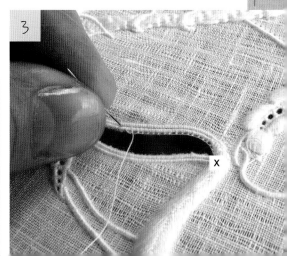

3

X

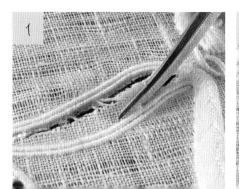

1

2

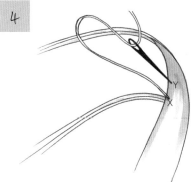

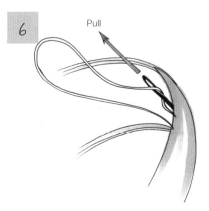

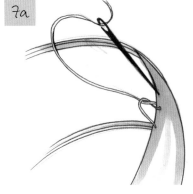

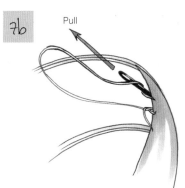

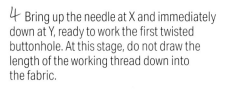

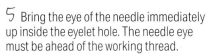

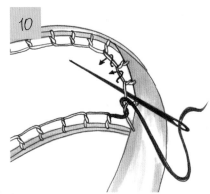

4 Bring up the needle at X and immediately down at Y, ready to work the first twisted buttonhole. At this stage, do not draw the length of the working thread down into the fabric.

5 Bring the eye of the needle immediately up inside the eyelet hole. The needle eye must be ahead of the working thread.

6 Twist the working thread once around the eye of the needle. Grab the needle eye and pull through in the same direction as the stitch, across the width of the leaf shape. Use your needle to tension the working loop formed, to settle the twisted buttonhole which is formed as you ease it into place. Pull until the twisted stitch sits firm and neat, protruding out from the trailed edge. This first process makes two stitches: one untwisted and one twisted.

7 Proceed to work the next twisted buttonhole spaced just under 1mm (1/16in) from the previous one.

8 Continue to work evenly spaced, single twisted buttonholes along the upper edge of the leaf, each a little under 1mm (1/16in) apart. The stitches initially bite into the edge of the fishbone leaf, but will later be stitched over the inner row of trailing.

9 At the left-hand tip of the design shape, work a stitch, just catching into the fabric rather than working over the trailing. Add an extra twist if required, to allow the stitch to sit comfortably and tightly at the corner. Continue along the lower edge, as for the upper edge.

10 On reaching the start again (marked in yellow), slip the needle down between the yellow starting stitch and first twisted buttonhole. Bring it immediately up, eye first, in the large centre hole. The ring of the first row is now linked (see thread marked in red).

11 Pass the needle down between every pair of twisted buttonholes around the ring; each time, emerge eye first in the centre hole. This puts a wrapping stitch between each pair of buttonholes (see thread marked in red in the diagram on the next page). Pull the wraps tight by pulling round in the direction of the ring, rather than across the leaf, to neaten, strengthen and define the effect. The row will now be strong enough to work into with further rows of needlelace.

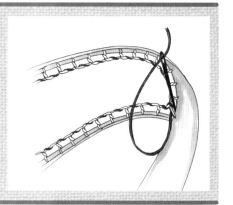

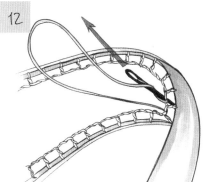

12 Start a new length of thread – 70cm (27½in) – by oversewing into the reverse of the fishbone again. Bring the thread to the surface at the right-hand corner and wrap around the first stitch as you did to finish the previous thread. Now work the second row of twisted buttonhole stitches. The needle emerges at the point shown; the first buttonhole is worked by taking the needle down into the next space and working the single twist around the eye of the needle as before (see yellow thread). Draw the needle through and pull across the design shape to tension.

13 Work one twisted buttonhole between each pair of stitches on the outer row around the full perimeter of the shape. If the second-row stitches are being squeezed too tightly together around the tighter curved section and at the point, miss out a stitch occasionally.

14 On reaching the start again, link the row and work a wrapping stitch between each pair of buttonhole stitches as for the first row: pull in the direction of the ring again.

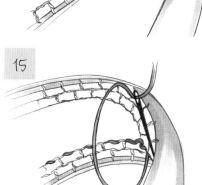

15 On completion of the wrapping row, seal off the current thread and take a new one again so that the thread is fresh for working the centre filling. Wrap once into the starting stitch of each row again to travel the thread out to the outer edge, finishing on the reverse as before (see blue thread).

16 Work tacking stitches across the leaf to prevent it spreading open. The central lace filling will then be easier to tension correctly, ensuring that the leaf retains its shape and does not gape. Work the tacking stitches back and forth across the shape as shown.

17 Secure a further 70cm (27½in) length of thread on the reverse. Bring the thread to the surface at the right-hand tip of the shape. Wrap around the existing stitches as before, travelling to the inner corner of the filling. Now divide the central space into triangles by working simple (rather than twisted) buttonhole stitches between the existing rows of needlelace. Rather than count the number of twisted buttonhole stitches between each triangle, judge their positions to keep them visually pleasing. The triangles should be acutely pointed rather than being too broad. As you work the central filling, pass the needle under the tacking stitches so that they do not become trapped in the filling.

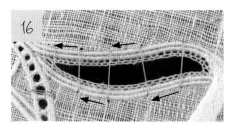

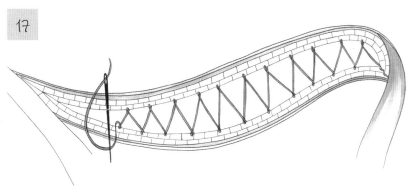

18 On reaching the left-hand end of the shape, do not attempt to squeeze tiny triangles into the narrow tip. At the position shown, the thread is thrown back to the top edge, slipping the needle into the row of twisted buttonholes again at the tip of the triangle, emerging to the left (see peach thread). Check that the tension of the triangle base stitches has remained tight; adjust if necessary.

19 Work the triangle with needleweaving. Slip the needle over the left arm of the triangle and under the right arm, before weaving back over the right and under the left.

20 Continue needleweaving back and forth between the two threads down the full depth of the triangle. The thread should be carefully tensioned as each weaving stitch is worked, to retain smooth edges and a crisp triangular form. The tension should be tighter at the tip of the triangle and slackened towards the base.

21 On completing the first triangle, pass the thread under the right-hand arm in the usual pattern of needleweaving; wrap it once over the right-hand base thread of the triangle. Then slip the thread down into the lower twisted buttonhole row to lock and complete the triangle. Emerging as shown, the thread will now be passed to the top of the next triangle, slipping into the upper row of twisted buttonhole as before (see also the diagram at step 18). The needle will emerge on the left to begin the needleweaving process again.

22 Work the remaining triangles in the same fashion. On completion, finish the thread by wrapping around the stitches at the right-hand point of the shape, to travel to the outer edge again. Secure the thread in the reverse of the fishbone stitching and remove the tacking stitches to finish.

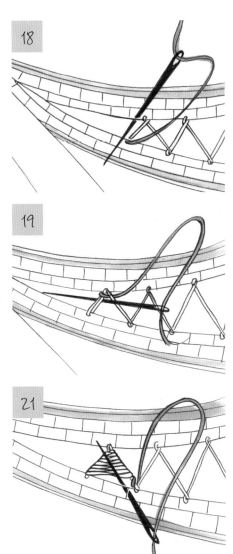

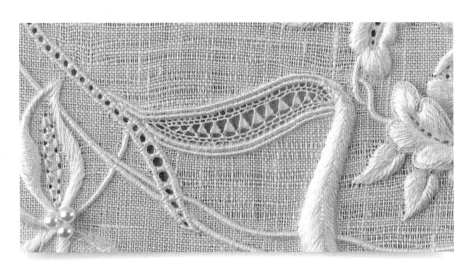

The completed needlelace-filled leaf.

WASHING YOUR WORK IN A SLATE FRAME

Whitework embroidery should always be washed when complete; this prevents yellowing over time, which results from contact with the skin. In fine whitework however, the washing stage is completed once the surface embroidery is complete and the piece therefore remains strong, before the net is revealed and three-dimensional shapes are added. Three-dimensional leaves should not be washed as they contain wire and rusting may occur.

Do not be concerned if the piece seems to look grey when wet: the piece will dry white.

Always take great care, when washing your piece, not to touch or rub the front surface of your embroidery as this may disturb your threads.

1 Keep the work tight in your slate frame while you clean it. However, it is advisable to open the frame to its furthest extent by unrolling the rollers, so that these will not get wet. Add more lacing at the sides if required.

2 Release the lacing along one side of the frame and slide a piece of flexible plastic tubing (with a slit along one edge) over the arm of the slate frame. Slide it under the lacing, with the slit at the outer edge of the frame. If you do not have tubing, slide a strip of plastic sheeting or cling film (plastic food wrap) around the arm instead. Re-tighten the lacing, and wrap the two corners of the slate frame thoroughly in plastic sheeting or cling film (plastic food wrap).

3 Stand the frame sideways, on its arm end (not the roller end) in the bath or in a sink. Keep the reverse of the work facing you and the rollers upright so that the water will run away from them. Wet the work from the reverse by pouring tap water gently from a jug. Avoid wetting the rollers.

4 Make up a solution of foamy detergent in a clean bowl. Use a clean, soft sponge or cotton cloth to sponge the solution evenly over the reverse of your work. Leave the detergent to soak into the piece for about an hour. If the work is discoloured, leave for longer, sponging for a second time. Do not allow the work to dry out while the detergent is present, as this can lead to watermarking. Keep applying water or detergent if the work appears to be drying out.

5 Rinse out the detergent by pouring water from the jug or using a shower head on a low pressure setting. Pour over a bottle of deionized water – this may help to prevent the formation of iron mould over time.

6 Blot the reverse of the piece with a clean towel to remove any excess water and then leave to air-dry naturally. Cover the piece with a clean white cotton cloth if there is any risk of debris falling onto the piece.

> ## Tip
> If the piece has become stained or discoloured during work, apply a stain remover spray after cleaning with the detergent – rinse out the detergent fully before applying the spray. Leave the solution on the work for the time recommended by the manufacturer and then rinse thoroughly before pouring through the deionized water.

YOU WILL NEED:

Flexible plastic tubing such as that used to retain and tidy electrical cables in the home, or, alternatively, plastic sheeting or cling film (plastic food wrap)

Detergent: mild liquid detergent for washing silk and wool garments, or conservation detergent (see suppliers' list on www.searchpress.com)

A soft sponge

Bottle of deionized water (usually available at the chemist or petrol station)

Jug

CALCULATING THE MOUNTING SIZE

Before the slate frame is slackened again to allow the net to be revealed, work out the size to which the piece will be mounted.

Place four strips of coloured card (or two L-shapes of card) around the design. Ensure that the placement of the strips is visually pleasing, and the space left around the design is balanced on all four sides. Also consider an allowance for framing:

a) If you plan to have a window mount around the framed design, this will need to sit into your piece by at least 0.5–1cm (³⁄₁₆–³⁄₈in) on all sides. The mount may be much wider, but the framer can hide supports beneath it.

b) If you plan to fit the design directly into a picture frame, you will need to consider the rebate of the frame, that is, the lip which allows the frame to sit over the piece. This is usually approximately 4–5mm (³⁄₁₆in). Include these measurements when deciding on the final size of mount board to cut.

Mark the centre points of the mount board position onto your piece with clean pins or tacking thread so that you can locate the position easily when you place the mount board later.

> ### Note
>
> When mounting this design I allowed:
>
> • 4.5cm (1¾in) to the left and right, measuring from the edge of the ladder-stitch circle;
>
> • 5cm (2in) at the top of the design, measuring from the edge of the ladder-stitch circle;
>
> • 4cm (1½in) at the bottom, measuring from the bottom edge of the lettering;
>
> This resulted in a final mount board size of: D: 26.7cm (10½in) × W: 22.5cm (8⅞in)
>
> These measurements are a guide only.

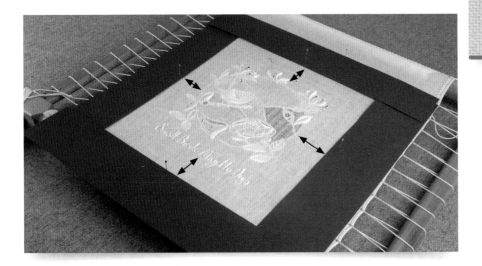

THREE-DIMENSIONAL OAK LEAVES

Three oak leaves are worked in a separate hoop onto silk organza with a wired edge, which allows them to be cut out on completion. When added to the nest, these create a greater sense of realism.

Use a no. 10 embroidery/crewel needle, with L60 thread for the couched edge, L50 for the ladder stitch and buttonhole edge, ST for the embroidery, and F for padding.

1 Place a piece of white silk organza in your shallow edged, 15cm (6in) embroidery hoop. Place the hoop down over the pattern provided on page 191 for the three-dimensional oak leaves. Trace the shapes using a pale grey marker pen.

2 Take the organza out of the hoop and replace the normal way around for work, with the drawn lines on the upper surface and the leaves in the same orientation as on the finished design (see page 129).

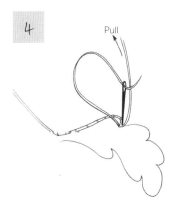

Pull

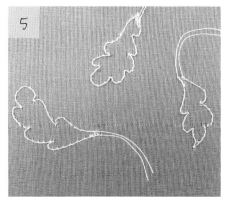

3 Using L60, cast on your thread WKT within the leaf. Take one of the 15cm (6in) lengths of fine craft wire. Leaving a tail of 2–3cm (1³⁄₁₆–1³⁄₁₆in), place this at the base of the leaf.

4 Couch the wire around the perimeter of the leaf, couching every 1–2mm (¹⁄₁₆in), i.e. close enough to control the delicate design shape. At each point around the shape, work the couching stitch at the tip. Pull on the stitch from below the work while bending the wire sharply back on itself. Pinch with tweezers to sharpen further. Secure the working thread with a tiny stab stitch worked within the leaf before continuing to couch.

5 On reaching the base again, secure the working thread with stab stitches within the leaf and leave the tail of wire, trimming to 2–3cm (1³⁄₁₆–1³⁄₁₆in).

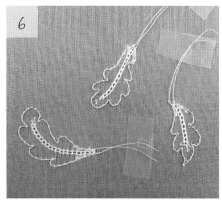

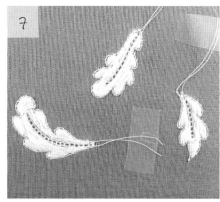

6 Using L50, work ladder stitch through the centre of the leaf. Use a loop of thread at the tip to create the edge (as for the tiny leaves in the nest – see page 171).

7 Pad the remaining area between the ladder stitch vein and the wire edge using long split stitches or satin stitch as appropriate (F).

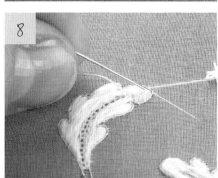

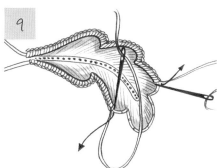

8 Starting at the tip of the leaf, fill the leaf with slanted satin stitch. Work the stitches by tucking the needle under the wire. When the leaf is edged, the buttonhole stitches will bite into the tips of the satin stitches, creating greater strength and cohesion.

9 Using L50 and starting at the base of the leaf, work a tight buttonhole stitch around the perimeter of the leaf, working over the wire and biting into the tips of the satin stitches. Secure threads to finish by darning through the reverse of the satin stitch. The diagram shows how the buttonhole edge can be worked in either a clockwise or anti-clockwise direction as you prefer.

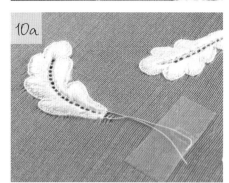

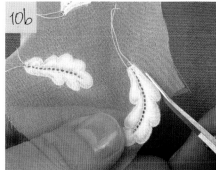

10 On completion of the three leaves, remove from the frame and cut out roughly leaving a border of excess organza. Use curved-tip scissors to carefully trim away the excess organza, up to the buttonhole stitch edge.

11 Brush a fingernail around the perimeter edge to loosen any trapped organza fibres before trimming these away.

179

12 Position the leaves on the main design. Once you are happy with the positions, use a fine awl to ease a hole for the wires. Push the wires through. Pin the leaves in place.

13 Turn to the reverse, fold the wire tails back on themselves. Secure by oversewing to the reverse of the stitching using L60 and trim the tails back to 8mm (⁵⁄₁₆in).

14 Return to the front and use L60 to secure each leaf at two to three points: work stab stitches over the buttonhole edge.

The completed leaves.

REVEALING THE NET

The linen can now be trimmed away from the front of the work to reveal the embroidered net beneath. Slacken the work in your embroidery frame again to do this effectively.

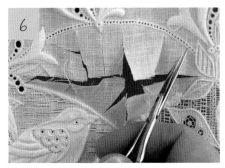

1 Slacken the lacing and move the pegs in by two to three positions. Work over a plain dark cloth or piece of card so that you can see the linen and net below more clearly.

2 Remove any remaining tacking securing the blue plastic film.

3 With a fine tapestry needle, lift a few of the vertical linen threads in the centre of the design area.

4 Using fine curved-tip scissors, snip these threads.

5 Insert the ball-ended tip of a pair of lace scissors into the opening made and cut out to the perimeter edge, sliding the ball tip over the protective plastic.

6 In the same way, cut the remaining linen into small flaps.

7 Pull gently on each flap before trimming it away flush against the perimeter stitching, using curved-tip scissors. Take great care as you do this as the net will be exposed at the perimeter edge. Look beneath each flap as you cut so that you can check that the net is not caught in your scissors.

8 In confined areas of the design, slide the eye of a large needle into the opening to force a space between the net and fabric. Remove the needle and trim into the space, exercising great caution.

The finished effect.

9 Once all the fabric flaps are trimmed away, carefully brush around the perimeter edge in both directions using the tip of your fingernail. This will loosen any remaining fibres of linen trapped in the edge. Flick these upwards, away from the net, and trim away with curved-tip scissors.

Tips

There will always be a tiny rim of linen visible around the perimeter edge. Do not keep trimming excessively and risk cutting the net!

If you accidentally cut one of your lace threads forming your needle-run net patterns, simply unpick the whole row and rework this.

WORKING THE HONEYSUCKLE STEM OVER THE NET USING NEEDLEWEAVING

Use a no. 10 embroidery/crewel needle with L36 thread.

1 Re-tighten the slate frame, exercising great caution. The stem of the central honeysuckle will be worked over the revealed net.

2 Re-insert the pegs to apply *gentle* vertical tension, but do *not* stand on the frame to apply more tension! Ease up the side lacing gently to restore some horizontal tension.

3 A pattern guide for working the stem with leaves is provided on page 191. Lay this beneath the net to gauge the position of the stem and mark the tips with pins.

4 Secure a length of lace thread into the reverse of the linen using oversewing, close to the base tip of the stem.

5 Using the pattern beneath the net as a guide, work along the line of the stem using a long running stitch. Avoid working small running stitches as this will produce an uneven curve.

6 On reaching the leaves, break away from the stem line and 'draw' the shape of a leaf using running stitch. Continue to work another two rows of needleweaving, spiralling in towards the centre of the leaf, creating density.

7 Complete the stem and secure the thread in the solid stitching at the perimeter edge.

8 Work back along the stem line, adding an equivalent leaf to form a pair.

9 Secure the thread at the base of the stem on the reverse of the work.

The completed design.

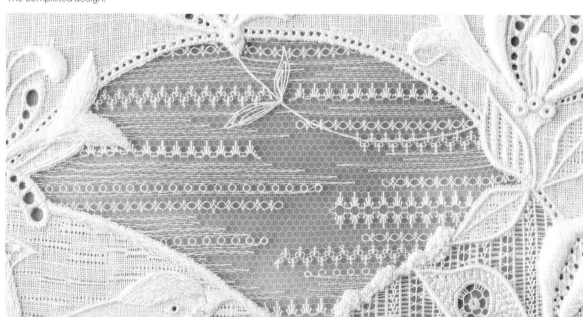

MOUNTING THE COMPLETED EMBROIDERY

PREPARING YOUR BACKGROUND FABRIC

Fine whitework is shown at its best when a coloured fabric is placed behind: this enhances the translucency of the fabric, the open areas and the contrast of the solid areas. When selecting your fabric, lay various pieces behind the finished work to see whether the fabric draws out the best qualities of the design, or flattens them.

Mid-tone blue fabrics work particularly well, as blue heightens the whiteness, and midtones enhance open and lace areas well without excessively darkening the overall effect – however, the choice is ultimately down to personal taste. Be advised that patterned fabrics can clash with intricate patterns and fillings and may confuse, rather than enhance, a design. Soft patterns can, however, be effective in some instances (see Florence Collingwood's *Art Nouveau Portrait*, page 124).

Smooth, matte or soft-sheen fabrics – such as fine cottons and silks – are ideal: textured or slub weaves and high-gloss finishes can be distracting and cause distortion. For the background of *Small Birds May Fly High*, I painted medium-weight habotai silk using silk paints to form a softly-shaded ground fabric. This enhances the sense of depth in the design by suggesting the colours of hedgerow and sky.

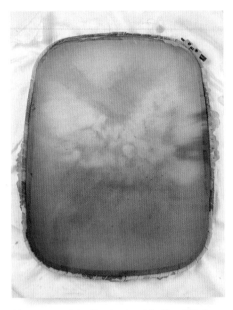

Above, my painted background for *Small Birds May Fly High*.

1 Take a piece of silk large enough to span the planned mounting size of the piece, with at least 5cm (2in) extra beyond this on all sides. Allow sufficient silk to fit a stretching frame.

2 Rinse the silk in a little detergent to remove any dressing, and allow to dry. Avoid creasing the silk as you wash it, and iron once dry to smooth the fabric.

3 Stretch the silk taut by pinning it over a silk painting frame or embroidery hoop.

4 Use a clean, soft watercolour brush to dampen the fabric all over with clean water.

5 Pour a selection of your chosen shades of silk paints or dyes into a palette. Mix and test colours on the side of your fabric until you find your preferred combination. Using large soft brushes, apply the paint to the fabric. Carry the paint right out to the perimeter edges of the piece of fabric to ensure a large enough area of consistent colour for mounting.

6 Repeatedly press a small pad of kitchen paper or similar absorbent paper (avoiding tissue paper, which will shed fibres) at intervals over the surface of the fabric. This will draw out some paint, leaving a pleasing mottled appearance. Similarly, if you dislike an area of the painting, press the kitchen paper over the area to suck out the colour before reworking it.

7 Finally, drip clean water onto the painted surface at intervals to enhance the mottled effect.

8 Once you are satisfied with the paint effect, remove the fabric from the frame and press with a warm iron to seal the paint.

> **Tip**
> Keep an outline copy of the design to hand so that you can adjust the placement of colour as required. Alternatively, photocopy the design outline onto paper, cut out the centre of the design and hold the 'window' over the painted fabric to gauge the finished effect.

CUTTING THE MOUNT BOARD

YOU WILL NEED:

- Metal ruler
- Set square
- Cutting mat
- Sharp craft knife
- Sandpaper
- Fine, sharp H pencil
- Approximately 3.5mm (⅛in) thickness high-quality, acid-free mount board, suitable for textiles (or a thinner equivalent)
- Firm, medium-weight cotton calico (muslin) or densely-woven linen
- Extra strong thread such as buttonhole thread
- Curved needle
- Good quality PVA, EVA or equivalent glue which is safe to use with textiles
- Brush suitable for gluing
- Fine, ideally short, clean, firm pins
- Dressmaking scissors
- Bubble wrap (or four small towels)
- Acid-free tissue paper

Tip

If you have only thin mount board, plot and cut two pieces and glue these together. Cut one piece lengthways along the sheet of board and one widthways. Sheets of card have a straight grain, so if both layers are cut in the same direction as this grain, when plied together, they may curl and warp. If cut in opposing directions, they will act against each other to stiffen the board.

183

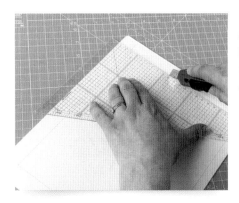

Plot your mount size onto the board using a fine, sharp pencil and ruler: use a set square to ensure that the corners are absolutely square. Working over a cutting mat, use a firm craft knife with a sharp, or new, blade, and a metal ruler to cut the card. Do not try to cut through in one run of the knife. Score the card surface, then work repeated cuts until you gradually cut through. Keep your hand and fingers well away from the cutting path of the knife.

Use fine sandpaper to smooth any roughness from the edges of the card.

COVERING THE BOARD WITH A BASE FABRIC

Most fabrics used to give colour behind fine whitework tend to be reasonably fine and are not sufficiently sturdy to support the mounting process alone. It is therefore best to cover the board with a layer of cotton or linen first.

However, if you do choose a sturdy fabric behind your piece, you can apply this here instead of the base layer.

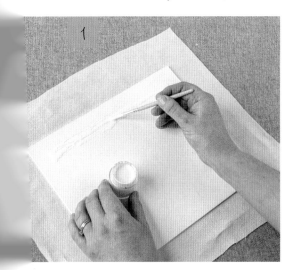

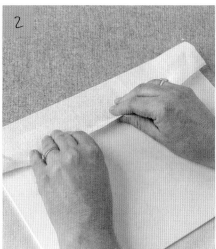

1 Cut a piece of calico (muslin) or linen to 5cm (2in) larger than the mount board on all sides, as straight to the fabric grain as possible. Place the fabric flat on a clean work surface and place the mount board centrally on top. Paste a strip of adhesive along the two long edges, 2cm (1³⁄₁₆in) in from the card edge. The glue strip should also start and finish 2cm (1³⁄₁₆in) from the edge of the card.

2 Working from the centre outwards along one edge, pull the fabric border onto the glue and press firmly in place. As you work out to the sides, pull the fabric outwards to tension.

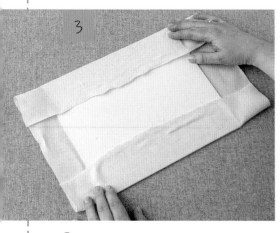

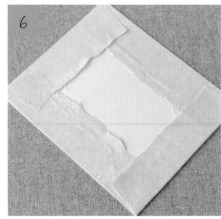

3 Rotate the card, and pull the second border of fabric over in the same fashion. This time, apply more tension – the first strip of fabric is already sealed and you can pull against this. Work from the centre out to the sides again, to achieve a taut surface across the front of the board.

4 Allow the glue to dry, then use dressmaking scissors to clip out the excess fabric at the corners as shown. Allow approximately 2mm (1/16in) of fabric to overhang the tip of the corner so that the card will not poke through.

5 Glue along the two remaining short edges in the same fashion, again leaving a 2cm (13/16in) gap. Pull one of the fabric strips over to the reverse and press into the glue as before.

6 Turn and pull over the final strip, pulling the fabric as tight as possible across the front of the board. Check the front is completely smooth and taut, adjust if necessary. Allow the glue to dry, then trim away any excess fabric beyond the glued bands on the reverse.

184

COVERING THE BOARD WITH THE BACKGROUND FABRIC

Now cover the board with your coloured background fabric, in exactly the same way as for the base layer (see above).

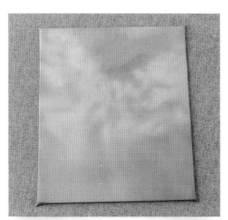

The front of the covered board.

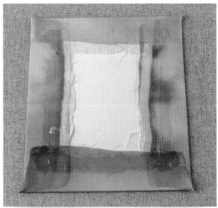

The reverse of the covered board.

PINNING THE WORK TO THE PREPARED BOARD

Take your completed embroidery in the slate frame, which will retain gentle tension after working the needlewoven design over the net. Place the prepared mount board beneath the design and align as close as possible with your pre-marked positions.

1 Pushing the board up against the reverse of the piece, insert a pin through the linen and into the edge of the mount card at the centre of each side. Along the top edge, add more pins in the same fashion 2cm (13/16in) apart and working from the centre outwards. Aim for the board to sit as closely aligned with the straight grain of the fabric as possible.

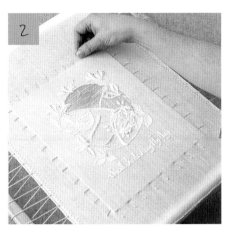

2

3

2 Repeat along the bottom edge and along each of the two sides in turn. Check that the design is correctly positioned, the measurements from the design to the edge of the card are as planned, and that the design is not distorted. Make any adjustments before adding further pins, approximately 4–5mm (³⁄₁₆in) apart along each edge in turn again, always working from the centre out to the sides.

3 Once the piece is correctly positioned and taut, cut the piece away from the slate frame, leaving a border of linen at least 6cm (2³⁄₈in) in depth around all edges.

MAKING A SUPPORT WELL

Make a padded support for your work to protect the three-dimensional front surface.

1 Roll four sheets of bubble wrap and tape them together to form a frame (alternatively, roll four small towels to form the same structure).

2 Cover the support with a piece of clean white tissue paper. Place the work face-down over the prepared well, supporting the edges with the padded frame.

3 At each corner in turn, fold in the excess fabric and finger-press the folds.

4 Fold in the fabric edges, producing a mitre. The mitre should not meet, but should remain open by a width of about 3mm (¹⁄₈in).

5 Unfold and trim away the excess fabric triangle, leaving just 1cm (³⁄₈in) depth from the point of the mount board. Re-fold the corner and pin.

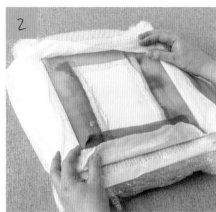

1

2

3

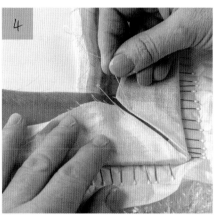

4

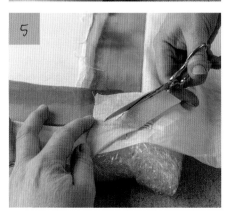

5

The pinned corners.

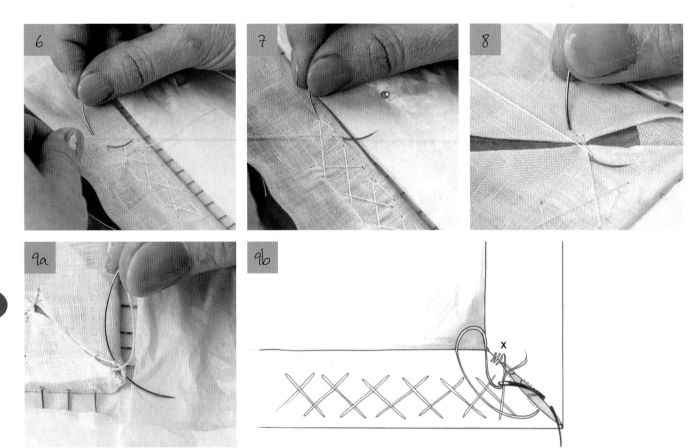

6 Thread a curved needle with a long length of buttonhole thread. Starting at the centre of one of the long edges, apply tension to the excess strip of linen while securing the thread into the perimeter edge using two to three oversewing stitches worked on top of each other (do not use a knot). Stitch down into the 2cm (1³⁄₁₆in) border of taut base fabric, which remains free from adhesive. Work herringbone stitch along this edge, working into the 2cm (1³⁄₁₆in) adhesive free strip to bind the linen of the embroidery to the taut base fabrics. Each stitch of the herringbone should be approximately 8–10mm (⁵⁄₁₆–³⁄₈in) long. Place consistent, firm tension on the flap of excess fabric throughout. Pull up the herringbone tightly with every stitch.

7 Every three to four stitches, take a second locking stitch over the top of the current stitch to lock the tension of the previous section and maintain tension throughout. If the fabric appears wrinkled as the stitches pull tight, this is a good sign that you are pulling tight enough.

8 On reaching the corner, work a locking stitch over the last herringbone stitch to secure. Pass a stitch across the corner to the far side and stitch across the join, digging down into the base fabric below.

9 Work two to three oversewing stitches across the mitre to pull it tightly together (see point X in the diagram above). Now work a slip stitch (ladder stitch) to seam the mitre together, carefully slipping the needle into the fold edge to the left and then to the right and pulling tight to ease the gap between them snugly together.

10 On reaching the corner tip, work a tiny catch stitch into the very tip of the fabric and pull the thread tight to finish. Then pass the needle back up under the mitred corner (be sure not to allow the tension of the ladder stitch to slacken as you do this and pull the thread to re-tighten if required) to emerge in the fabric to the left (see point Y in the diagram opposite).

Tip

Take a strip of paper or tissue paper and wrap this over the protruding pins as you work the herringbone (see photographs 6 and 7). This will prevent the working thread catching in the pins.

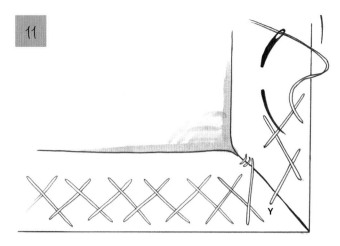

11 Throw the thread over to the right of the mitre and start the herringbone stitching along the new edge as before, working regular locking stitches. Each corner is completed in the same manner. On completion of the stitching, trim away any excess flaps of linen to within 1cm (⅜in) of the herringbone stitching.

> **Tip**
>
> When working ladder stitch, as you cross from one edge to the other, step back on yourself a little each time, rather than jumping straight across. This will help ease the seam together.

This completes this intricate design. I hope you have enjoyed this exploration of the art of fine whitework and that it will encourage you to attempt further pieces, perhaps even designing your own.

Remember that small birds may fly high!

TEMPLATES

These templates are reproduced at 100 per cent/ full size unless otherwise stated.

SCULPTURED TECHNIQUES

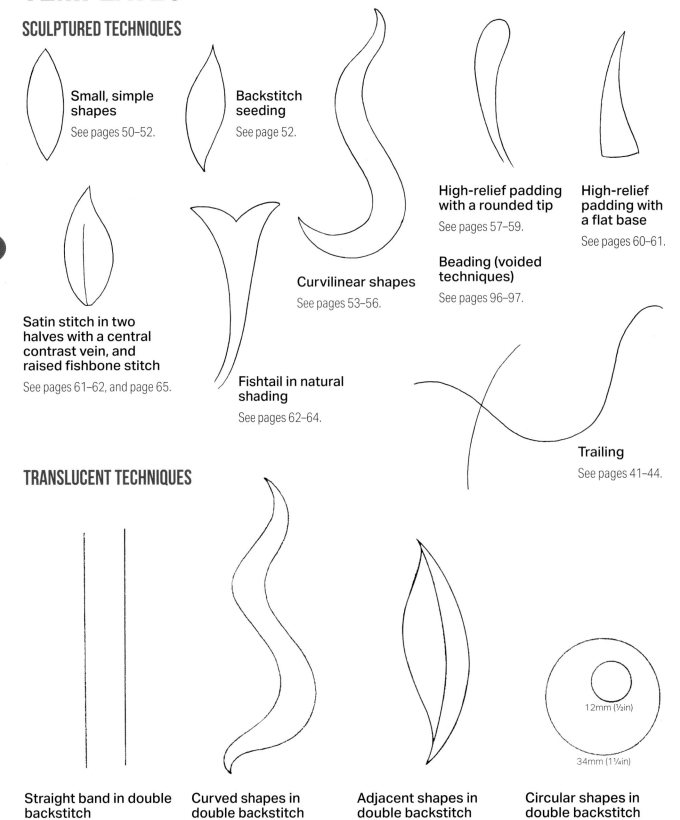

Small, simple shapes

See pages 50–52.

Backstitch seeding

See page 52.

High-relief padding with a rounded tip

See pages 57–59.

High-relief padding with a flat base

See pages 60–61.

Beading (voided techniques)

See pages 96–97.

Curvilinear shapes

See pages 53–56.

Satin stitch in two halves with a central contrast vein, and raised fishbone stitch

See pages 61–62, and page 65.

Fishtail in natural shading

See pages 62–64.

Trailing

See pages 41–44.

TRANSLUCENT TECHNIQUES

Straight band in double backstitch

See pages 66–67.

Curved shapes in double backstitch

See page 68.

Adjacent shapes in double backstitch

See page 68.

Circular shapes in double backstitch

See page 68.

12mm (½in)

34mm (1¼in)

Template for Ayrshire needlelace filling

See pages 99–102.

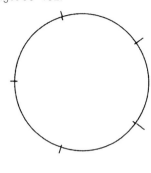

SCABIOSA DESIGN
Scabiosa template

See pages 108–119.

SMALL BIRDS... DESIGN
Template for Ayrshire needlelace filling

See page 154.

SCABIOSA DESIGN
Template for buttonhole scallops

See page 118.

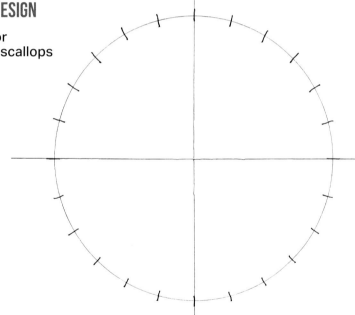

FILIGREE TECHNIQUES

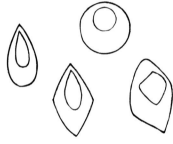

Shaded cut eyelets

See pages 94–95.

Template for *Small Birds May Fly High* design

See pages 128–187.

Template for clouds

See page 131.

Patterns for leaves in nest

See page 171.

Patterns for three-dimensional oak leaves

See page 178.

Pattern for needlewoven honeysuckle

See page 181.

INDEX